Christianity and Philosophical Culture in the Fifth Century

Other Books of Interest from St. Augustine's Press

Benedict M. Ashley, O.P, and John Deely, *How Science Enriches Theology*

Gerard V. Bradley and Don Demarco, *Science and Faith*

Ralph C. Hancock, Calvin and the Foundations of Modern Politics

Marion Montgomery, *With Walker Percy at the Tupperware Party: In Company with Flannery O'Connor, T. S. Eliot, and Others*

Marion Montgomery, *Making: The Proper Habit of Our Being*

Marion Montgomery, *Romancing Reality: Homo Viator and the Scandal Called Beauty*

René Girard, *A Theater of Envy: William Shakespeare*

Josef Pieper, *The Concept of Sin*

Josef Pieper, *Death and Immortality*

Klaus Vondung, *Paths to Salvation: The National Socialist Religion*

George William Rutler, *Principalities and Powers: Spiritual Combat 1942–1943*

Jeffrey J. Langan, (Translator and Commentary), *The French Revolution Confronts Pius VI: Volume I: His Writings to Louis XVI, French Cardinals, the National Assembly, and the People of France with Special Emphasis on the Civil Constitution of the Clergy*

Florent Gaboriau, *The Conversion of Edith Stein*

Ralph McInerny, *The Defamation of Pius XIIl*

James V. Schall, *On the Principles of Taxing Beer: And Other Brief Philosophical Essays*

James V. Schall, *At a Breezy Time of Day: Selected Schall Interviews on Just about Everything*

Rémi Brague, *Moderately Modern*

Josef Kluetgen, *S.J., Pre-Modern Philosophy Defended*

Étienne Gilson, *Theology and the Cartesian Doctrine of Freedom*

Barry Cooper, *Consciousness and Politics*

Christianity and Philosophical Culture in the Fifth Century

The Controversy about the Human Soul in the West

Ernest A. Fortin, A.A.

Translated by James C. Colbert

St. Augustine's Press
South Bend, Indiana

Manufactured in the United States of America.

1 2 3 4 5 6 25 24 23 22 21 20 19

Library of Congress Cataloging in Publication Data
Fortin, Ernest L.
[Christianisme et culture philosophique au cinquihme sihcle. English]
Christianity and philosophical culture in the fifth century:
the controversy about the human soul in the west / Ernest Fortin, A.A.;
translation by James G. Colbert. – 1st [edition].
pages cm
Includes bibliographical references and index.
ISBN 978-1-58731-110-9 (clothbound: alk. paper)
1. Philosophy, Ancient. 2. Church history – Primitive and early church, ca. 30–600. 3. Philosophical theology – History. 4. Soul. 5. Christian philosophy. I. Title.
B631.F6713 2014
128'.109015 – dc23 2013040170

∞ The paper used in this publication meets the minimum requirements of the American National Standard for Information Sciences - Permanence of Paper for Printed Materials, ANSI Z39.48-1984.

St. Augustine's Press
www.staugustine.net

Table of Contents

Introduction vii

Foreword xii

Chapter One – Life and Letters in the Lyonnaise Region on the Eve of the Great Fifth Century Invasions 1

I. Claudianus Mamertus: Formation – His "Triple Library," Apostolic Ministry, His Influence 1

II. A Witness of Philosophical Culture in Gaul, Rhetoric, the Soul in Neo-Platonism 17

Chapter Two – Opponents of the Spirituality of the Soul: Faustus of Riez 36

I. Third Letter of Faustus of Riez and the Problem of Anonymity 36

II. Bible and Spirituality of the Soul according to the Marseilles Authors 40

III. Divine Incorporeality and Omnipresence 49

IV. Divine Incorporeality and Incomprehensibility 56

V. Attitude of Cassian, Faustus of Riez, and Their Disciples toward Philosophy 62

Chapter Three - Claudianus Mamertus and the Neo-Platonic Concept of the Soul 76

I. The Cosmological Proof of the Existence of the Spiritual Soul, Its Platonic Origin 78

II. Divinity of the Soul: Attraction of This Doctrine for Plotinus and His Disciples 98

Chapter Four – Neo-Platonism and Union of Soul and Body 120

I. *Unio Inconfusa* [ἀσύχυτος ἕνωσις] in St. Augustine and *De Statu Animae* 120

II. The soul as "Place" of the Body in Paganism and Christianity 142

III. Separation of Soul and Body; Physical Death and Spiritual Death 157

IV. Drama of the Soul, Fall of the Soul, Fate of the Incarnate Soul, Return of the Soul 173

Chapter Five - *De Statu Animae*'s "Rhetoric" 182

Conclusion 194

Appendix - The Concept of *Paideia* in Aristotle 199

Bibliography 214

Index of Names and of Ancient and Medieval Authors 225

Index of Terms 230

Introduction

All the completed volumes of Father Ernest Fortin, A.A., have appeared in English, except his first and his last.[1] His last book, *Dantes Göttliche Komödie als Utopie* (*Dante's Divine Comedy as Utopia*), a lecture delivered at the Carl Friedrich von Siemens Foundation in Munich in 1989, centers on one of his great literary pursuits: understanding the author of the *Divine Comedy* as a political writer.[2] His first book, *Christianisme et culture philosophique au cinquième siècle: la querelle de l'âme humaine en occident* (*Christianity and Philosophical Culture in the Fifth Century: the Controversy about the Human Soul in the West*), was his reworked dissertation, published in 1959, that revealed the first fruits of what became his life-long passion: understanding the human soul in its yearning for the eternal.[3] A reader of this first book, presented here in translation by Professor James G. Colbert, might notice that *Christianity and Philosophical Culture* is both a meticulous historical and deeply philosophical reflection. As Fortin later remarked concerning this work: "My dissertation . . .

> . . . was on a treatise by Claudianus Mamertus, the only ancient Christian work to deal exclusively with the soul. I never regretted that topic, because it made me realize how important the teaching on the soul was. That's the core of the classical

1 For a complete list of the writings of Ernest L. Fortin, see *Gladly to Learn and Gladly to Teach: Essays on Religion and Political Philosophy in Honor of Ernest L. Fortin, A.A.*, ed. Michael P. Foley and Douglas Kries. Lanham, Boulder, New York and Oxford: Lexington Books, 2002, 303–316.

2 Ernest L. Fortin, *Dantes Göttliche Komödie als Utopie* (Themen 50). München: Carl Friedrich von Siemens Stiftung, 1992.

3 Ernest L. Fortin, *Christianisme et culture philosophique au cinquième siècle: la querelle de l'âme humaine en occident*. Paris: Études Augustiniennes, 1959.

> teaching, the centerpiece of ancient political philosophy. And so I wasn't wandering too far from what I was really looking for.[4]

Father Fortin kept looking and looking, and probing. His findings are revealed here and in all his other books and in the many articles he wrote over the years. These articles have been gathered recently in four volumes of his collected essays.[5] The germ and stimulus of all his reflections on the nature of the soul are found in the present work, the study of the *De Statu Animae* (*On the Nature of the Soul*) of Claudianus Mamertus. Many of Fortin's later essays grow out of his further efforts to understand the nature of the soul, often helped by the struggles of other authors of the Patristic era. We see this in his later essays on "Augustine and the Hermeneutics of Love," "Augustine's *De quantitate animae* or the Spiritual Dimensions of Human Existence," "The *Viri novi* of Arnobius and the Conflict between Faith and Reason in the Early Christian Centuries," and "The *Definitio fidei* of Chalcedon and its Philosophical Sources.[6]" Through these later essays we find that Claudianus, the only ancient Christian between St. Augustine and Boethius to write a work dealing exclusively with the soul, had a number of Christian and pagan predecessors and contemporaries who wrestled in varied contexts "with such notions as the divine, incorporeal, rational, immortal, and impeccable nature of the soul, its intermediary quality, its preexistence, its innate knowledge, the theory of reminiscence, union with the body and the impediments resulting from that union."[7]

4 Ernest L. Fortin, *Gladly to Learn . . .* 292–293.

5 Ernest L. Fortin, *Collected Essays*: Vol. 1: *The Birth of Philosophic Christianity: Studies in Early Christian and Medieval Thought*; vol. 2: *Classical Christianity and the Political Order: Reflections on the Theologico-Political Problem*; vol. 3: *Human Rights, Virtue, and the Common Good*: *Untimely Meditations on Religion and Politics*, ed. J. Brian Benestad. Lanham, Boulder, New York and London: Rowman & Littlefield Publishers, Inc., 1996. Ernest L. Fortin, *Collected Essays*: Vol. 4: *Ever Ancient, Ever New: Ruminations on the Soul, the City, and the Church*, ed. Michael P. Foley. Lanham, MD: Rowman & Littlefield Publishers, Inc., 2007.

6 These essays are found in volume I of his *Collected Essays*, 1–19, 41–59, 169–197 and 199–207.

7 *Ibid*. 173.

The terms "divine," "incorporeal," "rational," and "immortal" are philosophical terms; or, if they are Biblical terms, they were often given in the Christian circles, where Claudianus spent his life, specific philosophical or interpretative meanings. The barbarians in the late fifth century era occupied the Lyon region where Mamertus mostly lived. Yet, the letters of Sidonius Apollinaris, Claudianus's contemporary, speak of the strong culture of the region fed at this time by its *triplex bibliotheca*. In these letters he sees Claudianus and himself enriching the bilingual Greco-Roman literary culture with Christian contributions, especially the works of St. Augustine. The threefold library helped much to prepare Mamertus to bring philosophical precision to his discussions of the soul. Whereas most Christians today think that the spirituality and immortality of the soul seem to be inseparable from Christianity, there are some, like N.T. Wright, in his recent book, *Surprised by Hope* (New York: HarperOne, 2008, p. 28), who raise questions about the Biblical teaching:

> "Do we have immortal souls, and if so, what are they? Again, much Christian and sub-Christian tradition has assumed that we all do indeed have souls that need saving and that the soul, if saved, will be the part of us that goes to heaven when we die. All this, however, finds minimal support in the New Testament, including the teaching of Jesus, where the word *soul*, though rare, reflects when it does occur underlying Hebrew or Aramaic words referring not to a disembodied entity hidden within the outer shell of the disposable body but rather to what we would call the whole person or personality, seen as being confronted by God. As to immortality *1 Timothy* 6:16 declares that only God himself has immortality."

Yet, we may even today be confused when we hear references to the "whole person." Should it be understood as portrayed by Rousseau or an existentialist author like Sartre, or more vaguely as a synonym for "the individual"? The understanding of the words of the Old and New Testaments is not always self-evident. Nor historically has that understanding been without debate. It might be surprising to discover that many early Christian writers who closely read the Scriptures held that the soul, for them the chief component of the whole person, is material. In fact, the *De Statu Animae* of Claudianus is a response to Faustus of Riez whose *Letter 3* is a total defense of the corporeality of the soul. *Letter 3* is scriptural rather than philosophical. For Faustus, only God is incorporeal: incorporeality is a divine privilege. In similar fashion, many early Christian writers also held that the soul is not naturally immortal. Why? Because the Greek and Roman gods were immortals, so a naturally immortal soul implied a claim to divinity. For these Christians the immortality of the human soul was not a natural property, but rather a gift from God. Some of the needed philosophical clarifications found in the *De Statu Animae*, of course, came from the writings of St. Augustine. Still, as Fortin's work argues, Mamertus is not simply a disciple of Augustine. He offered his own reworking of the competing view of the soul, that of Neo-Platonism, drawn principally from Porphyry. The *De Statu Animae*, as well as the letters of Sidonius Apollinaris, reveal a strong Christian culture in the late fifth century. In these writings there is no sign of the Dark Ages. In the case of Mamertus, furthermore, it is, as Fortin establishes, not only a Christian culture but a Christian culture that is strongly philosophical and able to respond to the false claim of the divine character of the human person or the exaggerated Christian response of Faustus of Riez.

In Fortin's *Christianity and Philosophical Culture*, the case for the proper Christian view of the soul according to Claudianus is presented with well-contextualized historical accuracy and philosophical acumen. What is argued just as strongly is the importance of a solid assisting philosophy for discovering the meaning of the truths of the Christian faith as well as evaluating the truth and falsity of the declarations of authoritative philosophers. The latter is a thesis that Fortin argued in favor of for the rest of his life: various heresies and misunderstandings of the Scriptures needed to be unmasked, their errors refuted, and the intention of the divine Author better discovered; the authoritative teachings of the philosophers needed to be rightly understood and measured against the truth of things as grasped by faith and reason. Fortin might in the end not accept Mamertus's total position or all his arguments concerning the nature of the soul, but his judgments will teach the reader some worthwhile lessons concerning the nature of philosophy and its limits and importance for philosophical and theological issues. They are fruits Fortin gained from reading Claudianus

Mamertus and his sources, especially Augustine and Porphyry. From these teachers he learned, and shares with us, how to appreciate properly and, if necessary, to criticize rightly, all our teachers.

The more general conclusion to be drawn from the controversy between Claudianus Mamertus and Faustus of Riez is that Faustus attempted to force the Scriptures to answer a philosophical question, a question that Claudianus realized needed to be addressed in its own order. As the years moved on, Fortin came to realize more and more the deeper meanings of Augustine's discovery that: "Our hearts are restless until they rest in Thee" (*Confessions* I, 1). He also noted that Augustine underscored the soul's pull toward human community in the opening book of his *Soliloquies* (I, 13, 22): "What limit can there be to my love of that Beauty, in which I do not only not begrudge it to others, but I even look for many who will long for it with me, sigh for it with me, possess it with me, enjoy it with me; they will be all the dearer to me the more we share that love in common." These Augustinian references, taken from an article written some twenty years after the publication of *Christianity and Philosophical Culture*, are feeder texts to support his conviction that ancient authors, such as Claudianus, Augustine, and the Neo-Platonists, despite their limitations, have a lot more to teach us about our human soul than do Rousseau and Freud with their modern scientific attempts to derive the higher from the lower, or Spinoza, whose political program is rooted in man's supposed highest desire: self-preservation, or Hobbes's portrait of self-centered men who "measure not only other men, but all things, by themselves" (*Leviathan*, I, 1). What Fortin, however, learned earlier from Claudianus's engagement with his contemporaries and what he attempts to pass on in *Christianity and Philosophical Culture*, is that it is not enough to repeat doctrines, nor is it enough to hold the contrary to what is opposed to doctrines. There is further need of greater precision (*mikrologia*), while avoiding nitpicking. Even more, there is a need for a philosophical element in Christian culture to fight philosophical and theological distortions of Gospel teachings and appreciate the wisdom of the divine message.

Stephen F. Brown
Boston College

Foreword

Apart from a few dictionary articles, often old and necessarily a bit condensed, there is no comprehensive study of the doctrine of the human soul according to the Fathers of the Church. Yet, the question holds an important place in patristic literature. Few authors have failed to pose it at least once in their writings or to recur to it to illustrate some point or other of doctrine, and there are many who have devoted one or several whole treatises to it. By their admission, it is also one of the most difficult questions, to the point that it is said the great Origen[8] recoiled in modesty from the notion of writing a Περὶ ψυχῆς. The very idea of the spirituality of the soul appears to us to be inseparable from Christianity, but was a difficult acquisition, not definitively consolidated until a fairly advanced date. It is significant that in the fifth century, a number of prominent ecclesiastical writers still taught that the human soul was material and, by its own nature, mortal. For anyone interested in what has been called Patristic philosophy in recent years,[9] to use a term which perhaps would have astonished the Fathers themselves, here is a relatively unexplored territory, rich in promise.[10]

8 Pamphilius, *Apologia pro Origene*, c. 8 *Patrologia Graeca*, vol. 17, column 604: ". . . tanti sensus vir et tantae prudentiae, cum utique magister esset ecclesiae, et tanta ab eo dicta scribuntur, non est ausus id sibi auctoritatis assumere, ut proprie *De Anima* librum ederet scriptum."

9 It would be interesting to investigate what combination of circumstances has led our time to study ecclesiastical writers from the secular point of view, if one may so speak.

10 Nevertheless, let us mention the monumental commented edition of Tertullian's *De Anima*, produced some years ago by Professor Jan Hendrik Waszink (Amsterdam: J. M. Meulenhoff, 1947), as well as the splendid synthesis of Father André-Jean Festugière, *La révélation d'Hermès Trimégiste*, vol. 3: *Les doctrines de l'âme*, (Paris: Lecoffre, 1953).

The present study, centered on Claudianus Mamertus, attempts to make a modest contribution to this vast subject. In the Latin world, *De Statu Animae* is one of the most complete treatises we have on the incorporeality of the soul, in fact one of the rare treatises to pose the question in its totality. In this regard it is exemplary and merits a more detailed examination than it has received so far. Through it we can hope to grasp a little better the range of discussions and the groping to which the problem gave rise at the end of antiquity and even beyond.

The indifference, we might be tempted to call it "contempt,"[11] of which Mamertus has been the object until very recently is partly explained by the longstanding attitude of historians toward the so-called period of decadence at the end of our fifth century. Some years ago it would have been difficult to admit that in such a discredited, already semi-barbaric period, it would be possible to discern anything of positive value. Wedded to mediocrity, confused with the mass of his contemporaries, all more or less equally negligible, the author of *De Statu Animae* seemed not to merit great interest.[12]

11 See the harsh judgement of Émile Bréhier, *The History of Philosophy. The Middle Ages and the Renaissance*, trans. Wade Baskin (Chicago: University of Chicago Press, 1965), p. 5–6: "Through Claudius Mamertus, men of the late Middle Ages came to know the views on the incorporeality of the soul expressed in the *Phaedrus*, the *Timaeus*, and the *Phaedo*; his work also provided them with a model of a lamentable erudition, which consisted of disconnected extracts and was the last descendant of the doxographies which in the age of antiquity summed up the philosophical past as it was drawing to a close; in his work we find alongside the Greek philosophers (Pythagoreans and Platonists), the Roman philosophers (Sextius and Varro), then the barbarians (Zoroaster, the Brahmans, Anacharsis), and, of course, the Stoic Chrysippus, whimsically cited to prove the spirituality of the soul." In fact Chrysippus is simply cited for dialectical skill, following a commonplace of the period, and not at all as witness to the spirituality of the soul.

12 Such was the viewpoint of Martin Schulze, *Die Schrift des Claudianus Mamertus, Presbyter zu Vienne, über das Wesen der Seele*, (Dresden: Rammingsche Buchdruckerei), 1883. André Loyen's thesis, *Sidoine Apollinaire et l'esprit précieux en Gaule aux derniers jours de l'empire* (Paris: Belles Lettres, 1943), still suffers from that mentality (see, for example, the Foreword). Not until after World War I, when, to paraphrase Valéry, our civilization understood it was mortal, did this hitherto rather neglected period suddenly appear as one of the most exciting moments of history. Closer to us, the disenchantment of that impe-

This neglect is also and perhaps even more occasioned by the widely accepted idea that Mamertus's doctrine did little more than reflect that of his master St. Augustine. "The latter [Claudianus Mamertus]," Jean-Vincent Bainvel wrote,[13] "hardly does more than follow St. Augustine, although personal in orientation, manner, erudition. He orders arguments dispersed in the master's writings. He pushes them, he gives them form. Here and there, his reasoning has complete scholastic rigor." It was normal that those who only saw him as a disciple without originality never dreamed of developing his thought.

nitent optimist H. G. Wells, as reflected in his last work, *Mind at the End of Its Tether* (New York, 1946), can give us an idea of the upheaval felt by the most lucid spirits. The way in which civilizations die ought to interest us henceforth as much as the way in which they are born, if not more. Of all the examples of decadence recorded by history, the end of the ancient world is the only one whose documents are abundant enough to permit us to follow the progress of the sickness step by step, the only sufficiently well preserved corpse, it has been said, to allow a dissection. Eventually the historians of this period had to split into two camps: one maintained that the exhausted and sclerotic ancient culture was condemned to disappear slowly and inevitably ("L'Empire est mort de maladie interne," Ferdinand Lot, *La fin du monde antique*, Paris: A. Michel, second edition 1951), p. 275; others deemed that Roman civilization had conserved its vitality and that it finally foundered only because the cadres with which it was identified collapsed under the blows of the barbarians ("La civilisation romaine n'est pas morte de sa belle mort. Elle a été assassinée," André Piganiol, *L'Empire chrétien* (Paris: Presses Universitaires de France, 1947) p. 422.

For the history of this *Dekadenzidee*, cf. Walther Rehm, *Der Untergang Roms in abendländischen Denken* (Leipzig: Dieterich, 1930); and for a summary of recent discussions on the subject, N. H. Baynes, "The Decline of the Roman Power in Western Europe, Some Modern Interpretations," in *The Journal of Roman Studies*, vol. 33, 1943, pp. 29–35; André Piganiol, *L'Empire chrétien*, pp. 411–422; and irrespective of whether one accepts the author's philosophical assumptions, Santo Mazzarino, *Aspetti sociali del quarto secolo* (Rome: "L'Erma" di Bretschneider, 1951), pp. 7–31. See also the brilliant *retractatio* of Henri-Irenée Marrou, *Saint Augustin et la fin de la culture antiqu*e (Paris: E. de Brocard, second edition, 1949), pp. 663 ff, which illustrates well the efforts made over many years to exorcise the more than century old cliché of Roman decadence.

13 Jean-Vincent Bainvel, Article "Âme" in *Dictionnaire de Théologie Catholique*, vol. I, column 1004.

However, a more attentive reading of the work reveals that on many points Mamertus does not depend on Augustine and even clearly departs from him. Pierre-Paul Courcelle proved that he was in debt to Porphyry for at least part of his pagan erudition. We hope to show that it is legitimate to believe he took from pagan philosophers a good part of the doctrine that he presents as his own, not just some quotations which figure in *De Statu Animae*.

Posed thus, the problem goes far beyond the particular polemic which set Mamertus and his adversary, Bishop Faustus of Riez, at odds. The real interest of the work is elsewhere, in the conflict which for several centuries set Christianity against what Gregory of Nyssa called the "philosophy of the external."[14] The conflict was precisely on this question of the human soul, traditionally reserved to profane speculation, but whose links with Christian thought stand out more and more clearly in the measure in which the contents of Revelation were more profoundly understood.

It is necessary to begin with a word on the method followed, which has been imposed by the difficulties with which a study of this sort collides. Positing in principle that the first task of the historian of ideas is to rediscover the thought of the ancients as exactly as possible, we have made the effort to understand Mamertus as he understood himself and as he might hope to be understood by the readers to whom he directed himself. Such a task is more difficult than it seems at first sight; to begin, because we are dealing with a work composed by an author who lived in a very different time from ours, who had neither the same intellectual formation, nor the same methods of work, nor the same reflexes that we do. To grasp this, we must only consider that, for the Christians of the first centuries, the notion of the spirituality of the soul was above all a pagan doctrine to be treated cautiously, which often provoked quite unexpected reservations among them. The problem is no less real when we go on to ideas which basically present themselves to us in the same way as to the ancients. The snare here, being less evident, is all the more formidable. Even the most apparently

14 Ἔξω φιλοσοφία, *De Anima et Resurrectione*, *Patrologia Graeca*, vol. 46, column 49 B. Cf. Saint Basil, *Aux jeunes gens sur la manière de tirer profit des lettres helléniques* [Oratio ad Adolescentes], 2, 44, p. 43 Boulanger (Paris: Les Belles Lettres, 1935, 1952); 3, 9, p. 44; 4, 1, p. 44.

simple thought is rooted in a subtle play of analogies and images, to which it never ceases to remain subject. To pretend to grasp that thought independently of this ideological context would be to condemn ourselves to seriously misunderstand its sense and its scope. None of the precautions with which the historian could surround himself in this regard can be judged superfluous.

In the second place our task is complicated by the fact that we lack essential data for this period. Many texts have not come down to us, some of which, like the lost works of Porphyry, seem to have exercised considerable influence. Hence the need to fill in the gaps in our information by different forms of cross-checking, and in general, by philological techniques whose application is often delicate.

There is a final reason why it is not always easy to determine an author's thought precisely; his most important teaching is not necessarily the most obvious one. To make himself understood usefully by a contemporary, presenting the truth in a veiled manner is often indispensable. An author rarely says everything he thinks exactly as he thinks it. Nietzsche[15] affirms that only listening with the "third ear" do we fully understand what an author means. Even the spirituality of the soul seems to have been considered a doctrine that it was important to protect against the bad use to which it might be put. Everything occurs here as if certain writers believed themselves obliged to practice that "art of hiding the truth" by which St. Augustine in the past tried to absolve the Platonists, examined in *Contra Academicos*.[16] In this case, only a deeper reading of the work and attention to every detail can allow us to detect the secret thought of the author under the exterior which hides it.

* * *

We hope that the present research will be followed shortly by a study which will expand its base and which will deal with a certain number of treatises

15 Friedrich Nietzsche, *Jenseits von Gut und Böse*, article 246.

16 Augustine, *Epistula I*, p. 1, 14 Goldbacher (*Corpus Scriptorum Ecclesiasticorum Latinorum*, vol. 34, 1): "illa utiliter excogitata occultandi veri ars et ratio." Cf. *Contra Academicos*, II, (4), 10; II (10), 24; III, (7), 14; III, (17), 38; III, (20), 43.

often only implicitly taken into account in these pages. The present study never would have been brought to completion without the help of those who have been its inspiration from the beginning. I am particularly grateful to Professor Henri-Irenée Marrou of the Sorbonne, who has not ceased to shower me with advice and encouragement, and who has suggested many corrections. I must also specially thank Professor Pierre-Paul Courcelle of the Collège de France, who put at my disposition the opportunities for teamwork afforded by his courses at the École Pratique des Hautes Études, and who has shown unflagging interest in this research. To the courses of Father André-Jean Festugière, director of studies at the École Pratique des Hautes Études, and to the lectures of Professor Henri-Charles Puech of the Collège de France I owe numerous clarifications on Platonism and the particularly thorny question of the relations between neo-Platonism and the different Gnostic sects at the close of antiquity. During the final revision I have likewise kept in mind the remarks and suggestions of Professor Maurice de Gandillac of the Sorbonne.

Finally, it is a most pleasant duty to express my thanks to the Institut des Études Augustiniennes and the Institut Français d'Études Byzantines, whose splendid libraries have greatly facilitated my task and many of whose members have been associated with this project on an almost daily basis.

Chapter One
Life and Letters in the Lyonnaise Region on the Eve of the Great Fifth Century Invasions

I

We have little precise information about Claudianus himself.[1] He was a native of the Lyon region, which was severely tested in the vast fifth century barbarian invasions. The poet Orientius describes the troubles which marked this especially painful period in tones of an eyewitness: "In the towns, estates, countryside, the crossroads, the villages, and all along the roads wherever you looked, nothing is to be seen but only death, woe, destruction, disaster, fire, and mourning; in short, all Gaul is nothing but a smoking funeral pyre."[2] The city of Vienne, where Claudianus may have been born, was occupied twice, first in 423 and again in 438, the second occupation occasioning massive devastation.[3]

1 The only more or less certain date we possess is that of *De Statu Animae*, about 470. The dedication addressed to Sidonius alludes to the title of Patrician, which he received in 469 (or 468). Cf. André Loyen, *Recherches historiques sur les panégyriques de Sidoine Apollinaire* (Paris: Belles Lettres, 1943), p. 18. By contrast, it does not mention Mamertus as a bishop, the rank to which he was elevated shortly thereafter, in 470 or 471. Thus the work must have been written between the two dates. Since Claudianus met Eucher personally between 434 and 450, he must have already reached a certain age by that period.

2 *Commonitorium* II, 180, quoted by Pierre Gustave Labriolle-Bardy, *The History and Literature of Christianity from Tertullian to Boethius* (trans. Herbert Wilson, foreword by Cardinal Gasquet, New York: Barnes and Noble, 1924, 1968), p. 466.

3 The ancient metropolis of Allobroges had conserved all its importance under the Romans, despite the proximity of Lyon. Its privileged position at the in-

However, calm had returned. In particular, southeast Gaul was to enjoy a few years of relative peace and what must be called, for want of a more appropriate term, a kind of literary renaissance.[4] Installed in *Sapaudia* since 443, the Burgundians, distinguished by their mildness from other Germanic peoples, occupied part of the land under an autonomous political regime, with the title of "confederates" of the Empire. But they continued to be regarded as a mere garrison, which would soon depart for new conquests according to their custom.

Mindless of the menace that this officially sanctioned occupation represented for the empire,[5] Gallo-Roman society lived withdrawn into itself and its traditions, avoiding as much as possible any contact with the barbarians toward whom it generally felt only aristocratic repugnance. The lifestyle of rich landowners, already half-retired to their country homes, in a manner that presaged that of the great medieval territorial lords, is well known to us thanks to the *Letters* of Sidonius Apollinaris.[6] Centered on the past, spending their leisure in literary games which seem quite frivolous to us given the gravity of their circumstances – although how can we judge

tersection of many highways, and the fertility of the surrounding region, made it particularly blessed. The city was proud of the splendor of its monuments. "In all of Gaul, it was the noble city par excellence," Camille Jullian, *Histoire de la Gaule*, vol. 6 (Paris: Hachette, 1929), pp. 330–336.

4 The expression was employed by Pierre-Paul Courcelle, *Les lettres grecques in Occident* (Paris: Brocard, second edition 1948), p. 221.

5 Indeed, the Burgundians violated the *foedus* and seized Lyon in 457. Majorian, the first legitimate emperor to set foot in Gaul since Valentinian II, that is to say for 70 years, retook it the following year. But after his death (461) the barbarians made Lyon their capital and extended their domination over part of the Rhone Valley. However, they could not penetrate Provence, into which the Visigoths had moved first.

6 Regarding Sidonius and his friends, cf. André Loyen, *Sidoine Apollinaire et l'esprit précieux en Gaule aux derniers jours de l'empire* (Paris: Belles Lettres, 1943), and for a rapid overview, Gustave Bardy, *L'Église et les derniers romains* (Paris: R. Laffont, 1948), pp. 125–168. The abundance of Christian inscriptions provided by the Lyon region even in this period (cf. Pierre Wuilleumier, *Lyon métropole des Gaules*, Paris: Belles Lettres, 1953), p. 96, constitutes another witness of this Indian summer of ancient life in the Rhone valley, one of whose most remarkable products is *De Statu Animae*.

that? – these literati of decadence evade in any way they can a reality doubtless felt to be all too prosaic. The great questions of the day find only feeble echoes in the literature of this exquisite society which is indifferent to them, but its fidelity to the muses is touching and pays homage in its own way to their spirit! Under pressure of events, that society would learn how to demonstrate courage when its hour came. Sidonius and his brother-in-law Ecdicius organized the defense of Auvergne (*Civitas Avernorum*), the most important city of Prior Aquitania, assailed by the Goths toward 470.

But let us return to our Claudianus. The fact that he personally knew Eucher, Bishop of Lyon from 434-450, and that he heard him dispute,[7] allows us to suppose that he resided in Lyon during part of his youth and perhaps studied there. There too he would have established his friendship with Sidonius, rather than at Vienne, where the latter seems never to have lived.

We might wish to be better informed about the nature of the studies that were carried out in this period. Was Claudianus a student in the sort of ancient schools that existed in every corner of the empire up to the end of antiquity? Or, since the system of public schools in Gaul had collapsed at the beginning of the century during the first great invasions, did he receive the lessons of a rhetorician at home?[8] Were there clerical schools in this period, where laymen and future priests were initiated both in ecclesiastical sciences and secular subjects? Without further evidence, we are reduced to hypotheses. One thing seems certain: the efforts of St. Jerome and St. Augustine[9] to lay the foundations of a specifically Christian culture

7 *De Statu Animae*, p. 135, 12 Engelbrecht (*Corpus Scriptorum Ecclesiasticorum Latinorum*, Vienna, 1866, vol. 11): "haudquaquam tamen Eucherium praeterierim mihimet vivente doctrina et praesentaneis coram disputationibus cognitum."

8 Two formerly contending theses are known: Maurice Roger, *L'enseignement des lettres classiques d'Ausone à Alcuin, introduction à l'historie des écoles carolingiennes* (Paris: A. Picard, 1905), held that school organization crumbled in the fifth century; the almost abandoned position of Henri Pirenne, "De l'état de l'instruction des laïques à l'époque mérovingienne," in *Revue Bénédictine*, vol. 46, 1934, pp. 165–177, favored its survival until a fairly advanced date.

9 To tell the truth, in St. Jerome's case (*Epistula 107 ad Laetam* and *Epistula 128 ad Gaudentium*) the attempt had rather restricted scope, because these two letters only concern two young women destined for religious life. Thus the

had not observably modified traditional instruction, and whatever the type of school Claudianus may have attended, he must not have received a very different education from that obtained by a grammarian or rhetorician up to then.

It is difficult to form an idea of Claudianus's classical culture from just *De Statu Animae*. However, he seems to have distinguished himself very early by his knowledge of Greek, Latin, and Christian authors: *Triplex bibliotheca quo magistro Romana, Attica, Christiana fulsit; quam totam monachus virenti in aevo secreta bibit institutione*.[10] Sidonius's reference to this "triple library" is striking and suffices to reveal the deep transformation which had taken place in the intellectual customs of the period. In the bilingual world of the Roman Empire, there were double libraries. Caesar already resolved to put the best possible Greek and Latin libraries at the disposition of the public,[11] a project first accomplished shortly thereafter by Asinius Pollio.[12]

program outlined by the author does not necessarily address Christians in general. It is quite different in St. Augustine's *De Doctrina Christiana*, if we accept Henri-Irenée Marrou's interpretation, *Saint Augustin et la fin de la culture antique*, p. 394 ff. The issue of Christian education would have taken a decisive step forward here. While his predecessors were simply content to take the best of traditional education, without dreaming of replacing it with a specifically Christian system of education, Augustine for the first time would erect "a program of higher education which constitutes the complete formation of the spirit and which is conceived solely in function of the religious goal that Christianity assigns to intellectual life." (p. 398) On the limits of this program, cf. Marrou, *St. Augustin et la fin de la culture antique*, pp. 399–401.

10 Sidonius, *Letters* vol. II, Book IV, XI, 6 (Loeb Classical Library, Cambridge, Mass.: Harvard University Press, 1965, 1984, trans. W. B. Anderson), p. 108.

11 Suetonius, *Caesar*, 44; Isidore, *Etymologiae*, 6, 5, 1. On libraries, cf. René Cagnat, "Les bibliothèques municipales dans l'empire romain," in *Mémoires de l'Academie des Inscriptions et Belles Lettres*, vol. 38, 1909, p. 1 ff, and H. Leclercq, article "Bibliothèques," in Cabrol-Leclercq, *Dictionnaire d'archéologie chrétienne et de liturgie*, vol. 2, Paris, 1910, columns 842–904.

12 Suetonius, *Fragments*, p. 130, 14 ff. Refferscheid (*Suetoni praeter Caesarum Libros Reliquiae*, Leipzig, 1860): "Romam primus librorum copiam advexit Aemilius Paulus Perse Macedonum rege devicto, deinde Lucullus e Pontica praeda. Post hos Caesar dedit Marco Varroni negotium quam maximae bibliothecae construendae. Primum autem Romae bibliothecas publicavit Pollio hinc Graecas simul atque Latinas additis auctorum imaginibus in atrio [sc. Libertatis],

Later Augustus would create public libraries with both Greek and Latin works at the Porticum of Octavius and the Palatine,[13] and Sidonius himself mentions Greek and Latin libraries in Trajan's forum.[14] Likewise, we find a considerable number of this type of private library.[15] Sidonius's remark about Claudianus's "library"[16] acquires this full meaning, when we realize

quod de manubiis magnificentissimum instruxerat." Cf. Pliny, *Historia Naturalis*, 35, 2, 2, number 10; Ovid, *Tristia*, 3, 1, 71; Quintilian, *Institutiones Oratoriae*, 11, 3, 4; Isidore, *Etymolgiae*, 6, 5, 2, etc.

13 Suetonius, *Augustus*, 29; Dion Cassius, *Historia Romana,* 53, 1; 66, 24; 69, 43.

14 Sidonius, *Letters*, vol. II, Book IX, 16, 3, v. 25–28, p. 600, Loeb Classical Library; cf. Aulus Gellius, *Noctes Atticae*, XI, 17 (pp. 340–343 *The Attic Nights of Aulus Gellius II*, with English trans. by John Rolfe, Loeb Classical Library, Cambridge, Mass: Harvard University Press, 1927, 1982); Flavius Vopiscus, *Divus Aurelianus*, I, 7, p. 150, line 1 ff. Hohl (*Scriptores Historiae Augustae*, vol. 2, Leipzig, 1927).

15 E.g., Cicero, *Ad Quintum Fratrem*, III, 4; Petronius, 48, II: "Bybliothecas habeo, unam Graecam, alteram Latinam."

16 Strictly speaking, we could view Sidonius's text as a mere allusion to book II of *De Statu Animae*, which appeals successively to Greek, Latin, and Christian authors; cf. *De Statu Animae*, p. 129, 4: "Plurimorum in negotium praesens philosophorum plurimis testimoniis usi sumus multosque ex eadem Graecia, si vel causa posceret vel ratio sineret, proferre possemus. Sed ne localiter veritatem quaesisse videamur, ut haec eadem ab una tantum videri gente quiverit et aliis ignorata sit, cum veri compos humana substantia non sit regione, sed genere, Romanos etiam eosdemque philosophos testes citemus . . . ," and p. 131, 7: "atque ut ad ipsos caelestium voluminum fontes illis fere ducibus, qui ex eisdem largius hausere, veniamus, Gregorius Nazianzenus . . . ," etc. But it does not matter whether Sidonius employed the word "library" in a real or metaphorical sense. The expression should hold us here as much as the thing, and it is only meaningful in the context of the Roman Empire's double libraries. For the figurative use of the word "library," which was usual, cf. Origen, *In Genesim Homiliae*, II, *Patrologia Graeca*, Migne, Paris, 1857–1866, vol. 12, column 173 C; Jerome, *Epistula* 60, 10, 9, p. 561, 18 Hilberg (*Corpus Scriptorum Ecclesiasticorum Latinorum*, vol. 54): "lectione . . . adsidua et meditatione diuturna pectus suum bibliothecam fecerat Christi;" Cassiodorus, *Institutiones Divinae*, 5, *Patrologia Latina*, Migne, Paris, 1844–1964, vol. 70, column 1116 B: "tantos libros in memoriae suae bibliotecha condiderat;" Sidonius, *Letters* vol. II, Book VII, 9, 1(p. 334, Loeb Library): "bibliotheca fidei catholicae," etc. Furthermore, it should be noted that Sidonius often mentions his friends' private collections, some of which seem to have been well supplied, like Lupus's

that for a very long time aspirants to culture were recruited almost exclusively among the Roman aristocracy, which by and large remained loyal to the faith of its ancestors to such an extent that "culture" and "paganism" seemed to be identified. Little by little, however, the fishermen theologians whom Celsus[17] and then Julian[18] mocked acceded to the ranks of the literate. In the period we are considering, the times were past when higher education remained the monopoly of late representatives of paganism. The works of Church Fathers and ecclesiastical writers took their place on library shelves next to the great authors of classical antiquity.[19] Intellectual labor was carried on henceforth in a Christian atmosphere.

The same conclusion follows if we consider the literary genre of Sidonius's text, *ekomion* or funeral eulogy closely related to *ekomion*; the careful codification of its rules in rhetoric manuals which thereby perpetuated it, expected the orator to hold forth about the education of the personage whose merits were being celebrated.[20] In fact, despite the reticence Roman sensibility might feel in the presence of anything Greek, numerous portraits

"multiple library," (*Letters* vol. II, Book VIII, 11, 2, pp. 456–457, Loeb Classical Library), or that of Consentius (*Letters*, vol. II, Book VIII, 4, 1, p. 412 Loeb Classical Library), or again that of Ferreolus, which contained the works of St. Augustine, Prudentius, and Origen, the latter in Rufinus's translation (*Letters*, vol. I, Book II, 9, 4, p. 454 Loeb Classical Library). Ferreolus's library had the peculiarity that works of piety were near the seats reserved to women, whereas others, grouped by style, were set up on the men's side!

17 Cf. Origen, *Contra Celsum*, I, 62; Tertullian, *De Anima*, 3, 3.

18 Julian, *Epistula 79*, p. 606, 19 Hertlein. On the antithesis fisherman-philosopher in patristic literature, cf. Jan Hendrik Waszink, *Tertulliani, De Anima*, p. 119.

19 See the analogous case of Agapitus's library studied by Henri-Irenée Marrou, "Autour de la bibliothèque du Pape Agapit," in *Mélanges d'archéologie et d'histoire*, published by the École Française de Rome, vol. 48, 1931, pp. 124–169.

20 Regarding this *topos* of παιδεία, already noted by Aristotle, *Rhetoric*, I, 9, 1367 b 28, according to the Greek rhetoricians of the imperial period (Hermogenes, Theon of Alexandria, Menander of Laodicea, Aphtonios) and according to the Latins (*Rhetorica ad Herennium*, 3, 6, 10; 3, 7, 14; Cicero, *De Inventione*, 1, 25, 35; 2, 9, 29 etc.; Quintilian, *Institutiones Oratoriae*, 3, 7, 15; Laurentius Victorinus, Priscian.) Cf. Henri-Irenée Marrou, Μουσικὸς, *étude sur les scènes de la vie intellectuelle figurant sur les monuments funéraires romains*, Grenoble: Didier & Richard, 1938 pp. 226 ff.

or eulogies that we owe to Sallust,[21] Suetonius,[22] Plutarch,[23] and to the authors of *Historia Augusta*,[24] allude to their heroes' Greek and Latin culture. Precisely this same theme, with a care for suitable brevity, is found in the epitaph composed by Sidonius at Claudianus's death and addressed to his nephew Petreius. But the author was incapable of limiting himself to an allusion to the deceased's double culture. Though in the old tradition of rhetoricians, the eulogy has been enriched by a new element, characteristic of the *tempora Christiana*, as they are now called:[25] ecclesiastical culture, far from renouncing the other two, must, in transforming them, assure them a place in a new world under construction.

We will return below to the problem of Greek philosophers, a key but also an enigma in this period. As for the Latins, ancient or archaizing authors were the fashion: Cicero, Varro, Pliny the Younger, Apuleus, Fronto.[26]

21 Sallust, *Catilina*, 25, 2, on the subject of Sempronia, "litteris Graecis et Latinis docta, psallere et saltare elegantius quam necesse probae;" *Jugurtha*, 95, 3, on the subject of Sulla, "litteris Graecis et Latinis juxta atque doctissime eruditus."

22 Suetonius, *Caligula*, 3, 1–2, on the subject of Germanicus, "ingenium in utroque eloquentiae doctrinaeque genere praecellens." Cf. *Claudius*, 42, 1–2; *Augustus*, 89,1.

23 Plutarch, *Lucullus*, 1, 5

24 *De Vita Hadriani*, 1, 5, vol. 1, p. 3, 17 Hohl (*Scriptores Historiae Augustae*, Leipzig: 1927); *Severus* 1, 4, vol. 1, p. 136, 9: "Latinis Graecisque litteris . . . quibus eruditissimus fuit;" *Alexander Severus*, 27, 5, vol. 1, p. 271, 17; *Alexander Severus*, 30, 1, p. 273, 20; *Maximini Duo*, 27, vol. 2, p. 23, 28: "Litteris et Graecis et Latinis imbutus." When the occasion arises, the absence of this culture is remarked, *Vita Clodii Albini*, 5, 2, vol. 1, p. 172, 7: "eruditus litteris Graecis ac Latinis mediocriter.".

25 E.g., Optatus of Milevis, *Contra Parmenianum Donatistam*, 7, 1, p. 163, 4 and 10 Ziwsa (*Corpus Scriptorum Ecclesiasticorum Latinorum*, vol. 26); St. Augustine, *De Civitate Dei*, I, 1, 19 and 33 (*Corpus Christianorum*, vol. 47, p. 2); also V, 22.

26 Claudianus Mamertus, *Epistula ad Sapaudum*, p. 205, 30 Engelbrecht (*Corpus Scriptorum Ecclesiasticorum Latinorum*, vol. 11); *Epistula ad Sapaudum*, p. 206, 3: "Quisquis enim recentiorum aliquid dignum memoria scriptitauit, non et ipse nouitios legit. Illi ergo reuentilandi memoriaeque mandandi sunt, de quibus isti potuere proficere quos miramur." Cf. Sidonius, *Letters* vol. II, Book IV, 3, 1, pp. 68–70, Loeb Classical Library. Regarding this archaizing tendency, see André Loyen, *Sidoine Apollinaire*, pp. 4–5, and 174.

Claudianus even proposed Naevius and Plautus as examples of elegance.[27] Whatever other models he used,[28] there is undeniable influence of Cicero,[29] from whom Claudianus borrows several expressions and quotes two passages. Varro's influence is doubtless less obvious, but perhaps greater than is usually thought.[30] Among all the poets, *De Statu Animae* appeals most often to Virgil.[31] Only Gregory of Nazianzus is cited among the Greek Fathers.[32] As for the Fathers of the Latin Church, besides his compatriot Eucher, Mamertus knew Hilary, Ambrose, and Jerome but above all shows himself to be the disciple of St. Augustine, whom he often follows step by step and from whom he seeks a spirit and a method.[33] The fact that an

27 Claudianus Mamertus, *Epistula ad Sapaudum*, p. 205, 30.

28 According to August Engelbrecht, who has given us the critical edition of *De Statu Animae*, Claudianus's style was modeled on that of Apuleus; cf. "Untersuchungen über die sprache des Claudianus Mamertus," in *Sitzungsberichte der Wiener Akademie*, vol. 110, Vienna, 1885, pp. 423–542.

29 See the discovery of Einar Harleman, *De Claudiano Mamerto Gallicae Latinitatis Scriptore Quaestiones* (Uppsala: A. B. Lundequist Kabokhandheln, 1938), p. 76.

30 According to Willy Theiler, *Porphyrios und Augustin* (Halle: M. Niemeyer, 1933), p. 5, note 1, Mamertus took the ideas which he attributed to Varro (*De Statu Animae*, p. 130, 2 ff.) from Porphyry and St. Augustine, not directly from Varro himself. However, see below ch. 3, end of section I.

31 Five times altogether. The hemistich on p. 22, 2: "spreta paucitate doctorum inludunt inperitos, *quae maxima turba est*," not identified by the editor, is taken from *Aeneid* III, 611. Cf. St. Augustine, *Contra Academicos*, I, 1, 2: "si stultorum hominum, *quorum inmensa turba* est . . ."

32 *De Statu Animae*, p. 131, 8: "Gregorius Nazianzus in *Apologetico* magnum videlicet inter animam et corpus clamat esse discrimen atque ut corpus corporalibus pasci, sic animam incorporeis saginari." Mamertus contented himself with rather freely paraphrasing Gregory's text, which was available in Rufinus's translation. Cf. *Apologeticus*, I, 18, p. 20, 18 Englebrecht (*Corpus Scriptorum Ecclesiasticorum Latinorum*, vol. 46): "aequumque iudicium inter animam habeamus et corpus numquam deteriori naturae subicientes meliorem" etc.

33 *Nobilissimus tractator sanctarum scripturarum*, cited on p. 196, 7, is again St. Augustine, *De Doctrina Christiana*, I, 23, *Patrologia Latina*, vol. 34, column 27. In a note of *Texte und Untersuchungen, neue Folge*, V, 3, p. 147, Adolf Harnack tells how he unsuccessfully tried to identify the author of this quotation for many years. The notion of four rules of charity expressed there (*quattuor pones dilectionis regulas, quod supra nos, quod juxta nos, quod nos, quod infra nos*) are found

otherwise unknown passage from Eucher conserved by *De Statu Animae* is inspired almost completely in Augustine[34] makes us realize that in the first half of the fifth century in Gaul a group of intellectuals imbued with the ideas of the bishop of Hippo actively contributed to their diffusion.

Later we find Claudianus, a simple priest, exercising his ministry alongside his brother Candidus, who later became bishop of Vienne (toward 460).[35] Claudianus devotes himself to preaching, redeems captives, helps the afflicted and the needy. He assists and accompanies the bishop whenever the occasion arises.[36] Likewise, he seems to be interested in Church chant.[37] Lenain de Tillemont sums up this unceasing activity with what used to be called "unction" (today it would sound a bit ironic): "Indeed there was a second bishop, who bore the weight of the episcopacy with his brother, one had the honor and the dignity, the other the work and the fatigue."[38]

* * *

Besides *De Statu Animae* we have two letters of Claudianus, one to Sidonius, whom he amicably reproaches not having acknowledged receipt of the treatise dedicated to him; the other to the rhetorician Sapaudus of Vienne, in a slightly pompous style, but touching given its historical context. The author deplores his contemporaries' scant zeal for the liberal arts and for studies in general. He accuses them of being ashamed of their own language,

again in Goethe's *Wanderjahren*. Harnack, quite properly, is unwilling to admit that Goethe could have borrowed them directly from Claudianus Mamertus.

34 Text quoted below ch. 4, note 55. To our knowledge this dependence has never been noted.

35 The Church owes the institution of Rogations around 469 to St. Mamertus. Cf. Sidonius, *Letters* vol. II, Book V, 14, 2–3, pp. 216–218, Loeb Classical Library.

36 Sidonius, *Letters* vol. II, Book IV, 11, 4–5, pp. 104–106, Loeb Classical Library.

37 Sidonius, *Letters* vol. II, Book IV, 11, v. 13–15, p. 108, Loeb Classical Library: "Psalmorum hic modulator et phonascus, ante altaria fratre gratulante instructas docuit sonare classes."

38 Lenain de Tillemont, *Mémoires pour servir à l'histoire ecclésiastique des six premiers siècles*, vol. 16, Paris: 1712, p. 119.

and he attributes this state of things to negligence rather than to lack of good spirit.[39] Only Sapaudus and Claudianus struggle against an otherwise desperate situation. Greece in particular, proclaimed master of arts and sciences, seems worthy of praise.[40] In this regard, Mamertus holds forth on the topics of Plato's voyages and barbarian wisdom, whose popularity seems to increase during this period.[41] Among ancient authors whose works are known to us, he is even the only one to affirm that Plato reached India.[42] Sidonius speaks in laudatory terms of a hymn which has not come down to us.[43] Claudianus seems to have also been author of a lectionary, which is also lost. Dom Morin has formulated the hypothesis that the letter which prefaces the *Comes ad Constantium* refers to this lectionary.[44] Finally, Gennadius informs us that Salvianus dedicated a commentary on the last part of *Ecclesiastes* to Claudianus.[45]

39 "Unum illud procul ambiguo dixerim nostro saeculo non ingenia deesse, sed studia." Letter of Claudianus to Sapaudus, p. 204, 16 Engelbrecht.

40 "Disciplinarum omnium atque artium magistra Graecia idcirco maxime nobilibus studiis prouecta est atque orbem paene totum multiplicibus conplexa doctrinis, quoniam nemo illic omnium fuit, qui quidquam bonae frugis ferret, cui non par merito honos fiet, "Letter of Claudianus to Sapaudus, Englebrecht, p. 203, 3.

41 Regarding this commonplace, cf. F. Boemer, *Der lateinische Neuplatonismus und Neupythagorismus und Claudianus Mamertus in Sprache und Philosophie*, Leipzig, 1936, p. 104–109; Pierre-Paul Courcelle, *Histoire littéraire des grandes invasions germaniques* (Paris: Hachette, 1948), pp. 120–121.

42 Mamertus no doubt found this teaching in Porphyry; cf. F. Boemer, *Der lateinische Neuplatonismus*, pp. 96–103.

43 *Epistula IV*, 3, 8, p. 35, 29 ff., Lütjohann: "Iam vero de hymno tuo si percunctere quid sentiam commaticus est, copiosus dulcis elatus et quoslibet lyricos dithyrambos amoenitate poetica et historica veritate supereminet, idque tuum in illo peculiare, quod seruatis metrorum pedibus, pedum syllabis syllabarumque naturis intra spatii sui terminum uerba ditia uersus pauper includit nec arctati carminis breuitas longitudinem phalerati sermonis eliminat . . ."

44 Germain Morin, "La lettre préface du Comes, *Ad Constantium* se rapporterait au lectionnaire de Claudien Mamert?" in *Revue Bénénedictine*, vol. 30, 1913, pp. 228–231.

45 Gennadius, *De Viris Inlustribus*, 68, p. 85; 1 Richardson (*Texte und Untersuchungen*, XIV, 1, Leipzig: J.C. Hinrichs. 1896).

* * *

The lack of attention paid today to *De Statu Animae* should not make us forget that the treatise was one of the classics of psychology during almost the whole Middle Ages. Gennadius, who did not share the author's views about the spirituality of the soul, nevertheless paid homage to his merits as a philosopher and writer.[46] Mamertus seems to have been one of the favorite authors of Cassiodorus, who found inspiration not only in the former's *De Statu Animae*, but also in his commentaries on Holy Scripture.[47] Licinianus of Carthage borrowed some of his best pages from him in a parallel controversy with an unknown author on the subject of the spirituality of the soul.[48]

During the Carolingian period, Candidus of Fulda utilized him,[49] and

46 Gennadius, *De Viris Inlustribus*, 83, p. 90, 11 Richardson: "vir ad loquendum artifex et ad disputandum subtilis." Claudianus is no doubt one of the innovators considered by Gennadius, *Liber sive Definitio Ecclesiasticorum Dogmatum*, ch. 54, p. 99 Turner (*Journal of Theological Studies*, vol. 7, 1906): "Propter novellos legislatores, qui ideo animam tantum ad imaginem Dei creatam dicunt ut quia Deus incorporeus recte creditur etiam anima incorporea esse credatur, libere confitemur imaginem in aeternitate similitudinem in moribus inveniri."

47 Cf. Van der Vyver, "Cassiodore et son oeuvre," in *Speculum*, vol. 6, 1931, p. 270; L. W. Jones, *An Introduction to Divine and Human Readings by Cassiodorus Senator*, New York, 1946, pp. 19 and 31. Cassiodorus (Pseudo Primasius), *In Epistulam I ad Corinthios*, *Patrologia Latina*, vol. 68 column 511 A-B = *De Statu Animae*, p. 34, 9–17; *In Epistulam ad Romanos*, L. W. Jones, *op. cit.*, col. 466 B = *De Statu Animae*, p. 37, 4–7.For the significance of these passage see below ch. 3, note 56.

48 Cf. José Madoz, *Liciniano de Cartagena y sus cartas*, Madrid: 1948, and by the same author, *Segundo decenio de estudios sobre patrística española, 1941–1950*, (Madrid: Estudios Onienses, Ediciones Fax, 1951), pp. 95–97.

49 On Candidus and Claudianus Mamertus, cf. Franz Zimmerman, "Candidus, Ein Beitrag zur Geschichte der Frühscholastik, in *Divus Thomas* (Friburg), vol. 7, 1929, pp. 30–60. See, however, M. Cappuyns's reservations concerning beatific vision in *Bulletin de théologie ancienne et médiévale*, vol. 1, 1929–1930, n. 127. In the sixteenth century the monastery of Fulda still possessed a manuscript of *De Statu Animae*; cf. C. Scherer, "Der Fuldäer Handschriften-Katalog aus dem 16. Jahrhundert," in F. Falk, *Beiträge zur Rekonstruktion der alten Bibliotheca fuldensis und Bibliotheca laureshamensis, Beihefte zum Centralblatt für Bibliothekswesen*, vol. 26, Leipzig: 1902, p. 104.

Ratramnus of Corbie quotes him at length.[50] The fact that Mamertus had harshly singled out another Christian, a bishop in the bargain, no doubt harmed his reputation in certain circles: like the author of *De Diversa Animae Ratione* Alcuin and his disciple, Rabanus Maurus, ignored Claudianus, perhaps voluntarily, and based themselves rather on Augustine and Cassiodorus.[51] However, a letter in verse from Mico of Saint Riquier furnishes us a new indication of the favor *De Statu Animae* enjoyed in the same period. The author expresses the desire to borrow a manuscript of Claudianus's book from a friend, thanks to which he hopes to improve the copy his monastery possesses.[52]

Faithful to the teaching of Cassian, Faustus of Riez, and their disciples, the Spanish adversary of classical culture, Álvaro of Córdoba, has scant esteem for an author as open to philosophy as Claudianus, and he reproaches Claudianus for defending a position to which a Christian should never adhere, namely that the human soul is incorporeal and invisible even for God.[53] Shortly afterwards, Mamertus finds an eloquent defender in the

50 Ratramnus of Corbie, *De Anima*, p. 213, 130–180 Wilmart (*Revue Bénédictine*, vol. 43, 1931) = *De Statu Animae*, p. 185, 10 - p. 187, 8. By contrast, the same author's *Liber De Anima ad Odonem Bellovacensem*, recently edited by Dom Lambot (*Analecta Mediaevalia Namurcensia*, 2 Namur and Lille, 1951), raises an issue foreign to *De Statu Animae*, that of the universal soul, and seems to owe nothing to Claudianus Mamertus. The history of controversies about the soul during the Carolingian period is still rather badly known.

51 Alcuin, *Liber de Animae Ratione*, *Patrologia Latina*, vol. 110, column 639 ff; Rabanus Maurus, *Tractatus de Anima*, *Patrologia Latina*, vol. 110, column 1109 ff; Pseudo Hincmar, *De Diversa Animae Ratione*, *Patrologia Latina*, vol. 125, column 929 ff. The later treatise, which might be a reply to Ratramnus, insists on the localized character of the soul. Obviously the author did not follow Claudianus, who vigorously defends the opposite thesis.

52 Mico, *Poem 102*, 1, p. 355 Traube (Monumenta Germaniae Historica, *Poetae Latini Aevi Carolini*, vol. 3); cf. Max Manitius, *Geschichte der lateinischen Literatur des Mittelalters*, vol. I, p. 471 (Munich: C. H. Beck, 1911–1931).

53 Álvaro de Córdoba, *Epistula* 5, 7, *Patrologia Latina*, vol. 121, column 453 c: "Et iterum Claudianus contra opuscula suppresso nomine Cassiani tres libros de animae invisibilitate vel incorporalitate confecit, in quibus Beatum Hilarium probe sentientem ausus reprehendere fuit. In quibus subtili satis et pene incomprehensibili assertione, dialectica arte et ingenio elaborata, id multis et pene superfluis conatibus per geometricas formulas est nisus ostendere: quod

person of Samson of Córdoba, whose *Apologeticus* abounds in quotations taken from *De Statu Animae*.[54]

In the twelfth century Claudianus lost none of his popularity. Abelard salutes in him the friend of philosophy and quotes him in several works.[55] Abelard's disciples do the same.[56] One of them, Bérenger, will even regard Claudianus's attitude toward authors, specifically Hilary of Poitiers, some of whose ideas he reproves, as a model of the benevolence he demands in turn for his Master.[57] In a letter to Peter of Celle, Nicholas of Clairvaux, St.

nullus Catholicorum eum fecisse poterit conlaudare. Illud videlicet quod natura animae incorporea et invisibili etiam a Deo asseruit esse." On Mamertus et Álvaro of Córdoba, and on Álvaro's predilection for the Marseilles group, see José Madoz, *Liciniano de Cartagena*, pp. 49–53.

54 Samson of Córdoba, *Apologeticus*, II, ch. 8, pp. 411–415 in Enrique Flórez, *España Sagrada*, vol. 11 (Madrid: 1753, reprinted Hispanic Society of America, 1918): ch. 12, p. 429; ch. 20 p. 468; ch. 23, p. 486; ch. 25, p. 499; ch. 26, p. 503; ch. 27, p. 513; etc. Cf. Max Manitius, *Geschichte der lateinischen Literatur des Mittelalters*, vol. I, p. 430.

55 Abelard, *Introductio ad Theologiam*, I, ch. 15, *Patrologia Latina*, vol. 178, column 1005, C-D = *De Statu Animae*, p. 101, 4 ff; I, ch. 17, column 1012 D – 1013 A = *De Statu Animae* p. 122, 6 ff; *Sic et Non* , 44, *Patrologia Latina*, vol. 178, column 1407 D –1408 C = *De Statu Animae* p. 51, 22 ff, p. 53, 12 ff, p. 57, 13 ff; p. 58 11 ff; *Sic et Non*, 80, column 1464 D – 1465 A = *De Statu Animae*, p. 134, 17; *Sic et Non*, 81, column 1466 A = *De Statu Animae*, p. 161, 15 ff, and p. 158, 16. The first two references are noted by Manitius, *Geschichte der lateinischen Literatur des Mittelalters,* vol. 3, p. 112, who mistakenly remits to Abelard's commentary on the *Epistle to the Romans* (vol. 2, p. 349 Cousin).

56 E.g., Hermannus, *Epitome Theologiae Christianae*, ch. 11, *Patrologia Latina*, vol. 178, column 1712 D = *De Statu Animae*, p. 101, 4 ff.

57 Berenger, *Apologia pro Abelardo*, *Patrologia Latina*, vol. 178, column 1868 D ff: "His et aliis delinitus exemplis, Petrum, si errore sauciatus esset, jumento tuo deberes imponere, et sic ad stabulum universalis fidei revocare. Plures Catholici quaedam culpanda dixerunt, nec tamen ob id haereticorum collegio sunt ascripti. Duo dixit Hilarius erroris expugnator, propugnator ecclesiae, in quibus eum non audit sobrietas ecclesiae, primum, quod Christum nil in passione doloris sensisse asseruit. Contra quem sententiam Claudianus presbyter Lugdunensis, vir Christianissimus, et tam subtilis ad disputandum quam artifex ad loquendum, sic personat: 'Si Christus nil in passione sensit doloris, non vere passus est. . . .' Secundum, quod nullum incorporeum dixit esse creatum. 'Nec igitur,' inquit Claudianus, 'anima, cum sit incorporea, est creata. Quod

Bernard's secretary, praises Claudianus lavishly and compares him to St. Augustine in mental acuteness and extent of knowledge.[58] William of Saint Thierry dips freely into *De Statu Animae*, without acknowledging his debt to the author.[59] A beautiful passage *of De Cognitione Humanae Conditionis* about communication with God is taken almost word for word from Claudianus.[60]

si creata non est, nec creatura Dei est.' Sed non ob hoc, ut ait idem Claudianus, scientia doctoris perdit meritum confessoris, quia Ecclesia bono filio indulsit quod humana opinio minus caute disputavit. Procul dubio sic haec Petrus dixisset, eum esse lapidandum rigoris tui severitas sanxisset."

58 The text is found in the letters of Peter of Celle, *Epistula 52, Patrologia Latina*, vol. 202, column 499: "Habeo mecum plenam subtilitatis et sanctitatis animam et quae fronte non nomine solo praemineat, quam in auctoritatis arcem, tam scholasticorum, quam ecclesiasticorum chorus evexit. Claudianus hic est, qui totam Christianam, Romanam, Atticam bibliothecam in viridi aevo secretissimis institutionibus ebibens (cf. Sidonius, (*Letters*, vol. II, Book IV, 11, 6, p. 108 Loeb Library, cited above, note 10) et ingenii acumine et operis mole nobis alterum redidit Augustinum." This last phrase applies to Claudianus the praise that Claudianus had addressed to St. Augustine (cf. *De Statu Animae*, p. 133, 10). Peter of Celle, *Epistula 52,* column 501 B = *De Statu Animae*, p. 188, 5; column 503 A = *De Statu Animae*, p. 92, 25 etc. The best manuscript of *De Statu Animae* that we possess today, Codex Lipsiensis-Paulinus 286, which was the basis for Engelbrecht's editions, once belonged to Celle's monastery and was still there in the fifteenth century; cf. L. Schmid, "Beiträge zur Geschichte der wissenschaftlichen Studien in sächsischen Klöstern, in *Neues Archiv sächsische Geschichte und Alterumskunde*, vol. 18, 1897, pp. 227 and 255.

59 William of Saint Thierry, *De Natura Corporis et Animae*, II, *Patrologia Latina*, vol. 180, column 710 C – 711 A = *De Statu Animae*, p. 71, 20 – p. 73, 12; column 720 A = *De Statu Animae*, p. 82, 16 ff; column 720 B = *De Statu Animae*, p. 86, 7 ff; column 721 B –D = *De Statu Animae*, p. 95, 18 - p. 97, 5. Other passages from this work, which does not seem to be very personal, go back to Cassiodorus, *De Anima* (e. g. column 707) and to St. Augustine, *De Quantitate Animae* (e. g. column 723 A).

60 *Meditationes Piisimae de Cognitione Humanae Conditionis*, ch. 5, number 15, *Patrologia Latina*, vol. 184, column 495 (from Gilson's translation to French): "You are present to me, and I am present to you in prayer. If I say 'present,' do not be surprised. Because if you love me, I am as present to you, as you are to yourself. All that you are substantially, I am. Every rational soul is, indeed, God's image. So, he who seeks God's image in himself looks for his neighbor as well as himself, and when someone finds it in himself for having sought it there, it is such as it is in every man who knows it . . If then you see

Alain of Lille invokes Claudianus's testimony both in his *Theologicae Regulae* and in his *Contra Haereticos*.[61] Finally, if admirers of Claudianus exist, they will hear with delight that a century later he occupies a prominent place in Richard of Fournival's ideal library – *Biblionomia* – near Aristotle, with certain fourth and fifth century Fathers and the medieval Arab philosophers.[62] It would be

yourself, you see me, me who am none other than you; and if you love the image of God, it is me as image of God that you love; and in my turn, loving God, I love you. Thus seeking the same thing, we are always present one to another in God, in whom we love each other." Cf. *De Statu Animae*, p. 97, 21 ff. See Henri de Lubac, *Catholicism A Study of Dogma in Relation to the Corporate Destiny of Mankind*, trans. Lancelot Sheppard (New York: New American Library, 1964), pp. 33–34. Tradition has attributed this anonymous work to St. Bernard and to Hugh of St. Victor; cf. F. Cavallera, "Apocryphes attribués a saint Bernard," in *Dictionnaire de spiritualité ascétique et mystque*, vol. 1, column 1500. The ideas developed in this text are quite usual in the Cistercian school, as is evident by glancing through Étienne Gilson, *The Mystical Theology of St. Bernard* (London: Sheed and Ward, 1940, 1955 A.C. Downes trans.).

61 Alain of Lille, *Theologicae Regulae*, Regula XXI, *Patrologia Latina*, vol. 210, column 631 B: "Unde Claudius Claudianus in libro *De Anima*: Dicitur enim Deus poenitere, non passionis affectu, sed consequentis effectu." Cf. *De Statu Animae*, p. 30, 4, *Contra Haereticos libri quatuor*, Patrologia Latina, vol. 210, column 322 C: "Tamen Claudianus in libro *De Anima* de Hilario ait, 'Pictaviensis Hilarius inter nobilissima disputationum suarum genera in duobus errasse dicitur: in uno, quod dixit animam esse ex aliquo; et in hoc quod asseruit Christum nullum dolorem sensisse in patibulo; qui quamvis in vita sustinuerit reprehensionis stylum, in morte tamen poenitentia ductus, non sensit detrimenta meritorum.'" Cf. *De Statu Animae*, p. 134, 18 ff; Manitius, *Geschicte der lateinischen Literatur des Mittelalters*, vol. 3, p. 801. Regarding these references, see M. Baumgartner, "Die Philosophie des Alanus de Insulis," in *Beiträge zur Geschichte der Philosophie des Mittelalters, Texte und Untersuchungen*, II, 4, Münster: 1896, p. 67. – It would seem to be Bishop Mamertus and not Claudianus, as is sometimes said (e.g., Manitius, vol. 3, p. 142), to whom verses 265 ff of Peter de Cluny's poem *Adversus Calumniatores*, address themselves, *Patrologia Latina*, vol. 189, column 1010 A:

Ergo Viennensem jam nunc modulare Mamertum,
Quove docente pius servet ovile lupus.
Praesul Lugdunum patiens qui rexit aquosam,
Quanti sit meriti te referente patet."

62 Cf. Leopold Delisle, *Le cabinet des manuscrits de la Bibliothèque nationale*, vol. 2 (Paris, 1874; reprinted Amsterdam: Gérard van Heusden, 1969), p. 518.

easy to add to this list. We have only assembled scattered remarks of others, adding to them the results of almost chance soundings in medieval authors.

From the thirteenth century on, Claudianus's stock is clearly down. He is still known, as a certain number of manuscripts from this period prove. Alexander of Hales[63] and Albert the Great[64] allude to him. But he no longer has authority in advanced intellectual circles. An event of major importance is responsible for this recoil from neo-Platonic psychology: the penetration of Aristotle's works in the West. A more glorious name would have been necessary to withstand this impulse. Only an accident, such as the disguise that benefited Nemesius's *De Natura Hominis*, which was read in the Middle Ages under the name of Gregory of Nyssa, might have saved *De Statu Animae* from oblivion. When it begins to be read again in the Renaissance, it will be as a work from the past no longer felt to be binding. Then Claudianus only interests the learned[65] and historians of church literature. Yet, unlike the majority of their modern heirs, in the seventeenth and eighteenth centuries scholars were still committed to forming a personal notion of the author.[66]

63 Alexander of Hales, *Glossa in Quattuor Libros Sententiarum*, II, Distinctio 3, number 12 (Quaracchi edition, vol. 2, p. 29): "Mensura inest animae secundum suam capacitatem, numerus autem secundum virium aut virtutum numerositatem, pondus secundum appetitum in id quod tendit. Et omnis anima rationalis tribus individuis, memoria, consilio, voluntate subsistit, quibus capax est mensurae, numeri et ponderis." This text is a free rendering of *De Statu Animae*, p. 115, 16 ff, and a literal quotation of *De Statu Animae*, p. 119, 11 ff. It is likewise to be found in the author's *Summa Theologica*, II, 1 (Quaracchi edition, vol. 2, p. 39).

64 Albert the Great, In II P. *Summae Theologicae*, Tractatus 1, Quaestio 3, p. 53 Borgnet (*Beati Alberti Magni Opera Omnia*, vol. 32, Paris, 1895). The authenticity of this work, which is again attributed to St. Albert, was formerly disputed. The text in question is identical to that of Alexander and does not suppose direct knowledge of *De Statu Animae*. Cf. W. Schmid, "Claudianus Mamertus," in *Reallexicon für Antike und Christentum*, vol. 3, column 177.

65 E.g., Gaudenzi Paganino, *Quaestiones Exegeticae et Eruditae*, Vatican Library, Latin 1545, folio 23. For the legend that Descartes had been inspired by Claudianus Mamertus, cf. René Marie de La Broise, *Mamerti Claudiani Vita Eiusque Doctrina de Natura Hominis* (Paris: Retaux-Bray, 1890), p. 190 ff.

66 Egelbrecht's edition of *De Statu Animae* (*Corpus Scriptorum Ecclesiasticorum Latinorum*, vol. 11, 1885) was corrected, mostly on matters of detail, by Einar Harleman, *De Claudiano Mamerto Gallicae Latinitatis Scriptore Quaestiones*

II

Mamertus is certainly not a very original thinker, but it seems worthwhile to us to examine him as a representative of philosophical culture in Gaul at the end of the fifth century. *De Statu Animae* presents itself from the start as an explicitly philosophical work, perhaps the only one in the West during the whole period that goes from the death of St. Augustine to the first works of Boethius.[67] Furthermore, it deals with a major philosophical question, the human soul. If we wish to have an idea of the subject's importance, especially from the imperial period on, we can reflect on the impressive number of *De Anima* which antiquity has bequeathed to us under the form of treatises or commentaries; or we may simply reread the few lines that serve as an introduction to the third treatise of the fourth *Ennead*, a genuine exhortation, where Plotinus tries to shed light on the central place of the soul in the totality of neo-Platonic thought. The soul is the point of departure for the study of the intelligible world from which it comes and of the sensible world which comes from it. Furthermore, to study its nature is to obey the divine precept directing us to know ourselves. Before devoting ourselves to investigating things, studying the nature of the soul is to make the effort, as is only proper, to know that being which undertakes these investigations.[68] Did not St. Augustine himself as

(Uppsala: A. B. Lundquist Habokhandeln, 1938), *Pars Prima: Critica*. See also Harleman's supplemenatry remarks in *Eranos*, 1939, pp. 64–68. In René-Marie de La Broise, *Mamerti Claudiani Vita Eiusque doctrina de Natura Hominis*, p. V ff, gives a more complete list of earlier editions than Engelbrecht, p. v ff. Furthermore, let us note three manuscripts which have not yet been collated: Douai 749 (*excerpta*) thirteenth century; Avranche 226 (*excerpta*), twelfth-thirteenth century; Barberini Lat. 1952, fifteenth century, folios 1–55.

67 About seventy-five years, from 430 to the beginning of the sixth century. According to Pierre-Paul Courcelle, *Les lettres grecques en Occident*, pp. 257–304, there are grounds to believe that Boethius had the singular good fortune to study under Ammonius at Alexandria, the only center of importance in this late period. In large part this would explain the until now mysterious presence of a thinker of this stature in the West during the sixth century.

68 Plotinus, *The Enneads* IV, 3, 1, 4 ff (pp. 32–35, Plotinus IV, Loeb Classical Library, Cambridge, Mass.: Harvard University Press, 1984), p. 262 ff. The last two reasons are also invoked by Cassiodorus, *De Anima*, *Patrologia Latina*, vol.

a good neo-Platonist reduce all of philosophy to the study of God and of the soul?[69]

Let us add that Claudianus's contemporaries regarded him as a philosopher, specifically a Platonist, and that in their eyes he even passed for the wisest philosopher of his time in Gaul.[70] Sidonius, who was in a position to know, notes that he was distinguished from other Platonists only by his

70, column 1279 C ff: "Cum jam suscepti operis optato fine gauderem, meque duodecim voluminibus jactatum quietis portus exciperet, ubi etsi non laudatus, certe liberatus adveneram, amicorum me suave collegium in salum rursus cogitationis expressit, postulans ut aliqua quae tam in libris sacris quam in saecularibus abstrusa compereram de animae substantia, vel de ejus virtutibus, aperirem, cui datum est tam ingentium rerum secreta reserare; addens *nimis ineptum esse si eam, per quam plura cognoscimus, quasi a nobis alienam ignorare patiamur, dum ad omnia sit utile nosse qua sapimus* . . . Proinde nota esse debet quae sibi praesto est: quia tunc magis ante se ponitur cum subtilius de ipsa tractatur. *Nam dum a sapientibus praeceptum sit ut cognoscamus nosmetipsos, quemadmodum sustineri potest si nos habemus incognitos?* Cupimus enim nosse planetarum caelo contrarios cursus, signorum consentaneum lapsum," etc. It will be noted that these considerations are found also in the opening lines of Alexander of Aphrodisias, *De Anima*.

69 St. Augustine, *De Ordine*, II, 18, 47: "philosophiae disciplina . . . cujus duplex quaestio est, una de anima, altera de Deo." Cf. *Contra Academicos*, III, 17, 38 (Augustine, *Against the Academicians* and *The Teacher*, trans. & intro. Peter King, Indianapolis: Hackett, 1995, p. 88) : the soul is a subject "on behalf of which true philosophy is ever vigilant."

70 Sidonius, *Letters*, vol. II, Book V, 2,1, (p. 172, Loeb Library): "peritissimus Christianorum philosophus, et quorumlibet primus eruditorum." Cf. *Letters*, vol. II, Book IV, 11, 1 (p.102, Loeb Library edition): "hominum aevi, loci, populi sui ingeniosissimus." Even allowing for the exaggeration, these praises have indicative value. Claudianus had a taste for philosophy, Sidonius, *ibidem*: "indesinenter salva religione philosopharetur." Sidonius adds that he liked nothing so much as being able, on occasion of an apparently unsolvable difficulty, to display the treasures of his science, *Letters*, vol. II, Book IV, 11 2, (pp. 102–104, Loeb Classical Library): "Deus bone, quid erat illud, quoties ad eum [sola] consultationis gratia conveniebamus! Quam ille omnibus statum totum non dubitans, non fastidiens aperiebat, voluptuosissimum reputans, si forte aborta quarumpiam quaestionum insolubilitate labyrinthica scientiae suae thesauri eventilarentur."

dress and Christian faith.[71] So, if we want to understand him as he understood himself and obtain his testimony on the culture of this epoch, we must study him precisely in this perspective.

However, in order to grasp the work's significance it is important to determine precisely the sense of the expression "philosophical culture." To what reality did the terms "philosophy" and "philosopher" correspond in the thought of these late neo-Platonists? Plato returned too often to the question of "philosophical culture" for any of those authors who professed

71 Sidonius, *Letters*, vol. II, Book IV, 11, 2, (p. 102, Loeb Classical Library): "a collegio tamen Conplatonicorum solo habitu ac fide dissociabatur." In the end Sidonius's brief allusions teach us little about the other Gallo-Roman "philosophers" of the period. At least they permit us to get a glimpse of the milieu in which *De Statu Animae* was elaborated. Among these *Conplatonici* Sidonius also mentions Polemius, Poem XIV, 1 *Ad Polemium*, (vol. 1, p. 218 Loeb Library): "[philosophiae] talis ordo est, ut sine plurimis novis verbis, quae praefata pace reliquorum eloquentum specialiter tibi et Conplatonicis tuis nota sunt, nugae ipsae non valuerint expediri." Cf. *Epithalmium*, Poem XV, lines 118–119 (*Poems. Letters*, vol. I, p. 234 Loeb Classical Library): "Hoc in gymnasio Polemi sapientia vitam excolit adjunctamque suo fovet ipsa Platoni." One of them, Eutropius, was a disciple of Plotinus, *Letters*, vol. II, Book III, 6, 2, (p. 26, Loeb Library): "quibus [incitamentis] vix potuistis adduci, ut praefecturam philosophiae jungeretis, cum vos consectanei vestri Plotini dogmatibus inhaerentes ad profundum intempestivae quietis otium Platonicorum palaestra rapuisset, cujus disciplinae tunc fore adstruxi liberam professionem, cum nil familiae debuisses." Several of these literary men, like Probus, another correspondent of Sidonius, had studied philosophy under Eusebius who. among other things, taught Aristotle's *Categories*, *Letters*, vol. II, Book IV, 1, 3, (p. 62, Loeb Classical Library): "et vere inter Eusebianos Lares talium te quaedam moneta susceperat disciplinarum, cujus philosophica incude formatus nunc varias nobis rerum sermonumque rationes, ipso etiam qui docuerat probante pandebas, nunc ut Platon discipulus jam prope potior Socrate, sic jam tu sub Eusebio nostro inter Aristotelicas categorias artifex dialecticus atticissabas." On this subject see Pierre-Paul Courcelle, *Les lettres grecques*, pp. 240–246. This list, quite modest all things considered, emphasizes by contrast the continuity and quality of the Christian tradition in Orient, represented by a whole series of otherwise illustrious names in this same period, from Nemesius to Maximus the Confessor, passing through Eneus of Gaza, Cyril of Alexandria, Theodoret of Cyrrhus, pseudo-Dionysios, and John Philoponus.

philosophy themselves, claiming to be his legitimate heirs, whether they read his works assiduously or knew them indirectly, not to have formed an exact notion of their calling.

By "philosophical culture" we must understand here not only the more or less extensive baggage of knowledge that any writer might possess in philosophical subjects, but a certain way of envisaging and resolving problems, a genuine aptitude for philosophizing. Evidently, even the mind least gifted for speculation, however uncultivated, can acquire at school, by personal reading or in some other manner, notions for occasional use which we can consider philosophical culture. No one will go so far as to say that person has a philosophical mind. We here conceive of something deeper, one of the irreducible forms of intellectual activity, which of course supposes a certain knowledge of the philosophers, but above all a properly scientific cast of mind and method.

The ancients often saw the distinctive mark of this culture in the technicality, or to say it differently in that μικρολογία, which Aristotle claims is the condition of science.[72] Certain distinctions, with which no one can dispense, are necessary to understand even the simplest truths. With even more reason, these distinctions will be necessary when there are much more difficult questions, like those of the spirituality of the soul or of the divine nature. Faced with the difficulties which these problems pose for the mind, the philosopher, thus defined, is one who feels the need to recur to an appropriate technique, to a more or less elaborate dialectical apparatus, which alone is capable of adequately resolving the difficulties. How could a reality with many changing contours be grasped in its profound truth and in its nuances without a rigorous method adapted to its object, without that *philosophicae artis subtilissima disputatio*, of which Claudianus often speaks, and which permits one who has been able to master it, to perceive the hidden reasons of beings beyond appearances?[73] This is what it takes for the mind to arrive at the "origins

72 Aristotle, *Metaphysica* II, 3, 995 a 10.

73 *De Statu Animae*, p. 191, 7; cf. p. 121, 7: "multa . . . subtilissimaque disputatio;" p. 23, 13: "subtilissima rerum indagatrix ratio;" p. 120, 20: "nexuosissimae quaestionum minutiae," and *passim*.

of the primitive things" and to be able to penetrate "into their most secret recesses."[74]

This sort of move does not go naturally without some subtlety, without a sort of philosophical mannerism which some minds, disinclined by nature to enjoy this exactness, will only too easily see as verbiage and logomachy and which they will judge unworthy of a truly liberal education.[75] Also it is not astonishing that by itself this ideal has polarized all intellectual aspirations, and that another parallel and no less imperious voice makes itself heard almost from the outset.

To better grasp the originality of the philosophical culture that we have just described, let us confront it with another type of education, literary culture, which can be said to have shared antiquity with the former.[76] We find

74 *De Statu Animae*, p. 183, 8: "Et quoniam . . . nimis late patet in huiusce quaestionibus inmensum, principalium origines conplexa causarum inspici porro intus usque nequaquam potest, nisi duplicis creaturam substantiae . . . secernas . . ." Claudianus bubbles over in admiration for the Greeks, who were the first to discover this method, *Epistula ad Sapaudum*, p. 203, 7: "hinc nonnulli mortalis naturam paene supergressi mortalium extentis usquequaque excellentium ingeniorum viribus infatigabilibus curis rerum abdita rimantes repositas *originalium primordiorum causas* et temporaliter fluentium substantiarum praefixos aevo terminos indage et arte *conplexi* non modo intra mundanum, sed supercaeleste etiam introiere secretum." *De Statu Animae*, 23, 13: "causarum secreta;" p. 129, 16: "abstrusae rerum rationes;" p. 165, 12: "rationis abditum."

75 Cf. Aristotle, *Metaphysics* II, 3, 995 a (Books I-IX, trans. Hugh Tredennick, Loeb Classical Library, Cambridge, Mass.: Harvard University Press, 1980, p. 95): "Again, some require exactness in everything, while others are annoyed by it, either because they cannot follow the reasoning or because of its pettiness; for there is something about exactness [μικρολογία] which seems to some people to be mean [i.e. unworthy of well brought up people ἀνελεύθερον], no less in an argument than in a business transaction." In the same passage Aristotle notes that some minds only allow one to speak with mathematical rigor (μαθεματικο̂ς); others demand that we use examples (παραδειγματικως), or that we refer to poets. Cf. *Nicomachean Ethics*, I, 3, 1094 b 12, where not requiring more rigor in each subject than it allows is presented as one of the traits of an educated man (πεπαιδευμένος).

76 On this question, see Werner Jaeger, *Paideia, The Ideals of Greek Culture*, vol. 3, Oxford, 1947 pp. 46 ff. Henri-Irenée Marrou, *Saint Augustin et la fin de la*

Sidonius and his smart set contrasting with Claudianus, like him a friend of the Muses but more worldly and less austere. How is the second ideal distinguished from the first? At its extreme, which is not far from being reached in the period that interests us, it will take eloquence as its supreme value and subordinate even philosophy to it, and will take the orator as the most complete type of intellectual. Without necessarily ceasing to care for truth, it is uneasy with the heaviness and interminable twists of the philosopher, is more comfortable in the realm of the plausible and of opinion, is more careful of immediate effectiveness and speaking well. At this level, we can say that it represents the rights of the honest cultivated man who is put off both by ignorance and the invasive technicality of strictly philosophical disciplines; he represents the independence of the spirit of subtlety, better adapted to the multiple circumstances and the thousand contingencies of daily life, or simply the healthy reaction of good sense before the lack of flexibility which dialectic reveals in certain thinkers. The position assumed by the sophist Hippias at the end of a famous conversation, whether or not justified *in toto*, illustrates this different point of view well:

> . . . but that other ability is beautiful and of great worth, the ability to produce a discourse well and beautifully in a court of law or a council-house or before any other public body before which the discourse may be delivered, to convince the audience and to carry off, not the smallest, but the greatest of prizes, the salvation of oneself, one's property and one's friends. For these things, therefore, one must strive, renouncing the petty arguments, that one may not, by busying oneself, as at present, with mere talk and nonsense, appear to be a fool. (*Greater Hippias*, 304 AB, p. 421, *Cratylus, Parmenides, Greater Hippias, Lesser Hippias*, trans. by H. N. Fowler, Loeb Classical Library, Cambridge, Mass.: Harvard University Press, 1970.)

culture antique, pp. 169 ff; *A History of Education in Antiquity* (New York: Sheed and Ward, 1956), pp. 61, 89, 95, and *passim*. The classical description of the history of the quarrel between the two types of culture is still that of Hans Friedrich August von Arnim, *Leben und Werke des Dio von Prusa* (Berlin, Weidmannos, 1898), pp. 4–114.

Let us not believe that these reproaches involve only the struggle between Socrates and the first sophists. We find the same grievances under multiple forms and in very different contexts up to the end of antiquity. There are few ideas so ambiguous but whose history is more instructive for us than this notion of μικρολογία, which can mean scientific rigor and precision, detailed application and care for exactness, but which also very often means pettiness of spirit, trifles, congenital incapacity to grasp a question as a whole, or a nitpicking obsession of old men who always repeat themselves.[77] For the Fathers (who in general knew Aristotle very badly),

77 Isocrates, *Against the Sophists*, XIII, 8 (p. 167 *Isocrates II*, with English trans. by George Norlin, Cambridge, Mass.: Harvard University Press, Loeb Classical Library, 1929, 1992): ". . . when he [the layman] puts all these things together and observes that those who follow their judgements [δόξα] are more consistent and more successful than those who profess to have exact knowledge [επιστήμη], then he has, I think, good reason to contemn such studies and regard them as stuff and nonsense [μικρολογίαν] and not as a true discipline of the soul." *Antidosis*, 262 (*Isocrates II*, p. 331): "Most men see in such studies [astronomy, geometry] nothing but empty talk and hair-splitting [μικρολογία]; for none of these disciplines has any useful applications either to private or to public affairs; nay, thy are not even remembered for any length of time after they are learned because they do not attend us through life nor do they lend aid in what we do, but are wholly divorced from our necessities." *Lysias*, 33 (*Olympic Discourse*), 3: "For me, I did not come to discourse on vain objects [μικρολογησόμενος] nor dispute about words. I judge that this task is good for frivolous sophists who have great need to earn their living, but the duty of a good citizen, of a person of merit, is to make others clear about their essential duties . . .." Plato, *Republic*, VI, 486 a 1, G. M. A. Grube trans., revised by C. D. C. Reeves (Indianapolis: Hackett, 1992), p. 159: "And of course there's also this to consider when you are judging whether a nature is philosophical or not. – What's that? – If it is at all slavish (ἀνελευθερία), you should not overlook that fact, for pettiness (σμικρολογία) is altogether incompatible with a soul that is always reaching out to grasp everything both divine and human as a whole." Cf. *Republic* 558 b and *Symposium*, 210 d 4. Xenophon, *Hellenica*, 3, 1, 26; Dionysios of Halicarnassus, 6, 1015, 10; 1041, 13; Heraclides, *apud* Atheneus, 525 a; Plutarch, *Moralia*, 171 B; 730 B; 822 A; Plotinus, *Enneads* I, 4, 7 etc. The word μικρολογία is rendered in Latin as *minutiloquium*, Tertullian, *De Anima* 6, 7: "Sed nemo unquam cunctanti de exitu animae mulsam aquam de eloquio Platonis infudit aut micas de minutiloquio Aristotelis infersit." See Waszink's commentary, p. 141; Ireneus *Adversus Haereses*, 2, 18, 4: "et minuti-

Aristotle himself is usually only a subtle dialectician, μικρολόγος, someone who obstinately splits hairs in four and discusses all sorts of real or imaginary problems as far as the eye can see.[78]

Recently, the validity of this distinction between philosophical and oratorical culture has been challenged and its applicability denied for ancient and medieval literary history. Unable to quote everything, let us emphasize at least a few characteristic passages of this brilliant brief, whose literary qualities one must admire:

> This amounts to disputing a simplistic distinction, convenient but disastrous, which historians often make between literary or oratorical culture and philosophical culture. The rivalry between these two types of culture is possibly "one of the most constant traits of ancient civilization." Let us grant that, without insisting on the naively rationalistic character of such a distinction apparent above all at the stage of Aelius Aristides, though it is said to have held from the beginning! . . . Ancient social pressure naturally favored such a differentiation at school and in the forum, like the contemporary and unlike the medieval situation. But the need for *antagonism* is not apparent, and still less the existence of two opposed currents which would perpetuate themselves in history. Sometimes leading minds cultivate wisdom and rhetoric with equal felicity, and the two then lend each other mutual and fertile support.[79]

In support of his thesis, the author cites the example of St. Bernard, who presents "a system where thought and word (Scripture still more than

loquium, et subtilitatem circa quaestiones, cum sit Aristotelicum, inferre fidei conantur." In the same sense we find the expressions *subtililoquentia* peculiar to Tertullian, *Adversus Marcion*, 5, 19, and *subtililoquium*, Ireneus, *Adversus Haereses*, 3, 14, 4; Cf. Waszink, *Tertulliani De Anima*.

78 E.g., Gregory Nazianzus, *Orations*, 27, 10: Ἀριστοτέλους τὴν μικρολόγου πρόνοιαν. For other references, cf. Jan Hendrik Waszink, "Aristoteles," in *Reallexicon für Antike und Christentum*, vol. 1, columns 657–664. Regarding Aristotle and the Fathers, André-Jean Festugière, *L'idéal religieux des grecs et l'Evangile*, Paris: Gabalda, 1932, pp. 222–263.

79 F. Chatillon, "Dracontiana," in *Revue du Moyen Age latin*, vol. 8, pp. 209–211.

rhetoric) are so closely associated that they cannot be separated," and suggests that perhaps "with the spread of the religion of the Word, the old antagonism of word and thought has reached its end." But that is only a concession of which he soon repents: "But perhaps also this antagonism always had only illusory existence. Was not Plato an artisan of style and a philosopher? Hesiod a poet and theologian?"

The problem could not be posed in more vigorous terms, nor could it be better indicated, without trying, how a solution may appropriately be sought. It did not escape the ancients that the relations between philosophy and rhetoric constitute a real problem, difficult to resolve at least in practice. If we want to be fair, we need to first see what they themselves thought. We might be modest enough to ask whether they still have something to teach us in this respect. Evidently, in the narrow framework we have chosen, it is not appropriate to treat this problem in all its extension. In order to dispel any ambiguity it is still necessary to indicate the solution at which we have arrived on our own, and insist henceforth on certain notions to which we will appeal in the course of this account.

What must be kept in mind in this whole debate is that the author of the *Dialogues* had too high a concept of philosophy to believe it was accessible to all comers.[80] As the great classical tradition conceived the philosophical ideal, it will never be achieved by more than a small number of exceptionally endowed minds who have received in their youth an education suitable to make their natural gifts flower. Nothing is more foreign to the ancient mentality than the ideas which have surfaced on the subject at a relatively recent date and which find their logical outcome in our modern ideal of *philosophy for the millions*. To forget or ignore this fundamental principle exposes us to the constant risk of being blind to the practical consequences that ancient authors drew from it and which deprive us at the same time of an essential aspect of their thought.

80 On the small number of true philosophers see Plato, *Republic*, 491 a ff (Book VI, p. 164 Grube trans.): "I suppose that everyone could agree that only a few natures possess all the qualities that we just now said were essential to becoming a complete philosopher and that seldom occur naturally among human beings." Cf. *Republic*, 503 b 7 ff, and *passim*; *Timaeus*, 51 e; *Letter VII*, 344 a; *Philebus*, 52: *Laws*, 890 d-e etc. On discerning philosophical natures, see especially *Letter* VII, 340 b ff.

Once this is recognized, the goal of Socratic rhetoric will of course be partly to select candidates for high culture, to discover true philosophers and lead them in gradual stages to the knowledge of intelligible being.[81] In proposing to young minds ideas or more precisely opinions that common folk accept without careful scrutiny, and by inviting them to pose difficulties (ἀπορεῖν) on the subject, they are led to awareness of themselves and to think philosophically. This is all familiar and presents no special difficulty.

What is less often said but is no less important, is that this rhetoric has the parallel goal of screening out those whom nature has not predisposed for such a high pursuit. Not everyone is equally able to understand the highest truths. It would be a serious mistake to try to expose certain persons to a teaching whose consequences would only be disastrous for them. Plato returned too often to the dangers of dialectic and the ravages that it could make[82] for us to be able to conclude that he is categorically opposed to a kind of literary culture, which by definition is more within the reach of average intelligences. In this sense, it is not exaggeration to say that rhetoric tries not to reveal but to *hide* certain truths from those whose insufficient preparation or lack of intelligence renders them unsuited to comprehend them usefully.

Hence Plato's constant recourse to what we could call the oblique path, the posture of hiding his thought while allowing it to be glimpsed, the perpetual invitation to go beyond what is purely and simply expressed and to seek its secret themes.[83] Like it or not, there is a *de facto* esotericism inherent

81 E. g. *Republic*, 390 a 8 ff.

82 Abuse of dialectic, Plato, *Republic*, 539 b ff; *Phaedo*, 89 c 8 ff; *Philebus*, 15 d and 17 a (distinction between true and false dialectic), etc.

83 No doubt the most formal text is *Letter* 7, 34 b 7 ff, especially e 1 (Plato, *Timaeus, Critias, Cleitophon, Menexenus, Epistles*, trans. R. G. Bury (Loeb Classical Library, Cambridge, Mass.: Harvard University Press, 1961), p. 533: "But were I to undertake this task it would not, as I think, prove a good thing for men, save for some few who are able to discover the truth themselves with but little instruction; for as to the rest, some it would most unseasonably fill with a mistaken contempt, and others with an overweening and empty aspiration, as though they had learnt some sublime mysteries." Hence the superiority of oral teaching to written teaching, which always contains much that is entertainment, *Phaedrus*, 277 e 5, and is unable to teach the truth appropriately, *Phaedrus* 276, c 9. That is why a serious person can never be completely serious when he is forced to write, *Phaedrus* 276 d 1. Thus it is not astonishing that

in any culture to which Plato more than anyone was sensitive. But from here spring possible misinterpretations, often fertile ones, moreover, in attempting to establish his thought on some precise point. Notably this occurs when we try to discover his attitude about rhetoric. We should not conclude too quickly on the strength of certain apparently unilateral expressions in *Gorgias* or *Phaedrus* that there is hostility on principle. Far from being opposed to rhetoric, the philosopher himself will be obliged to recur to it whenever he does not direct himself to his peers, which is to say most of the time. The insistence with which Plato always preached about the need for higher culture does not imply at all the rejection of the other kind. On the contrary, it postulates it, although higher culture remains the only judge in the last analysis. His position in this respect is much closer to Aristotle and even Isocrates than might be believed.[84] Is not the very art of the *Dialogues*, perhaps the most subtle and nuanced that we know, already proof of this? Some might say that this art testifies against the author; it seems much more natural and in conformity to his own principles to believe it testifies for him!

Accordingly, we do not misrepresent Plato's thought by affirming that there are two well determined types of culture, although one is subordinate to the other, each of which fulfills different and complementary functions in

true discourses are not written discourses, but are "written in a soul," *Phaedrus* 278, a 3 p. 573, Plato, *Euthyphro, Apology, Crito, Phaedo, Phadedrus,* trans. H. N. Fowler, Loeb Classical Library, Cambridge, Mass.: Harvard University Press, 1966). In these and many other similar texts we must see the origin of the pedagogical method that St. Augustine attributes to the Academicians, whose antecedents are sought in sometimes very obscure writers (e.g., Diocles of Cnidus, Émile Bréhier, *The History of Philosophy. The Hellenistic and Roman Age*, trans. Wade Baskin (Chicago: The University of Chicago Press, 1965) , p. 117. Cf. , *Contra Academicos*, II, 10, 24 (Augustine, *Against the Academicians* and *The Teacher*, p. 47): "I don't think the Academicians were the sort of men who didn't know how to give names to things. On the contrary, these terms seem to have been chosen to conceal their view from the unintelligent and to reveal it to the more penetrating."

84 Considering the feebleness of the evidence on which it rests, the rivalry between Isocrates and Plato has assumed gigantic proportions in the mind of certain modern historians like Werner Jaeger. See on this matter the prudent reservation of Henri-Irenée Marrou, *A History of Education in Antiquity*, p. 376, note 2.

its own sphere. Our Mamertus seems to have understood just this when he congratulates Cicero for having required that the orator have genuine knowledge of his subjects and contrasts Cicero's attitude with that of Lysias, in whose regard he takes up the criticisms of the *Phaedrus*.[85] It matters little that Claudianus, who had not read Plato himself, only knew this passage indirectly. The mere fact that he depends on an intermediary attests to the persistence of a tradition, which is already interesting. A closer examination of *De Oratore* would no doubt reveal that, despite his efforts to bridge the gulf which had opened between rhetoric and philosophy, the Ciceronian ideal remained quite utopian.[86] His encyclopedic program is usually unachievable in practice because of the amount of knowledge it requires, but it is easy to perceive in it the seeds of an on-going dissension whose existence Cicero deplores bitterly.[87] At least he avoids making the rhetorician as such the philosopher's adversary.

85 *De Statu Animae*, p. 123, 3 ff: "Et quid hominibus fiat, quos cum eo usque inscitia teneat, ut indoctos se esse nesciant, scientiae nihilo minus privilegium sibi vindicant, dumque in inperitas aures verborum puerilium spumas exspuunt, uno eodemque mendacio semet scientiae fallunt, alios docendo decipiunt Lysiae similes, quem Platon idem cassa rerum verba fundentem in *Phaedro* eatenus increpat, ut esse deterius adstruat gnarum verborum, ignarum esse causarum, quam nescientem rerum verba nescire, potius arbitrans inperitum silentium loquaci inperitia." Λυσίου ψόγος to which this text alludes is found in *Phaedrus*, 235 a ff. A quote from *De Oratore* I, VI, 20 follows: "For it is from knowledge that oratory must derive its beauty and fullness, and unless there is such knowledge, well grounded and apprehended by the speaker, there must be something almost empty and childish in the utterance." (*De Oratore* Books I and II, trans. E. W. Sutton, into. H. Rackham, Loeb Classical Library, Cambridge, Mass.: Harvard University Press, 1942, 1988, p. 23).

86 For a survey of the question and recent bibliography, see the report by Pierre Boyancé, "Le platonisme à Rome, Platon et Cicéron," published in the *Acts of the Guillaume Budé Association Tours and Poitiers Congress*, Paris, 1954, p. 206 ff.

87 Cicero, *De Oratore* III, 16, 61. Cicero makes Socrates and the sophists responsible for this "the undoubtedly absurd and unprofitable and reprehensible severance between the tongue and the brain, leading us to have one set of professors to teach us to think and another to teach us to speak." (*De Oratore* Book III, *De Fato*, *Paradoxa Stoicorum*, *De Partitione Oratoria*, trans. H. Rackham, Loeb Classical Library, Cambridge, Mass.: Harvard University Press, 1942, 1992, p. 49)

We know well that the sophist is the real adversary. It is curious to see how Mamertus's reproaches against Faustus of Riez are often little more than what Plato directed to the sophists of his time. Here again, we must take stock of certain nuances. In one respect the sophist, far from being the special enemy, is simply that adult who, against what we ought be able to expect, has never attained intellectual maturity. He is the inoffensive and slightly ridiculous being who has not gone beyond the youthful stage of ideas and who should be treated accordingly. Viewed from this angle, sophistry is anything but a false philosophy. It is rather a particular mode of the absence of philosophy in someone who might be hoped to be better informed. Rather than severity, humor is called for. Nothing is more amusing than to see Claudianus, who boasts of having stripped away the ideas of youthful years as he grew, treat his adversary as a child and attack his notions about the nature of the soul as inanities that the adversary would have done better to abandon as Claudianus has.[88]

Unfortunately that *enfant terrible* is also a dangerous child, who adds formidable productivity to ignorance of which he is not even aware, and who furthermore assumes superficial wisdom the better to induce others to error.[89] In this situation it would have behooved him more to be ignorant simultaneously of the truth and the art of speaking, which at least would have kept him from harming others.[90] We see this type of person scorn the teaching of the learned, prefer the body of words to the "soul of reason"[91]

88 *De Statu Animae*, p. 156, 10: "hanc me opinionem qua corpus creditur anima cum puerilibus annis evasisse delectat." Cf. p. 175, 11: "Non ergo hisce frivolis solliciteris amplius;" p. 176, 6: "aliquorumpiam qui interimunt animas garrientibus nugis . . . lentamur;" p. 21, 7: "nam plerique mortalium aut per sensus corporis corporearum rerum haustis imaginibus veluti quibusdam rerum umbris obtutu mentis inluduntur, aut tenellis adhuc infantiae quondam suae persuasionibus in senectute puerascunt."

89 *De Statu Animae*, p. 106, 22: "magna videlicet rerum ignoratio et scientiae mira praesumptio;" Cf. p. 105, 22; p. 182, 15; p. 157, 3 and *passim*.

90 *De Statu Animae*, p. 123, 9.

91 *De Statu Animae*, p. 21, 11: "si qua illis dicendi copia est, neglectis rerum causis rationis animam spernunt et verborum corpora diligunt, cumque duplici ad veritatem veniatur via, ut aut praeiudicatae auctoritati credulitate subdamur aut ad scientiam ratiocinatione tendamus, nihil quod vel auctoritas iubeat vel ratio suadeat potissimum dicentes spreta paucitate doctorum inludunt inperitos, quae maxima turba est."

and, what is still more inexcusable, obstinately defend his point of view even when he is convinced of an error.[92] Praise, rather than the truth of the cause he sustains, attracts him.[93] When accused he defends himself by appealing to reason against authority as often as to authority against reason.[94] "If it occurs," Claudianus says, "that those whom they pursue with unjust hatred advance some truth of common interest, they hasten to affirm the contrary, even when they are of that opinion. Thus in their relations with persons whom they have decided to detest, they feel no scruple to make light of truth, so implacable and profoundly rooted is their hatred."[95] Besides, their aversion makes them more harmful to themselves than to their adversaries, and it ends by constituting a real danger for faith.[96] Such are the ideas that the first chapter of *De Statu Animae* develops and which set the work's general tone from the start.

Summing up, we might say that it is really between philosophy and sophistic, which can be defined by contrast to philosophy, that there is profound and irreducible antagonism, not between philosophy and its irreplaceable complement, rhetoric, or more generally if one prefers, literary culture. The ancients often spoke of formation of the spirit, what we usually call *culture* today (παιδεία and earlier, μουσική). Needless to say, they established a distinction between the several intellectual disciplines. But from there it is a great leap to speak of "cultures," as if there were several equally self-governing ones, to which each person could adhere according to his tastes and temperament, which would ultimately make for an

92 *De Statu Animae*, p. 23, 4.

93 *De Statu Animae*, p. 22, 4: "Laudantur namque falsoque laudantur et credunt, quo mentis sanitas maxime periclitatur."

94 *De Statu Animae*, p. 23, 11: "Si auctoritatem quaeras, subiciunt istius modi causarum secreta adiri nequaquam posse, nisi subtilissima rerum indagatrice ratione. Si eandem in articulo reposcas, adiciunt auctoritati potius oportere concedi, neque naufragiosum propter argumentorum latentes quosdam scopulos pelagus disputationis intrare. Ita auctoritate rationem, ut auctoritatem obiectu rationis eludunt et utroque horum ad id utuntur, ut neutro utantur."

95 *De Statu Animae*, p. 22, 7.

96 *De Statu Animae*, p. 23, 1: "Illud multo maximum longeque periculosius crimen est, quod catholicae sanitati opiniones inimicas stulte concipiunt, vane proferunt, superbe adstruunt, cum temeritate scribunt, cum intentione defendunt . . ."

involuntary option. Even the existence of ideals like καλοκἀγαθία and φιλοσοφία, those two great ways of conceiving happiness, however distinctly they may be characterized, has never allowed the best minds to erect an independent rhetoric in opposition to philosophy, free of any norms other than those of aesthetics or immediate efficacy.

The very term *philosophy* formerly did not have the specialized, technical sense we give it today, but rather, in conformity to its etymology, designated the pursuit of truth under all its forms, and invites us to see things this way. The educated person, πεπαιδευμένος, is not one who has sacrificed rhetoric to philosophy. In the full sense of the word, he is one who possesses the formation normally acquired during youth; this formation encompasses all the disciplines, which often presuppose each other and which were situated as the foundation of ancient education. The formation ended precisely with the study of philosophy properly speaking, or at least that part of philosophy deemed accessible to a young man of that age. The example of St. Augustine, the authentic heir of a tradition that remained very much alive, is there to remind us that true philosophy is the last to scorn poetry or rhetoric, and that though it has attained knowledge of the highest causes, it cannot help but recur to a literary culture each time it comes to grips with the reality of the innumerable shadows in the midst of which it lives.[97]

Once the legitimacy and rights of this "literary culture" are acknowledged, we should affirm with no less insistence the need for higher principles that judge in the last instance its value and utility and, if necessary, prevent it from degenerating into a minor art and into vain exhibition, or from sterilizing itself by becoming a mere mental game, a refinement of intellectuals who have lost all contact with reality. Nothing is further from the purest classical ideal than the notion of autonomous literature, absolutely free to dispose of itself, which our period has often tried to recognize.

Nevertheless, it is very necessary to confess that the connection which basically unites the different disciplines and assures their continuity, does

97 The question of order of the disciplines, of moral dispositions, and of natural gifts required of the students, as well as of the pace to follow in the pursuit of the highest truths, is the particular object of the whole last part of *De Ordine*; cf. II, 7, 24 ff.

not always appear with the same clarity in practice and that it often is weakened to the point of becoming almost indiscernible. Our fifth century offers remarkable examples of minds whose literary ideal was affirmed at the cost of philosophy, whose influence was felt less and less. Can one imagine more purely literary work, which by contrast emphasizes more one of the essential aspects of *De Statu Animae,* than that of a Sidonius Apollinaris or a Ruricius?

* * *

This distinction between philosophical and literary culture is only one side of our problem. It considers one difference situated on the level of culture, considered in both kinds of culture as a good. We must not forget that for a Christian in antiquity, abstracting from the particular form that this culture adopts, it is not something taken for granted. Before opting for one or the other type, supposing that such an option is necessary, we must ask ourselves about the value of profane culture as such. Thus, our philosophical culture will be opposed more radically by the absence or rejection of any culture, whose consequences we will soon be able to observe in the work of Faustus of Riez.

The Fathers soon realized that the philosophers' beloved dialectic was a double-edged sword; that it could be put at the service of error and of truth and that it constituted a real danger because of this fact. Gregory of Nyssa notes this judiciously at the moment when he prepares to examine the opinions of the pagans on the nature of the soul:

> We all know with certainty that the refinements of dialectic serve with equal facility to refute truth and denounce error. Hence it occurs that we often hold truth itself suspect when it is pursued by that art, in the persuasion that the skill which is employed there is capable of deceiving our judgment, and that perhaps it has been turned away from the true.[98]

98 Gregory of Nyssa, *De Anima et Resurrectione*, *Patrologia Graeca*, vol. 46, column 49 B. See similar remarks by St. Augustine on the subject of rhetoric this time in *De Doctrina Christiana*, (*On Christian Doctrine*, Book IV, ch. 2, 3, *Select Li-*

If such was the attitude of a Christian man of letters, himself a philosopher, we can imagine without difficulty the extent to which a monk who had renounced profane culture in the name of a purely religious ideal had to feel disarmed faced with that formidable dialectic which discussed every question with unbending rigor, ἡ τεχνικῶς περὶ τούων διαλβοῦσα.[99] Was not this reticence justified with regard to a skill (δεινότης) that could only have the goal of tending a subtle snare to his good faith? Let us simply recall the distrust that the sage inspired in the time of Socrates and Plato, whom the abundance of texts lets us judge better than anyone else. What was more natural for common people, who understood nothing about the true nature of wisdom, than to confuse the philosopher with the sophist and to suspect him of weaving some unknown plot against the city? But here it was a question of protecting an infinitely more precious good than the freedom of citizens, namely revealed faith. Aristotle already noted that this skill, δεινότης, had no component linked to virtue, ἀρετή, and that according to the good or bad use made of it, it was worthy of praise or blame.[100] Simple good sense invited prudence.

brary of the Nicene and Post-Nicene Fathers of the Christian Church, edited by Philip Schaff, vol. II, *St. Augustine's City of God* and *Christian Doctrine*, Grand Rapids, Michigan, William B. Eerdmans, 1983, p. 575): "Now the art of rhetoric being available for the enforcing either of truth or falsehood, who will dare to say that truth in the person of its defenders is to take its stand unarmed against falsehood? . . . Since, then, the faculty of eloquence is available for both sides, and is of very great service in the enforcing either of wrong or right, why do not good men study to engage it on the side of truth, when bad men use it to obtain the triumph of wicked and worthless causes, and to further injustice and error?"

99 Gregory of Nyssa, *De Anima et Resurrectione*, vol. 46, column 49 B.

100 Aristotle, *Nicomachean Ethics*, VI, 12, 1144 a 25. The word δεινός is often used pejoratively since Herodotus, e.g., V, 23: "Oh King, what have you done permitting a sharp and skillful (δεινός) Greek to found a city in Thrace." It frequently refers to oratorical skill; Ulysses is characterized as a "skillful and sly speechifier" in Sophocles, *Philoctetus*, 440. Cf. *Oedipus at Colonna*, 806. See also Isocrates, *To Demonicus*, 4, (p. 7, *Isocrates I*, with English trans. By George Norlin, Loeb Classical Library, Cambridge Mass.: Harvard University Press, 1928, 1991), where oratorical skill is contrasted with honorable morals. Cf. Plato *Theaetetus*, 177 a 4, *Euthyphro*, 3 c, etc. In the Aristotelian classification

This attitude of reticence ultimately explains that the doctrine of the incorporeality of the soul did not manage to impose itself everywhere despite the patronage of illustrious names like Ambrose and Augustine. As much as, or more than, a defense of the spirituality of the soul, *De Statu Animae* is a brief in favor of philosophy. Moreover, Mamertus is not unaware of the reproaches to which he exposes himself. Otherwise, would he have felt the need to justify himself and explain why he needed three books to refute what his adversary had said in a page? Error is not like truth. A word suffices to deny what someone has spent much time and effort to establish.[101] Precisely those notions which must be used to refute an error are often more difficult than the allegedly clear propositions in whose name they are rejected; it is accordingly easier to turn them into manifestly strange talk. That there has been a multitude of distinctions as useless as they are annoying, is completely evident. Besides, they are often the same ones. But it does not follow that all distinctions are such, and the truth sometimes demands that someone assume the laborious task of defending it.[102]

δεινότης is the quality of practical intelligence which permits one to discover rapidly the best way of attaining any goal. For the order of acting, it is what ἀγχίνοια (liveliness of mind, aptitude for discovering the middle term, cf. *Posterior Analytics*, I, 33, 89 b 10) is in the speculative order. In Latin the two concepts are rendered by the word *sollertia*; cf. Cicero, *De Officiis*, I, 44, 157: "agendi cogitandique sollertia."

101 *De Statu Animae*, 188, 4: "Quid tu igitur, ait aliquis, per haec tria volumina adversum brevem paginam spatiatus es si verbum verbo satis? Sed non id negotii est fallaciam struere, quod destruere. Neget quispiam sphaeram esse mundum: uno quidem hoc ille verbo negaverit, sed non id uno item verbo vel Timaeus adstruxerit. Proinde quidquid illud ampliuscule sermocinati sumus, non modo sola falsi confutatio, sed veri etiam coegit adstructio."

102 *De Statu Animae*, p. 18, 9: "haud temere suscepissem [hoc negotium], nisi id spernere periculosius quam agere laboriosius iudicassem, quamquam pro virili parte meum quoque fuerit vel non admonitum, prout posse subest, adserere veritatem." God permits error so that by contrast, thanks to the discussions it provokes, the truth may shine forth more, p. 100, 8: "omnia scilicet dinoscuntur melius contrariorum comparatione. Sic equidem lumen tenebris, sic vita morti, sic veritas falsitati conposita plus delectat. Oportuit igitur hasce distantias pro suis qualitatibus sibi compotes sortiri patronos, ut nec falsi lateret defensor nec veri vacaret adsertor itaque fieret, ut nec ille magis noceret oc-

In all these reflections, we must see an authentic defense of philosophy, a clear-cut stand taken against a tendency that manifests itself loudly, thanks especially to the increasing influence of Marseilles, and that was firmly opposed to any intervention of profane reason in the elaboration of an authentically Christian ideal. We can grasp the nature of this tendency better, and, by contrast, the originality of the efforts of Claudianus, by more closely examining the doctrine of his adversary, Faustus of Riez.

cultus, nec otiosus iste torperet." Cf. p. 181, 6. To these reflections he adds a psychological reason: it is that we cherish more what we have conquered with more effort; cf. p. 101, 4: "Et quoniam mortalium generi natura datum est ut abstrusa fortius quaerat, ut negata magis ambiat, ut tardius adepta plus diligat, eo flagrantius ametur veritas quo vel diutius desideratur vel laboriosius quaeritur vel tardius invenitur, hinc factum est ut philosophi quoque excellentibus ingeniis, multimodis doctrinis, pugnantibus sententiis, longis saeculis de eadem veritate quaerentes ab usque Pythagora Italico vel Ionico Thalete semper exstiterint, qui dissidentibus aliis vel in parte operis aliquid dignum tanta indage sentirent."

Chapter Two
Opponents of the Spirituality of the Soul: Faustus of Riez

> For if many things had not been known to me about [the nature of] a body, the form which is in a body, time and place and motion, which points are keenly discussed, by reason of their bearing on this very question, I indeed would have been inclined to give the palm of victory to those who say that the soul [life principle] is a body. St. Augustine, *De Quantitate Animae*, XXXI, line 63 (p. 173 Francis Tourscher trans., Philadelphia: Peter Reilly, 1933)

I

Faustus of Riez's *Letter 3* provoked *De Statu Animae*. The letter answers questions put to Faustus by a priest whose identity[1] we do not know. The letter's particular significance resides in its being the only more or less thorough exposition of the doctrine of the corporeality of the soul extant from this period. Understandably, writers unfamiliar with profane thought or at odds with it for different reasons were not attracted by purely philosophical subjects and presented their thought only in occasional writings, aimed at refuting ideas they judged erroneous or harmful to faith. Surprising as it may be to us, erroneous or harmful is what the doctrine of the spirituality of the soul seemed to them.

Let us recall that only the third part of this letter, which is by far the longest and differs clearly from the others in tone,[2] deals with the question

1 Lovers of hypotheses can turn to those of Bernard Rehling, *De Fausti Reiensis Epistula Tertia*, Münster, Westphalia, 1898, p. 36.

2 Louis Sébastien Lenain de Tillemont, *Mémoires pour servir à l'histoire ecclésiastique des six premières siècles*, vol. 16, (Paris: 1712), p. 419 already noted this:

of the soul. The first two are devoted respectively to the problems of the Trinity against the Arians and of divine impassibility. The letter circulated without the author's name and seems to have provoked the curiosity which quite frequently attaches to disputed questions.[3] Mamertus tells rather picturesquely how one day he surprised a group reading the letter and was then invited to become acquainted with its content.[4]

Did Claudianus know who was the author of the anonymous letter he undertook to refute? It is legitimate to think so, although he constantly pretends not to know.[5] Rehling noted several exact parallels between *Letter 3* and Faustus's *De Spiritu Sancto*.[6] But these similarities, as valuable as they may be, prove simply that Mamertus might have guessed who wrote the letter in question, supposing he had read *De Spiritu Sancto* and had thought to crosscheck. Given the fame of the bishop of Riez, the hypothesis is eminently plausible, but we would like to see it confirmed by positive evidence.

"He [Faustus] is believed to have written the letter less to defend his own perceptions than to combat a work given or published by someone he disliked." In the manuscripts, only the third part of Faustus's letter, unquestionably added by a copyist toward the end of the seventh century, figures at the head of *De Statu Animae*. Cf. Bernard Rehling, *De Fausti Reiensis Epistula Tertia,* p. 5.

3 *De Statu Animae*, p. 19, 6: "Sane opusculum illud sine auctore proditum et usquequaque proquiritatum, toto agmine sui in acie eductum et conserta nobis manu congressum viceritne cesseritne, tu, potissime disertorum [he refers to Sidonius], ferto sententiam."

4 *De Statu Animae*, p. 24, 3 ff: "Nuper etenim offendi in quosdam, qui chartulam quandam oppido studiose lectitabant, et quia mortalium generi mos est, novi operis agnitione pellecti ad id percipiendum sedulo animo intenderant: hoc idem mihi ac si cognitu necessarium ultro ingerentibus inspicere plane non abnui."

5 *De Statu Animae*, p. 189, 4: "Tu nunc, *quisque ille es* adversus cuius scripta nosmet iniuria scriptorum tuorum dicere conpulit," etc. Cf. p. 20, 10: "nec conflictum metuit adversantis ignoti;" p. 24, 16: "percontor de nomine: nec responso nec scripto proditur;" p. 26, 1: "Enimvero illud, quod ista pagina propalatur eiusdemque auctor occultatur, evidens facit indicium eandem scilicet, a quo sit conposita, fuisse damnatam. Nemo enim studet occultari, nisi qui formidat agnosci. Ego tamen satis mirari nequeo, cur in eodem vitandae noxae non fuerit studium, in quo subprimendi nominis potuit esse iudicium."

6 Bernard Rehling, *De Fausti Reiensis Epistula Tertia*, pp. 44–45.

Perhaps this evidence exists. In fact at the beginning of *De Statu Animae*, we find a passage to which nothing corresponds in *Letter 3*, and which can be thought to refer directly to another work by Faustus of Riez. In it Mamertus combats at length an idea which he explicitly attributes to his adversary, but which that adversary developed, it seems, only in *De Spiritu Sancto*. It is here, and not in *Letter 3*, that considerations about the double nature of Christ figure importantly, invoked by the author to resolve the problem of divine impassibility:

De Spiritu Sancto, II, 4, p. 140, 3 (c, *Corpus Scriptorum Latinorum Ecclesiasticorum*, vol. 21)	*De Statu Animae*, p. 34, 9
Si requiras, quomodo potuerit inviolabilis pati et incomprehensibilis *crucifigi personae unitas* facit, ut, quod homo pertulit, Deus pertulisse credatur.[7]	. . . quoniam Christus homo verus et Deus verus ex duplici substantia una persona et Deus homo et homo Deus est, idem gloriae dominus et non sit *crucifixus* pro *inviolabili* divinitate et *crucifixus sit in homine pro unitate personae*.

The text of St. Paul on which this passage from *De Spiritu Sancto* is based (I *Corinthians*, 2: 8: *numquam Dominum gloriae crucifixissent*), whose interpretation Mamertus strongly contests, appears nowhere in *Letter 3*. It is possible, moreover, that the author of *De Statu Animae* wanted to deliberately and rather subtly take the position opposite to what his adversary affirmed, when instead of reverting here, like him, to the Biblical analogy of head and body to explain the union of two natures in Christ, he appeals, as we will show below, to the neo-Platonic doctrine of the union of soul and body:

7 The text quoted from Claudianus can also be compared to this other passage from Faustus, *Epistula* 7, p. 203, 8 Engelbrecht (*Corpus Scriptorum Ecclesiasticorum Latinorum*, vol. 21): "nos unum eundemque *verum hominem* et *verum Deum* intellegimus . . . nos *verum hominem* et *verum Deum* nullo modo ambigimus confitendum."

De Spiritu Sancto, II, 4, p. 139, 15	*De Statu Animae*, p. 37, 4
De duabus rationabilibus diversisque substantiis, praesertim de Dei et hominis, de creatoris et creaturae una fieri non potest, de duabus vero personis una fieri potest, sicut legimus caput et corpus, Christum et ecclesiam unam tenere personam . . .	. . . sicut anima et corpus ex diversa substantia unus est homo, ita Deus et homo ex diversa substantia unus est Christus.

Thus, at the same time that these comparisons let us suppose that Mamertus knows very well with whom he is dealing, they also permit us to perceive the intellectual distance which separates the two thinkers.

Furthermore, we will not be surprised that Claudianus pretended to be unaware of his adversary's name. Faustus's rank and especially the aggressive tone that this controversy had taken from the beginning made silence preferable in this respect. It was certainly not very flattering for a distinguished teacher within the Church in Gaul to have a simple priest label him *patentium causarum doctor ignarus*.[8] It is perhaps for a similar reason that the Bishop of Riez chose not to reveal his identity when he sustained the thesis of the corporeality of the soul at the risk of displeasing some of his confrères. There is a literary problem at this point which has not been completely clarified, but which we must at least mention here. It would certainly be interesting to study this tactic of anonymity for its own sake some day, a tactic used deliberately, and often successfully, in every epoch and especially in antiquity.[9]

8 *De Statu Animae*, p. 42, 2; cf. *De Statu Animae*, p. 51, 20: "Sic . . . pronuntias tamquam potissimorum scitus, qui minimorum probaris ignarus." These words do not lack audacity, given the increasingly pronounced distance between different ranks of the ecclesiastical hierarchy in this period, especially in the West. Claudianus does not show any concern to spare his adversary. See the ironic remarks, p. 41, 9; 52, 4 ff; 47 10: "quo me vertam acutissimi et doctissimi disputatoris ingenio et arte praeventus," etc. He will not be accused of placing persons above truth.

9 The reason which immediately comes to mind is that the author does not care to send his possible readers back to a work where they would find the thesis

II

What strikes us above all when we go through Faustus of Riez's *Letter 3* is the importance given to scriptural data, and inversely, how little space is given to purely rational elements in a question that we have come to consider typically philosophical. Such elements are patently reduced to a few very simple notions from which it would be difficult to reconstruct a solid, clearly articulated pattern of thought. To establish the soul's materiality, the author is content to say that the soul has been inserted into our members and connected to our entrails, in such a way that it is quantitative and therefore corporeal just like the body in which it is enclosed.[10] True, our thought seems to be freed of spatial conditions at first sight. We are transported by thought to faraway places; it reunites us with absent friends. But that does not imply that the soul has left the body. It does not suffice to imagine St. Peter or St. Paul for our soul to join them in heaven, or to evoke the punishments of the bad rich man to experience his torments ourselves.[11] Indeed, one thing is the essence of the soul and another the operations which come from it.[12] The latter can vary, deal with different objects; properly speaking, they do not leave the soul. The proof is that we can represent a faraway city like Jerusalem or Alexandria in our imagination, but in no way do we know how to describe these places and tell what is

he works to refute presented in a favorable light. But let us also imagine the massive impact which the attacks produce, in Arnobius, for example, directed against several adversaries, none of whom is named, and which bring to bear the weight of different criticisms all at the same time, so to speak.

10 *Epistula 3*, p. 175, 7 Engelbrecht (*Corpus Scriptorum Ecclesiasticorum Latinorum*, vol. 21): "Quomodo non localis est, quae inserta membris et inligata visceribus solis motibus vaga conditione substantiae tenetur inclusa?" Cf. *Epistula 5*, p. 188, 24: "Deus non alicubi est; quod alicubi est continetur loco; quod continetur loco corpus est."

11 *Epistula 3,* p. 175, 18: "cum verbi gratia Petri aut Pauli speciem intra mentis arcana depingit, numquid statim intimas paradisi sedes, ubi eos esse novimus, penetravit? Aut cum sibi in corde divitis illius flammas ex lectione proposuit, numquid iam ad tormentorum eius loca ac vivis inaccessibilia inferi profunda descendit?"

12 *Epistula 3*, p.175, 11: "primum intellegendum est, quod aliud sit animae status, aliud is, qui de anima nascitur, cogitationis affectus."

happening in them, or even say what an absent friend is doing at the moment we think about him.[13] The soul abandons the body only once, at the moment of death, which clearly shows that it resides in it and is enclosed in it as in a place.[14]

Rather than belonging to a determined system like Tertullian's Stoicism, these considerations pertain to simple common sense, or to what is believed to be such, and to very ordinary experience. Furthermore, it is easy to see the unfinished character of the demonstration. To demolish the thesis he attacks, Faustus proposes to show that, whatever the defenders of the spirituality of the soul say, the soul is subject to place and quantity.[15] In fact, he does not breathe a word about this latter category, and Claudianus, who attaches particular importance to it, will take pleasure in reproaching him with having found nothing to say about his subject.[16]

This letter is interesting less for the ideas we discover there than for what it reveals to us indirectly. Thanks to it, we can form an idea of what a mind unbiased and free of any philosophical "prejudice" might derive

13 *Epistula 3*, p. 176, 9: "Cum ergo anima Alexandriam vel Hierosolymam cogitavit, si vere illic tota sui praesentia, ut arbitraris, interfuit, referat nobis situs locorum, vultus hominum, motus actusque populorum . . . Ecce per haec praesentis temporis momenta vos cogito et animo reminiscente vos video et quorum <reminiscor> omnimodis, quid geratis et utrum quieti an lectioni vel orationi vacetis, ignoro."

14 *Epistula 3*, p. 177, 2: "unde hoc magis ipsa conscientiis nostris ratio loquitur, quod unaquaeque anima aut multiplicia cogitata rerum causis intra se concepta parturiat aut sensus suos velut quaedam officia aut ministeria diversis necessitatibus occupanda dispergat, ipsa vero in conclavi corporis sui semel de eo exitura requiescat."

15 *Epistula 3*, p. 175, 2: "Nunc vero in hoc tractatus nostri status habita discussione pendebit, ut si nec localis sit nec quantitati subiaceat, esse eam [sc. animam] haud dubie incorpoream concedamus. Si vero demonstraro eam quantitate determinari locovi concludi, consequenter eam etiam corpore contineri nec ipse iam dubites."

16 *De Statu Animae*, p. 182, 17: "de quanitate autem cur te disputaturum spoponderis nihilque de eadem disserueris, non possum oblivionis fuisse dicere, cum satis constet ne nomen eius nisi ex memoria potuisse proferri. Illud ergo magis credendum est te non noluisse aut oblitum fuisse dicere, sed nihil quod diceres invenisse. Quid itidem congruit vel in disputationem vocare reticenda vel reticere proposita?"

from Scripture on the problem of the soul. It is all too evident that we most often read the Bible with thoughts and concerns that have become familiar after many centuries of speculation, but which, as such, remain foreign to the sacred text. We unhesitatingly introduce notions which, to say the least, are not explicitly found in Scripture. An imaginative effort is now necessary to represent the almost insurmountable difficulties encountered by minds preoccupied above all with knowing, not what men taught, but what God had revealed on the subject.

Now Scripture is disconcertingly reticent on this point. It nowhere says in so many words that the human soul is spiritual. One thing stands out clearly in the *Epistle to the Colossians* and some parallel texts in St. Paul: God created all beings, visible and invisible.[17] But on what authority should we conclude that invisible creatures are in fact incorporeal? Thinkers were not lacking who remarked that invisibility and incorporeality are two quite distinct notions, not at all interchangeable: *nonnulli eruditissimi patrum alia adserunt esse invisibilia, alia vero incorporea*."[18] Air is not visible; it is no less

17 St. Paul, *Ad Colossenses*, 1, 16: "quoniam in ipso condita sunt universa in caelis et in terrra, visibilia et invisibilia."

18 Faustus, *Epistula 3*, p. 173, 17 Engelbrecht. Who are those *eruditissimi patres* to whom the text remits us? In a passage of the *Liber Testimoniorum*, published by Jean-Baptiste Pitra, *Analecta sacra et classica spicilegio solesmensi*, vol. 5 (Paris and Rome: A. Juby et Roger, 1888), we read under the name of St. Augustine what is surely by one of Faustus's disciples, if not by Faustus himself: *Sicut scientissimi Graecorum doctores asserunt, quorum ita sententia est . . .* A Quote from Cassian's *Conlationes* (VII, 13) follows, which also figures in Faustus, *Letter 3* (p. 174, 8).Thus, we would therefore be tempted to believe that the doctrine in question goes back to the Fathers whose position Cassian reports in his interviews. A difficulty remains, however, that the expression *sapientissimi Graecorum* ill suits these Fathers who, with one exception, did not speak Greek (cf. Pierre-Paul Courcelle, *Les lettres grecques in Occident*, p. 213 and note 1). Perhaps it is explained by the fact that Cassian, who did not know Coptic, must have learned their teaching in Greek. One thing seems certain: that Faustus is conscious of the eastern origin of the doctrine whose interpreter he becomes. This would prove once more that there is no immediate link between Tertullian and the defenders of the corporeality of the soul in the fifth century. On the influence of Tertullian's *De Anima*, which seems to have been minimal in the West, see Jan Hendrik Waszink, *Tertulliani De Anima*, p. 48. – I owe my acquaintance with this text of the *Liber testimoniorum* to G. Mathon.

material. Nothing prevented their believing that the soul, although imperceptible, is a body, no doubt more subtle than other bodies, but of the same nature.[19]

Of course, Fathers like Origen or St. Augustine who defended the soul's incorporeality were led to acknowledge a convergence between the invisible creatures of which St. Paul spoke and the philosophers' incorporeal beings: *Nam Graeci* ἀσώματον *eam [substantiam], id est incorpoream, dixerunt, divinae vero scripturae invisibilem nominarunt*.[20] Still, the very word "incorporeal" has the air of a philosophical term, neo-Platonic to be exact,[21]

19 *Epistula 3*, p. 174, 12: "Licet enim pronuntiemus nonnullas spiritales esse naturas, ut sunt angeli, archangeli, ceteraeque virtutes, ipsa quoque anima nostra vel certe aer iste subtilis, tamen *incorporeae nullatenus aestimandae sunt*. Habent enim secundum se corpus, quo subsistunt, licet multo et inconparabiliter tenuius, quam nostra sunt corpora . . ." (Cassian, *Conlationes*, VII, 13, p. 192, 24 Petschenig, *Corpus Scriptorum Ecclesiasticorum Latinorum*, vol. 13).

20 Origen, *De Principio*, IV, 3, 15, p. 347, 11 Koetschau (*Die griechischen christlichen Schriftsteller der ersten drei Jahrhunderte*, vol. 22); Origen, *De Principio* I, 7, p. 86, 18: "Manifeste ergo in Christo et per Christum facta esse omnia et creata pronuntiat [sc. Sanctus Paulus, *Ad Colossenses*, 1, 16] sive visibilia *quae sunt corporalia*, sive invisibilia, *quae non alia arbitror quam incorporeas substantivasque virtutes*." The problem is already clearly posed in the *Prologue*, p. 14, 16: "Appelatio autem ἀσωμάτου [id est incorporei] non solum apud multos alios, verum etiam apud nostras Scripturas inusitata est et incognita." Cf. St. Augustine, *Epistula 238*, 15, p. 544, 4 Goldbacher (*Corpus Scriptorum Ecclesiasticorum Latinorum*, vol. 57): "omnis incorporea natura spiritus in Scripturis appellatur; unde non tantum Patri et Filio et Spiritui Sancto sed omni rationali creaturae et animae hoc vocabulum congruit."

21 Methodius of Olympus, *De Resurrectione*, III, 18, 1, p. 414, 20 Bonwetsch (*Die griechischen christlichen Schriftsteller*, vol. 27]: How can he [Origen] declare in the fashion of the Platonists [πλατωνικῶς] that the soul is incorporeal [ἀσώματον]? No doubt the term *neo-Platonic* (or *middle Platonic*) would be more suitable here. Indeed, even if the soul is certainly incorporeal for Plato, he himself never employs the word ἀσώματον to describe it. On this term, which only appears five times in the Dialogues (*Phaedo*, 85 e; *Philebus*, 64 b; *Sophist*, p, 246 b; and 247 c; *Statesman*, 286 a), see Heinrich Gomperz, Ἀσώματος, in *Hermès*, vol. 57, 1932, pp. 155–167. St. Augustine points to the word *incorporeum* as current among the neo-Platonists, *De Civitate Dei,* X, 29, 2: "facilius quippe in fidem recipiendum est . . . *ut verbis utar, quae in usu habetis*, incorporeum incorporeo, quam corpus incorporeo cohaerere." In Latin *incorporeum* is found

and to say that the soul is incorporeal by nature was to depart visibly from the letter of Scripture, to interpret it in function of a pagan doctrine, which there were good reasons to distrust.

Moreover, this interpretation, far from imposing itself on us, seems to directly contradict the Bible's teaching. Does not every text of Scripture which deals with the soul rather suggest that it is corporeal? How should we explain that Lazarus died and was resurrected except by the fact that at a given moment his soul left his body and later rejoined it, which only a being subject to place, and hence material, has the possibility of doing?[22] Christ himself gave up his soul on the cross, and during the whole time that his body rested in the tomb, the soul remained separated from the body.[23] Similarly, if we do not admit that the soul occupies a particular place, we will be obliged to admit that the souls of the elect and those of the damned are found in the same location; and then Scripture would lie when it speaks of the unbridgeable abyss which separates the former from the latter.[24] The same remarks apply to the angels whom the Patriarch saw in a well known vision descend from heaven on a ladder and go back up, to the archangel Gabriel, messenger of the Incarnation, to the fallen angels,

first in Aulus Gellius, *Noctes Atticae*, V, 15, 1–2 (p. 426, *The Attic Nights of Aulus Gellius I*, with trans. by John C. Rolfe Cambridge, Mass.: Harvard University Press, 1984): "Vetus atque perpetua quaestio inter nobilissimos philosophorum agitata est, corpusne sit vox an incorporeum. Hoc enim vocabulum quidam finxerunt proinde quod Graece dicitur ἀσώματον." Cf. Claudianus Mamertus, *De Statu Animae*, p. 106, 3: "Enim vero quod est et absque corpore est, incorporeum esse necesse est, quod Graeci elegantius ἀσώματον vocant."

22 *Epistula 3*, p. 177, 9: "Nonne anima Lazari morante vita intra corpus fuit, recedente autem vita de habitaculo corporis exulavit et rursum intra exanimum refusa corpus illo, unde absentaverat, evocat remeavit?"

23 *Epistula 3*, 177, 14: "Sed quid ego haec de corruptibili homine loquar, cum ille, cuius caro non vidit corruptionem, inmaculatam quidem animam possederit, sed localem, quam utique intra se habuit, quando adfixus est in patibulo, extra se procul dubio emisit, quando iacuit in sepulchro. Quomodo non est localis, quam caro continet, coniungit vita, mors separat?" The same example is in Tertullian, *De Anima*, 7, 3.

24 *Epistula 3*, p. 177, 22: "Dic, quaeso, si locales non sunt, quomodo peccatores a coetibus consortiisque iustorum vastum illud chaos tristi interiectione discriminat, ut neque hinc illuc possint accedere neque inde huc transmeare?"

hurled into hell.[25] Besides, how should we conceive that the latter are tortured by flames if they have no body?[26]

In the face of such clear affirmations, may one admit that the doctrine of the spirituality of the soul or even of the angels conforms to revealed truth, without taking liberties with the sacred text, that is to say without doing what it was thought should be avoided at all costs? At most Faustus accepts that the soul can be called incorporeal by opposition to the density of the external body and thus in a completely relative sense.[27] Others try rather clumsily to reconcile the two opposed theses by affirming that the soul considered in itself is incorporeal, while remaining corporeal in the eyes of God. Mamertus rightly sees this move as a violation of the principle of non-contradiction.[28] It is most explicit only in Arnobius the

25 *Epistula 3,* p. 178,7 "Ego autem ne angelos quidem locales esse dubitaverim, quos certum nunc in caelestibus contineri, nunc per aeris vacuum ferri, nunc ad terrena dimitti, quos sermo divinus ascendentes et descendentes in patriarchae visione describit . . . Ipse beatissimus Gabriel, qui se ante Dominum adstare testatur, cum caelorum dominum Mariae infundendum visceribus nuntiaret cumque sub dominicae oculis genetricis adsisteret, sine dubio caelo deerat, maria non supervolabat, vacua atque diffusa vasti aeris non inplebat, sed illum tantum locum, in quo aderat, occupabat."

26 *Epistula 3,* p. 180, 12: "Sed absque dubio non aliud est quam substantia corporis, ubi dominari poterit vis doloris." Tertullian reasons in the same way, *De Anima*, 7, 4. On this whole question, which provoked many controversies in antiquity, see the commentary of Waszink, *Tertulliani De Anima*, pp. 146–149.

27 Faustus, *De Spiritu Sancto*, II, 1, p. 132, 14 Engelbrecht: "Crassitudini enim exterioris hominis comparata anima incorporea dici potest." Cf. Ireneus, *Adversus Haereses*, 5, 7, 1: "sed incorporales animae quantum ad conparationem mortalium corporum." Origen, *De Principio*, prologue, (p. 15, 15 Koetschau), presents this as the opinion of simple or uneducated people, *simpliciores vel imperitiores*.

28 *De Statu Animae*, p. 176, 10 ff.: "Et cum audio dicere quospiam qui et corporeas esse volunt animas et easdem incorporeas negare non possunt, aliud ipsas animas sibi, aliud esse creatori: Deo, inquiunt, animae corporeae sunt, verum sibimet incorporeae, quod ita est ac si dicant animas et corporeas esse et incorporeas." Especially, we will retain the fundamental reason why such a position is declared unacceptable: it is because God's knowledge is the cause of creatures. Whether we consider them in themselves or in relation to God, their mode of being is always the same. Cf. p. 178, 12: "non enim ex rerum

Young, whose thought is related in some aspect to that of the group of Lérins.[29]

But there is more. Here we touch on a difficulty that, even when not always stated explicitly, still underlies this whole debate: to affirm that the soul is spiritual, is not only to express an idea seemingly contrary to revelation, it is to claim for a created being the privilege of divinity. Our authors do not cease to repeat that God alone is incorporeal: *unus Deus incorporeus*,[30] they make incorporeality the exclusive prerogative of divinity to the exclusion of all creatures, including angels. Spirituality seems to them the notion which most adequately expresses the inner essence of God, as it were, the

notitia est creatoris scientia, sed existentia rerum ex notitia creatoris." Cf. St. Augustine, *Confessiones*, XIII, 38, 53: "Nos itaque ista quae fecisti videmus, quia sunt, tu autem quia vides ea, sunt . . . tu autem ibi vidisti facta, ubi vidisti facienda." *De Civitate Dei*, XI, 10, 80 (*Corpus Christianorum*, vol. 48, p. 332).

29 Arnobius the Younger, *Conflictus cum Serapione*, II, 5, *Patrologia Latina*, vol. 53 column 276: "Omnis quaecumque invisibilia et incorporea sunt, Deo soli secundum hoc, quae ab eo creata sunt, visibilia et corporea sunt." Evidently, this is the same idea that is found in a less paradoxical expression in Faustus of Riez, *Epistula 3*, p. 180, 2: "Equidem nobis ea, quae supra nos sunt, invisibilia sunt, sed omnia illi, sicut conprehensibilia, ita et corporea sunt, qui ex nihilo fecit omnia." Cf. *Epistula 5*, p.189, 2. *De Spiritu Sancto*, II, 1, p. 132. The idea seems to go back to Tertullian in the last analysis, *De Anima*, 8, 5, "Est adeo alteri quid invisibile, alteri non, quod non ideo incorporale sit, quia non ex aequo vis valet. Sol enim corpus, siquidem ignis; sed quod aquila confideatur, neget noctua, non tamen praeiudicans aquilae."

30 Faustus of Riez, *Epistula 3*, p. 180, 23 cf. *Epistula 5*, p.188, 20; Cassian, *Conlationes*, VII, 13, p. 193, 5 Petschenig (*Corpus Scriptorum Ecclesiasticorum Latinorum*, vol. 13); Hilary according to Claudianus Mamertus, *De Statu Animae*, p. 135, 2: "nihil incorporeum creatum dixit;" *Tractatus super Psalmum 118*, 19, 8, p. 527, 8 Zingerle (*Corpus Scriptorum Ecclesiasticorum Latinorum*, vol. 22); *Commentarium in Evangelium Matthei*, V, 8, *Patrologia Latina*, vol. 9 column 946: "Nihil est quod non in substantia sua et creatione corporeum sit;" Gennadius, *Liber sive Diffinitio Ecclesiasticorum Dogmatum*, 11, p. 91 Turner (*Journal of Theological Studies*, vol. 7, 1906): "nihil incorporeum et invisibile natura credendum nisi solum Deum:" Gennadius, *Liber sive Diffinitio Ecclesiasticorum Dogmatum*, 12, p. 92: "creatura omnis corporea." Arnobius the Young, *Conflictus cum Serapione*, II, 5, *Patrologia Latina*, vol. 53, column 276; *Commentarii in Psalmos*, *Patrologia Latina*, vol. 53, column 437 B.

stuff of which he is made.[31] Indeed this was the word St. John used to define him: *Deus spiritus est* (John 4, 24), and at least apparently, it had the advantage of giving positive content to the idea we can have of divinity. Job 25, 5-6 was interpreted in the same sense: ". . . the stars are not pure in His sight. How much less man that is rottenness, and the son of man, this vile insect?"

This conception was so powerfully implanted that even an author like Origen, who declares himself completely in favor of the existence of spiritual creatures, will not dare to maintain that they could do without a material element.[32] Incorporeal and invisible, they still make use of a body: *utuntur tamen corporibus*,[33] because no creature can live without a material substance.[34] Only the Trinity is incorporeal in the most absolute sense: *ex toto incorporea est*. In all these discussions we keep finding the origin of the doctrine of universal hylomorphism, which still had many defenders in the Middle Ages, and which some authors occasionally give the impression of wanting to timidly resurrect in our time.

Of course, the term *spiritus*, πνεῦμα, had philosophical ties. For Christians who wanted to reserve it for God, it had the special disadvantage of being used by the Stoics to designate a material principle, although an infinitely subtle one. Hence the need to insist on the strictly spiritual character of this divine element. But this fact already proves that we are not dealing with a simple quarrel about words, as might have been

31 See the texts assembled by George Leonard Prestige, *God in Patristic Thought* (London: S.P.C.K., 1952) p. 17 ff. Cassiodorus, *De Anima*, *Patrologia Latina*, vol. 70, column 1282 B: "Spiritus triplici modo dicitur. Appellatur enim veraciter et proprie spiritus Deus."

32 *De Principio*, I, 6, 4, p. 85, 18 Koetschau (*Die griechischen christlichen Schriftsteller*, vol. 22): "solius Dei . . . naturae id proprium [est], ut sine materiali substantia et absque ulla corporeae adiectionis societate intellegatur existere"

33 *De Principio*, IV, 3, 15, p. 347, 18 Koetschau.

34 *De Principio*, II, 2, p. 111, 28 ff. Koetschau.

35 Augustine considers and discards the hypothesis: *Epistula 166*, 4, p. 550, 11 Goldbacher (*Corpus Scriptorum Ecclesiasticorum Latinorum*, vol. 44): "Sed ne verbi controversiam vel superfluo faciam vel merito patiar, quoniam, cum de re constat, non est opus certare de nomine, si corpus est omnis substantia vel essentia vel si quid aptius nuncupatur id, quod aliquo modo est in se ipso, cor-

thought.[35] By affirming that the soul is material, the point was not simply to emphasize its status as a real being or shed light on the eminent purity of the divine essence. They were contrasted as two branches of a clearly grasped dichotomy whose existence is posited with full knowledge of the facts.

Therefore, a Faustus of Riez is understandably wary about a doctrine like the spirituality of the soul and eager to label it impious or even diabolical. To what did the doctrine lead but to make this "worm" which is man equal to God and even a part of his substance?[36] We know the punishment Lucifer deserved for having wanted to make himself equal to God.[37] The only way for man to imitate God is to practice virtue. In the absence of ontological similarity, we will have moral similarity, which we must regard with utmost seriousness, because of what we have just said. To become through irreproachable conduct that *homo spiritualis* of whom St. Paul speaks is indeed to belong to God in a very special way. In the measure in which a mere creature can do so, it participates in "the spirit," that is to say, in the very life of God, and in recompense deserves that immortality that only He possesses by nature.[38]

pus est anima. Item si eam solam incorpoream placet appellare naturam, quae summe incommutabilis et ubique tota est, corpus est anima, quoniam tale aliquid ipsa non est."

36 *Epistula 3*, p. 179, 18 Engelbrecht: "Quae cum ita sese habeant, qui incorpoream dicunt animam, vide, in quam profundum se crimen inmergant. Iam primum cum auctor universitatis Deus omnia in numero et pondere fecisse referatur, ergo anima a materia universae creaturae excepta esse creditur . . . non iam res Dei, sed pars Dei aestimanda iungitur."

37 *Epistula 3*, p. 180, 18: "Si bene requiramus, ad quos rerum exitus animum referas, haec vel maxime diabolum credulitas ex illa beatae sedis statione devolvit et propter hoc angeli perdidit dignitatem, dum se Dei praesumit habere naturam."

38 *Epistula 5*, p. 189, 24 ff: "Sciendum ergo est, quia ideo mors ad animam non pervenit, quia in eam Dominus imaginem suam et similitudinem conlocavit. Nam sicut Deus inmortalis, misericors, iustus, patiens est, ita harum dona virtutum in faciem nostri interioris infundit." The idea that we resemble God by immortality is found just once, it seems, in St. Augustine, *De Quantitate Animae*, II, 3 (pp. 6–9 Tourscher).

III

These remarks, however, only pose the problem in very general terms. If we want to see all its ramifications, we need to determine the properties of this corporeal being more precisely than we have done so far. After the word, the thing: what is a spiritual being for an author like Faustus of Riez, and how are its attributes incompatible with those of a creature? Because if it is true that the notion of "spirit" manifests the divine nature better than any other, it ought to be more accessible, better known in some way, than the being whose essence it expresses.

Here there is still no need to recur to philosophers. God has revealed everything man needs to know; it is enough to open the Bible. Now the Bible teaches that what characterizes a spiritual being and distinguishes it most clearly from others, is the fact of not being limited either in time or space, in other words, immortality and omnipresence: *Quod temporibus non includitur nec locorum terminis cohercetur, quod soli Deo conpetit, hoc tantum incorporeum esse cognosce* (*Epistula 5*, p. 188, 19 Engelbrecht).

In what concerns immortality, there is no possible hesitation. St. Paul expressly reserves it to God: *solus habet immortalitatem*.[39] So, if the human soul is also immortal, it is not by nature, but in virtue of a free gift by God. Scripture also teaches that all beings have been created by God "in measure, number, and weight."[40] Therefore, all creatures are quantitatively extended, possess corporeal dimensions, occupy a determined point of space. By contrast, spiritual being is not circumscribed by any place and is entirely liberated from all created categories. Unlimited in every respect, it is nowhere and still it is everywhere, filling and penetrating all things at the same time, without suffering any diminution and losing nothing of its eminent perfection.[41] These prerogatives of spirit are found summarized in a manner that leaves nothing to be desired in a passage from the book of *Wisdom*, often quoted explicitly or implicitly.

39 I *Timothy*, 6, 16.

40 *Wisdom*, 11, 21. Cf. Faustus, *Epistula 3*, p, 179, 20.

41 Faustus, *De Spiritu Sancto*, II, 1, p. 131, 15: "Dic mihi, si umquam ex creaturis ullam legeris potestatem atque virtutem, quae multos simul inpleat atque possideat et, quod maius est, indeminuta atque indivisa permaneat."

> For in her [wisdom] is the spirit of understanding: holy, one, manifold, subtle, eloquent, active, undefiled, sure, sweet, loving that which is good, quick, which nothing hindereth, beneficent, gentle, kind steadfast, assured, secure, having all power, overseeing all things, and containing all spirits, intelligible, pure, subtle. For wisdom is more active than all active things: and reacheth everywhere by reason of her purity. (*Wisdom*, 7, 22-24, Douay-Confraternity version)

Our fifth-century authors are evidently not the first to make the most of this passage and the numerous texts which echo it as well in both the Old and New Testaments. The whole patristic tradition saw omnipresence as a divine attribute par excellence. The classical formula *ubique simul totus*, in all its variants, captured the essence of this doctrine of capital importance from both the theological and purely religious point of view in a striking phrase.[42] A property of divinity as such, omnipresence ought to be affirmed of the three persons of the Trinity, whose equality it guarantees in some manner.[43] It took on new vigor under the pressure of controversies with heretics, when the Fathers were led to develop the idea of the compenetration of the divine persons and their simultaneous presence in each created being.[44]

42 Cassian, *Conlationes*, VII, 13, p. 193, 7 Petschenig (*Corpus Scriptorum Ecclesiasticorum Latinorum*, vol. 13); *Contra Nestorium*, I, 5, p. 243, 25 Petschenig (*Corpus Scriptorum Ecclesiasticorum Latinorum.*, vol. 17); Ambrose, *De Spiritu Sancto*, I, 7, *Patrologia Latina*, vol. 16 column 753 B; Cassiodorus, *De Anima*, 4, *Patrologia Latina*, vol. 70, column 1289 B; Arnobius, *Adversus Nationes*, VI, 4, p. 312, 1 Marchesi: "Hoc est enim proprium deorum, conplere omnia vi sua, non partialiter uspiam sed ubique esse totos, non adesse non abesse, non cenatum ad Aethiopas pergere et post dies bis senos privatum ad domicilium redire."

43 Faustus, *De Spiritu Sancto*, II, 1, p. 131, 5 ff; Cassian, *Conlationes* VII, 13, p. 192, 16 ff; Ambrose, *De Spiritu Sancto*, I, 7, *Patrologia Latina*, vol. 16, column 753 A-B; Gennadius, *Liber sive Diffinitio Ecclesiasticorum Dogmatum*, ch. 11, p. 92 Turner (*Journal of Theological Studies*, vol. 7, 1906: "Nihil incorporeum et invisibile in natura credendum, nisi solum Deum, id est Patrem, et Filium, et Spiritum Sanctum; qui ideo recte incorporeus creditur quia ubique est, omnia inplet atque constringit."

44 Cf. George Leonard Prestige, *God in Patristic Thought*, p. 34.

Cassian and Faustus of Riez insist more particularly on the intimate character of this total and undivided presence of divinity. He who says spirit, says interiority. Since any compenetration is forbidden to bodies by reason of their opacity, what is characteristic of spirit, that is to say of God, is to insinuate itself into what is deepest in beings, to sound out the most secret corners.[45] This mode of presence is unknown in angels, and *a fortiori* in men, by the mere fact of their corporeal nature.[46] The same must be said of the actions of demons upon humans. At worst, the demons can penetrate by breaking into the interior of bodies during sleep or in a moment of fatigue, but they do not reach the soul.[47] If they manage to discover our secret thoughts, it is thanks to our own complicity.[48] God alone reads the recesses

45 Faustus, *De Spiritu Sancto*, II, 1, p. 131, 21: "Solus Deus, in quo intellegitur et Spiritus Sanctus, simplex, subtilis et purus in facturam vel angelicam vel humanam virtute incorporeae divinitatis inlabitur, quae sola sui operis penetratrix occulta humani cordis ingreditur;" Cassian, *Conlationes*, VII, 13, p. 193, 5: "Quibus manifeste colligitur nihil esse incorporeum nisi Deum solum, et idcirco ipsi tantummodo posse penetrabiles omnes spiritales atque intellectuales esse substantias, eo quod solus et totus et ubique et in omnibus sit, ita ut et cogitationes hominum et internos motus atque adyta mentis universa inspiciat atque perlustret."

46 Faustus, *De Spiritu Sancto*, II, 1, p. 131, 18: "Impossibile est, ut spiritalis et rationabilis creatura cognatae sibi naturae umquam valeat infundi. Ita res materialis materialem nescit penetrare substantiam." *De Spiritu* Sancto, II, 1, p. 132, 13: "Ita substantia animae utpote materia corporalis aliae rationabili creaturae penitus nescit infundi."

47 Faustus, *De Spiritu Sancto*, II, 1, p. 132, 23: "Nam corporis latebras intrare possunt, animae vero interiora adire non possunt." This doctrine lends itself to certain convergences with pagan demonology, which does not in general admit that demons can act on the soul other than by mediation of the body. Cf. Porphyry, *De Abstinentia*, II, 36, and the commentary of Fr. Festugière, "Un source hermétique de Porphyre: l'Egyptien du *De Abstinentia*, II 47," in *Revue des études grecques*, vol. 49, 1936, p. 592. St. Augustine shares his doubts on this subject in *Retractationes*, II, 30, where he reproaches himself for having spoken in *De Divinatione Daemonum*, "of something very mysterious with greater assurance and boldness than necessary." In this regard, we can likewise read the remarks of Jean Pépin, "Saint Augustin et le symbolisme néoplatonicien de la vêture," in *Augustinus Magister*, vol. 1, Paris, 1954, pp. 296–300.

48 Faustus, *De Spiritu Sancto*, II, 1, p. 133, 5: "Manifestum itaque est, quod penetrare animarum substantias nequeunt, quarum conscientias scire non possunt.

of hearts; alone, as creator, he acts within us, to such an extent that if he should withdraw himself, the being thus deserted would remain empty and fall into nothingness.[49]

These views, commonly received and very often repeated, do not seem to have given rise to any special difficulty. The danger was elsewhere in the pantheistic interpretation to which they might lend themselves, given their affinity to certain pagan doctrines like Stoicism. They accounted for the immanence of God in the world. By contrast did not divine transcendence turn out to be somewhat irrelevant? This danger was generally circumvented by multiplying distinctions, by insisting on the peculiar character of this divine presence, totally different from that of bodies. God is not in the world like a liquid in a recipient; on the contrary, it is He who contains the world and maintains it in the most strict dependence. Thus, He is distinguished from it and He remains superior to it in all regards.

Some saw a surer way of safeguarding this transcendence in denying the existence of any spiritual creature and making incorporeality an exclusive attribute of God. The question was thus settled peremptorily. No ambiguity was henceforth possible.

Furthermore, it could seem that this radical step had become necessary for the period we consider. More than any earlier philosophy, triumphant neo-Platonism insisted on the divinity of the soul, elevated it above all spatial and temporal categories, proclaimed, from longing, its natural spirituality and immortality. In this regard it appeared to be the culmination and most virulent expression, if one may dare to say so, of a tendency which began with the dawn of Greek philosophy.[50] We can not insist more on this point without anticipating ideas which will be developed later, but we need to acknowledge its importance already. It is this fact that gives the materialist theses of Cassian or Faustus of Riez their peculiar character and best permits us to distinguish them more clearly from those we find in a

Quod si aliquando daemonibus nosse contigerit, de proditione est coniventiae, non de potestate naturae."

49 Faustus, *De Spiritu Sancto* II, 1, p. 132, 11 ff.

50 The origins of this idea were studied by Werner Jaeger, *The Theology of the Early Greek Philosophers* (Oxford: Clarendon Press, 1947), ch. 5 p. 73 ff: "Origin of the Doctrine of the Soul's Divinity."

previous period. Above all they are – what they were not yet in Tertullian, for example – a vigorous and excessive reaction against a doctrine which could be thought to make the Christian faith risk the greatest dangers. So we come to this paradoxical realization, namely that neo-Platonism, thanks to which the doctrine of the soul's spirituality was imposed in large measure, was also responsible in an unforeseen manner for the rejection of the same idea in other circles. We could indicate many examples of this phenomenon. To speak of a case which is more familiar to us: who does not know the distortion which heresy causes, not only by the errors it propagates, but also by the necessary and sometimes unilateral hardening which it risks provoking?

* * *

However, we ought to reflect for an instant on another aspect of the question which will make us see all its impact, which is considerable: it is the constant use in this matter, during all of antiquity and roughly up to the Renaissance, of concepts borrowed from physics: notably the notions of space and place are constantly employed in these discussions. The problem is all the more interesting, since this way, generally less current today, of conceiving God as filling the universe and being in some way the space and magnetic field in which the universe subsists and moves, has curious analogies with certain theories of modern physics. Therein lies part of the interest that we witness in research on these ideas in the ancient philosophers and the Fathers of the Church. It is not up to us to criticize or to justify the method employed, but it is evident that it ought to be approached with caution. In fact it does not seem that efforts in this direction have always been felicitous. We could ask ourselves whether such parallels do not end simply by distorting one or the other term of the comparison, so different was the perspective of the ancients from that of modern physicists. Without entering into all the details, let us at least try to extricate some essential ideas.

To what clear or confused intention did the interest in these concepts of space and place respond in ancient thought? More precisely, to what did that need to express the essence of divinity with the aid of spatial notions respond? Assuming the standpoint of the ancients, we discover very quickly that what characterizes this approach from its first manifestations is not the concern to elaborate a scientific theory in the modern sense, or an effort to substitute a rationalist conception of the world for the belief in divinity; it is quite precisely the search for a first principle or, what amounts to the same thing, a "sapiential" order. Unlike Homer, Hesiod was not content to narrate about the gods; he made an effort to establish a hierarchy among them and to explain by them the genesis of the world that we have before our eyes and of which we are a part ourselves.

Now the primitive way to conceive this order is precisely an appeal to the notion of place. Perhaps it is not entirely by accident that the first real poet-theologian placed what he calls Chaos at the origin of all things.[51] The modern physicist would cut a fine figure approximating his theories to such a crude doctrine. A recent historian of science[52] writes in substance that Hesiod formed a poor idea of space; his Chaos is not even a place, it is a void! But do not such considerations let what is essential slip away? Examined in the perspective of the truth that motivates them, the still crude approximations of the author of the *Theogony* appear under an entirely different light. Hesiod's void is not our void, any more than Thales's water is like the water in our faucets. In the poet's mind, it is a reality of "admirable power," θαυμαστὴ δύναμις, just as Aristotle noted, because it exists independently of all things and nothing exists without it.[53] As much as and more than a physical principle, it is a metaphysical principle, and Aristotle, who does not mistake its true nature, will speak of it both in the *Physics* and in the *Metaphysics*.[54] Of all the concepts borrowed from concrete reality, place seems most successfully to unite the two conditions required

51 *Theogony* lines 116–118 in Hesiod, *Works & Days. Theogony*, trans. Stanley Lombardo, intro. Robert Lamberton (Indianapolis: Hackett, 1993,) p. 134 "In the beginning there was only Chaos, the Abyss, But then Gaia, the Earth, came into being, Her broad bosom the ever-firm foundation of all."

52 Max Jammer, *Concepts of Space* (Cambridge, Mass.: Harvard University Press, 1954), p. 6.

53 Aristotle, *Physics*, IV, 1, 208 b 27.

54 Aristotle, *Metaphysics*, A, 4, 984 b 23 ff. On the idea of God in the first Greek philosophers, a little known but in many ways remarkable book is R. K. Hack, *God in Greek Philosophy to the Time of Socrates*, (Princeton, NJ: Princeton University Press, 1931).

of a truly first principle: that of interiority or immanence in the world, whose existence it must explain, and that of independence or superiority in regard to the beings which follow from it. That is why, even when a more perfect idea of divinity is formed and entirely separated from matter, the analogy of place will remain fertile and will continue to be important in theological thought.

These few remarks on Hesiod would apply to many other ancient thinkers, allowing for individual peculiarities.[55] Likewise, the ideas whose dynamic we have tried to recapture will enjoy considerable diffusion later on until about the seventeenth century, thanks probably to medieval Jewish thought.[56] Seen from this vantage point, our doctrine of ubiquity as a primordial characteristic of divinity ceases to appear purely gratuitous; it is rooted in a profound need of the human mind and can be a prelude to the highest metaphysical concepts.

On the one hand, this recourse to physical concepts has the advantage of giving a very solid definite base to the idea that mankind can have about God. In his classical work on the idea of God in Patristic thought, Prestige quite aptly notes that the slight hold that the notion of divinity exercises upon our contemporaries perhaps stems from the fact that we dispense too readily with the help of these images that can easily be assimilated.[57] But it suffices to think about the Manichaean theory of a spatial God, conceived like a kind of "infinite sea" in which the world soaks like a sponge—an idea to which St. Augustine adhered to for a period of his life[58]— to see at the same time the abuse to which these images lend themselves.

55 E.g., Archytas, *apud* Simplicius, *Commentary on the Physics of Aristotle*, 108 a: "Perhaps place is the first of all beings because everything that exists is in a place and cannot exist without a place." (Quoted by Jammer, *Concepts of Space*, p. 8).

56 Cf. Max Jammer, *Concepts of Space*, ch 2: "Judeo-Christian Ideas about Space," p. 25 ff. Thanks to isosephy, the name of God had come to be identified with the word designating place (p. 30). In the seventeenth century, Henry More still defended the same ideas vigorously (p. 38 ff.).

57 George Leonard Prestige, *God in Patristic Thought*, p. 35.

58 St. Augustine, *Confessions*, VII, 5, 7, Frank J. Sheed trans. (Indianapolis: Hackett, 1993) p. 111: "And I made one great mass of God's creation distinguished according to the kinds of bodies in it, whether they really were bodies,

Cassian and Faustus of Riez would doubtless not go so far. We wonder, however, whether in some measure their representation of divine infinity did not remain captive of imaginative thought. A more precise notion of the nature of spiritual being would no doubt have kept them from the extreme consequences that they believed they had to draw from their doctrine. We can do no better than to compare St. Ambrose's *De Spiritu Sancto* on this point with Faustus of Riez's work of the same name to which we have often referred ourselves. Like his imitator, the bishop of Milan sees omnipresence as a privilege reserved to God alone;[59] but he carefully refrains from concluding from that that every spiritual being is infinite. Even if such a being is not circumscribed by a place, it remains limited in its substance by the very fact that it is created, and an immeasurable distance always separates it from the divine being: *Cum igitur omnis creatura certis naturae suae sit circumscripta limitibus; si quidem et illa invisibilia opera, quae non queunt locis et finibus comprehendi, substantiae suae tamen proprietate clauduntur* (*De Spiritu Sancto*, I, 7, *Patrologia Latina*, vol. 16, column 723 A). By turning his back on philosophy, Faustus renounced the elements which might have provided this key problem with a solution capable of satisfying the demands of faith without contradicting those of reason.

IV

Throughout this polemic we find the notion of divine incomprehensibility paralleling that of omnipresence and closely related to it. This new problem is really only the epistemological side of the former. Being infinite, God can not be apprehended adequately by a created intelligence. He is strictly indefinable, since, as the name indicates, define – ὁρίζειν, *definire* – is to

or only such bodies as I imagined spirits to be. I made it huge, not as huge as it is, which I had no means of knowing. And I saw You, Lord, in every part containing and penetrating it, immeasurable everywhere, though still only a sea: and within it there were some mighty but not infinite sponge, and that sponge filled in every part with the immeasurable sea."

59 Ambrose, *De Spiritu Sancto*, I, 7, *Patrologia Latina*, vol. 16, column 723 B: "[Spiritus Sanctus] non habet circumscriptam determinatamque virtutem; quia et in omnibus et ubique semper est, quod utique divinitatis et dominationis est proprium."

assign boundaries, delimit in some way. Thus the divine essence necessarily surpasses on every side the concepts in which we would be tempted to enclose it. To know it perfectly, we ourselves would have to be God. To want to say now that the human soul is incorporeal would be to pretend that it is not only infinite but ungraspable in its turn, and to make oneself guilty of the crime of divine lese-majesty, claiming for it the soul, what properly belongs to God: *Vide, quo tendat imprudens et inperita persuasio, quae incorporeum cum loquitur, etiam incomprehensibilem confidetur ac sic condito adscribit operi, quod soli conpetit conditori, ac rebus creatis communicat privilegia maiestatis et indebitam facturae potentiam usque ad factoris extendit iniuriam* (Faustus of Riez, *Epistula 3*, p. 180, 14 Engelbrecht).

Given that we do not see the soul and that in this sense it escapes us, it may indeed seem ungraspable, but this fact does not imply that it is truly ungraspable. Its invisibility, we are assured, is simply due to its nature, more subtle than that of the beings to which our senses are habituated. Above all it stems from the feebleness of our sight, comparable to that of the owl's eye which an ever so weak light dazzles, as Tertullian noted.[60] The proof is that the soul is beautiful and quite perceptible for God, from whose sight no creature escapes: *non est creatura invisibilis in conspectu ejus* (*Hebrews* 4, 12).[61] Furthermore, it happens that in certain circumstances the soul

60 Tertullian, *De Anima*, 8, 4–5: "Ceterum etsi invisibilis anima, et pro condicione corporis sui et proprietate substantiae et pro natura etiam eorum quibus invisibilis esse sortita est. Solem noctuae nesciunt oculis; aquilae ita sustinent, ut natorum suorum generositatem de pupillarum audacia iudicent; alioquin non educabunt, ut degenerem, quem solis radius averterit. Est adeo alteri quid invisibile, alteri non, quod non ideo incorporale sit, quia non ex aequo vis valet. Sol enim corpus, siquidem ignis; sed quod aquila confiteatur, neget noctua, non tamen praeiudicans aquilae. Tantundem et animae corpus invisibile carni, si forte, spiritui vero visibile est."

61 Cassian, *Conlationes*, VII, 13, p. 193, 16 Petschenig. The idea is constantly found from Tertullian on. Cf. *Adversus Praxeam*, 7, p. 237, 13 Kroymann (*Corpus Scriptorum Ecclesiasticorum Latinorum*, vol. 47): "Spiritus enim corpus sui generis in sua effigie. Sed si et invisibilia illa, quaecumque sunt, habent apud Deum et suum corpus et suam formam, per quae soli Deo visibilia sunt, quanto magis quod ex ipsius substantia emissum est sine substantia non erit?" Lactantius, *Divinae Institutiones*, VII, 20, 11, p. 650, 13 Brandt (*Corpus Scriptorum Ecclesiasticorum Latinorum*, vol. 19): "anima enim cum divortium fecit a corpore,

becomes visible even to man. This is Tertullian's interpretation of *Apocalypse* 6, 9, where St. John affirms that in ecstasy he has seen the souls of the martyrs offered in sacrifice on the divine altar.[62] At the beginning of the fifth century, St. Augustine still took the trouble to refute the idea held by Vincentius Victor according to which the soul came to see itself during sleep.[63]

This tendency could take us very far, as is apparent. The soul came to be regarded as a veritable double of the body, possessing a form, color,

est, ut ait idem poeta, 'par levibus ventis volucrique simillima somno,' quia spiritus est et ipsa tenuitate inconprehensibilis, sed nobis, qui sumus corporales, Deo autem, cui subiacet posse omnia, comprehensibilis;" Arnobius the Young, *Conflictus cum Serapione*, II, 5, *Patrologia Latina*, vol. 53, column 276 C: "Omnia quaecumque invisibilia et incorporea sunt, Deo soli secundum hoc, quod ab eo creata sunt, visibilia et corporea sunt." Fulgentius of Ruspe, *Ad Trasimundum*, II, 1 *Patrologia Latina*, vol. 65, column 245 C: "Hinc etiam protinus moneretur quanto infinitatis atque incomprehensibilitatis culmine creatrix omnium virtus et sapientia modum creaturae intellectualis excederet, cum ipsam rationalem creaturam plena suae comprehensibilitatis agnitio, creatori quidem comprehensibilis et finita, sibi tamen incomprehensibilis et infinita, lassaret." Cassiodorus, *De Anima*, ch. 4, *Patrologia Latina*, vol. 70,. column 1289 D, etc.

62 Tertullian, *De Anima*, 8, 5; 9, 8.

63 St. Augustine, *De Natura et Origine Animae*, IV, 21, 34, p. 412, 13 ff. Urba-Zycha (*Corpus Scriptorum Ecclesiasticorum Latinorum*, vol. 60): "Dormi, et videbis; sed cum evigilaveris, vigilanter discerne quod videris. In somnis enim tibi velut corporeus apparebis; neque id corpus tuum, sed anima tua, nec verum corpus sed similitudo corporis erit. Iacebit enim corpus tuum, ambulabit ipsa; silebit lingua corporis tui, loquetur illa; clausi erunt oculi tui, videbit illa; et utique viventia iacebunt tui corporis membra, non mortua. Ac per hoc nondum extracta est velut de vagina sua gelata illa forma, sicut putas, animae tuae et in ea tamen tota atque integra cernitur similitudo carnis tuae." Cf. *De Genesi ad Litteram*, X, 25, p. 329, 4 Zycha (*Corpus Scriptorum Ecclesiasticorum Latinorum*, vol. 28, 1): "Ecce, quibus auribus et quibus oculis debuit audire et videre Deum populus, quibus anima in somnis fungitur, cum, si ipsum Tertullianum quispiam videret in somnis, numquam se diceret ab eo visum et cum eo locutum, quem vicissim ipse non vidisset. Postremo, si anima se ipsam videt in somnis, cum iacentibus utique uno loco membris corporis sui ipsa per varias imagines evagatur, quas videt, quis eam vidit aliquando in somnis aerii coloris et lucidi, nisi forte ut cetera, quae similiter falso videt? Nam et hoc potest videre."

dimensions, and members analogous to those of the latter.[64] At the extreme, God himself appeared as an exact replica of man. Let us recall Cassian's charming anecdote of the old desert Father, who learning one day that divinity had no human form, complained that they had taken his God from him: *heu me miserum! Tulerunt a me Deum meum!*[65]

The critique of our fifth century authors coincides, without expressly wanting to, with that of the Stoics regarding the spirituality of the soul. Plato, we should say, nowhere labeled the soul ἀσώματος, but from that period we generally find the idea that the soul is invisible.[66] Subsequent

64 Tertullian, *De Anima*, 9, 7–8: "Recogita enim, cum Deus flasset in faciem homini flatum vitae, et factus esset homo in animam vivam, totus utique, per faciem statim flatum illum in interiora transmissum et per universa corporis spatia diffusum simulque divina aspiratione densatum omni intus linea expressum esse, quam densatus impleverat, et velut in forma gelasse. Inde igitur et corpulentia animae ex densatione solidata est et efficies ex impressione formata. Hic erit homi interior, alius exterior, duplicitur unus, habens et ille oculos et aures suas, quibus populus dominum audire et videre debuerat, habens et ceteros artus, per quos et in cogitationibus utitur et in somniis fungitur. Sic et diviti apud inferos lingua est, et pauperi digitus, et sinus Abrahae. Per has lineas et animae martyrum sub altari intelleguntur (cf. St. John, *Apocalypse*, 6, 9)." This conception of the soul as a double of the body seems to have been more widespread than Jan Hendrik Waszink, *Tertulliani De Anima*, would make us think, p. 177. We find it not only in Vincentius Victor (*apud* St. Augustine, *De Natura et Origine Animae*, p. 61 note 4, but similarly in Methodius of Olympus, *De Resurrectione*, III, 18, 5, p. 415, 16 ff. Bonwetsch (*Die griechischen christlichen Schriftsteller,* vol. 27, Leipzig, 1927; cf. Methodius of Olympus, *De Resurrectione*, p. 413, 17 ff) where the souls of Lazarus and the evil rich man are presented as having tongue, fingers, and members identical to those of the body, and in Macarius, *Homiliae*, IV, 9, *Patrologia Graeca*, vol. 34, column 480 A-B: "Each of these beings, namely, angel, soul, and demon, is a body according to its own nature . . . Thus, despite its subtlety, the soul possesses an eye by which it sees, an ear by which it hears, a hand, in short, a whole body . . ."

65 Cassian, *Conlationes*, X, 3, 4, p. 289, 12 Petschenig.

66 Plato, *Phaedo*, 79 a; Laws, X, 898 d; Xenophon, *Memorabilia*, I, 4, 9; *Cyropedia*, VIII, 7, 17, where the existence of the soul guarantees in some measure the existence of an invisible God. See likewise Pseudo-Aristotle, *De Mundo*, 6, 399 a, 30 ff. When later, under the influence of the new Academy, ideas concerning the nature of the soul will undergo momentary eclipse, it is the notion of the invisible God which will confirm the existence of the soul; e.g.,

Platonists drew an argument in favor of the soul's incorporeality from this affirmation, which might seem formidable and one to which the Stoics would see themselves obliged to respond. Whence the distinction, banal at first glance, between what is invisible and what is incorporeal,[67] but which must be considered as of the utmost importance. Even if it is agreed – and how can it not be? – that the soul is imperceptible, its corporeality must be maintained at all costs, for, in this perspective, invisibility is only a mode of being of things which, once they exist, are all corporeal.[68]

Cicero *Disputationes Tusculaneae* I, 28, 70 (*Tusculan Disputations*, trans. J. E. King, Loeb Classical Library, Cambridge, Mass.: Harvard University Press, 1927, 2001, pp. 82–83). On these texts see André-Jean Festugière, *La révélation d'Hermès Trismégiste*, vol. 2: *Le Dieu cosmique* (Paris: Lecoffre, 1949), p. 83 ff.

67 Cf Alexander of Aphrodisias, *De Anima*, p. 113, 31 Bruns; Pseudo Maximus, *De Anima*, *Patrologia Graeca*, vol. 91, column 353 D; see furthermore remarks by Jan Hendrik Waszink, *Tertulliani De Anima*, p. 159.

68 Everything that exists is corporeal: ταὐτὸν σῶμα καὶ οὐσία, *Stoicorum Veterum Fragmenta* II, p. 123, 16; Jan Hendrik Waszink, *Tertulliani De Anima*, p. 359; Plutarch, *De Communibus Notitiis Adversus Stoicos* 30 (*Against the Stoics on Common Conceptions*) in Plutarch *Moralia* XIII, Part II, trans. by Harold Cherniss, Loeb Classical Library, Cambridge, Mass.: Harvard University Press, 1976, 1993, pp. 772–779); Sextus Empiricus, *Adversus Mathematicos*, IX, 211; Cicero, *Academica* I, 39 (Cicero, *De Natura Deorum. Academica*, Loeb Classical Library, Cambridge, Mass.; Harvard University Press, 1979, *Academica* I, chapter XI, 39, pp. 448–449) Tertullian, *De Anima*, 7, 3: "Nihil enim, si non corpus;" *De Carne Christi*, 11, p. 220, 1 Kroymann (*Corpus Scriptorum Ecclesiasticorum Latinorum*, vol. 70): "Omne, quod est, corpus est sui generis. Nihil es incorporale nisi quod non est." *Adversus Hermogenem*, 35, p. 165, 3 Kroymann: "ipsa substantia corpus [est] rei cuiusque;" St. Augustine, *De Natura et Origine Animae*, IV, 12, 17, p. 397, 3 Urba-Sycha, (*Corpus Scriptorum Ecclesiasticorum Latinorum*, vol. 60): "Sed me rursus sollicitum facis, ubi dicis; 'si anima caret corpore, ut sit, sicut quibusdam placet, cassae inanitatis aeria futilisque substantia.' His enim tuis verbis videris credere omne quod caret corpore inanis esse substantiae." Once the Stoic thesis is admitted, God himself must be conceived as a corporeal being: Tertullian, *Adversus Praxeam*, 7, p. 237, 13 Kroymann (*Corpus Scriptorum Ecclesiasticorum Latinorum* vol. 47): "Quis enim negabit Deum corpus esse, etsi Deus spiritus est?" Cf. again St. Augustine, *De Natura et Origine Animae*, IV, 12, 17, p. 397, 3 Urba-*Zycha; De Genesi ad Litteram*, X, 25, p. 328, 11 Zycha (*Corpus Scriptorum Ecclesiasticorum Latinorum*, vol. 28, 1): "Denique Tertullianus, quia corpus esse animam credidit non

But to connect the thought of an author like Faustus of Riez to a definite philosophical current, even Stoicism, is to do him great honor – or perhaps injure him. At the very most, the similarities that we have just highlighted make us see this view in a less unusual light and permit us to approach it from the types of solution to which the ancients thought they could reasonably adhere. Nothing in these pages obliges us to believe that the doctrine of the bishop of Riez is directly inspired by any system. We certainly find several allusions in Faustus to what was Stoicism's principal argument in favor of the corporeality of the soul, namely the impossibility that a spiritual being should suffer any influence whatever from a body,[69] as well as some technical terms proceeding from the same source. Their presence in these discussions ought not to mislead us. To bring up only a typical example, it is evident that at this late period notions like that of incomprehensibility had passed into common parlance and, detached from their original roots, had a life of their own for long time.[70] Besides, in order

ob aliud, nisi quod eam incorpoream cogitare non potuit et ideo timuit, ne nihil esset, si corpus non esset, nec de Deo valuit aliter sapere: qui sane quoniam est acutus interdum contra opinionem suam visa veritate superatur. Quid enim verius dicere potuit quam id, quod ait quodam loco [sc. *De Anima*, 7]: 'omne corporale passibile est?' Debuit ergo mutare sententiam, qua paulo superius dixerat etiam Deum corpus esse." – For Stoicism things which have merely ideal existence are incorporeal; such things are simply expressable (λεκτά) like space, the void, or nothing; cf. Plutarch, *Moralia*, 119 e; Diogenes Laertes, VIII, 53; Stobaeus, *Eclogae*, I, 392, etc.

69 Faustus of Riez, *Epistula 3*, p. 180, 13 (*Corpus Scriptorum Ecclesiasticorum Latinorum*, vol. 21): "Sed absque dubio non aliud est quam substantia corporis, ubi dominari poterit vis doloris;" Tertullian, *De Anima*, 7, 4: "incorporalitas . . . nihil patitur." Cf. ch. III, 1 below.

70 In Stoicism κατάληψις designated the act by which the faculty of knowledge grasps its object; cf. Max Pohlenz, *Die Stoa, Geschichte einer geistigen Bewegung* (Göttingen: Vandenhoech & Ruprecht, 1948, pp. 60–62. According to Plutarch, *Cicero*, 40 (in *Plutarch's Lives*, vol. VII, *Demosthenes and Cicero. Alexander and Caesar*, Loeb Classical Library, Cambridge, Mass.: Harvard University Press, 1919, 1986, pp. 184–185). Cicero would have introduced the term into Latin; cf. *Academica* II, vi (*De Natura Deorum, Academica*, trans. H. Rackham, Loeb Classical Library, Cambridge, Mass.: Harvard University Press, 1933, 1979, p. 488) : "(si verbum e verbo volumus) comprehensio quam κατάληψιν illi vocant . . ." [translator's note: Fortin cites a slightly different version ma-

to realize the extent to which Faustus shows himself indifferent about philosophy, it will be sufficient to examine a little more closely the position he believed he should to take regarding it.

V

A doctrine like the one we have just studied is only in fact fully intelligible, if it is situated in the framework of the centuries-old debates between Christianity and pagan thought. The doctrine offers a more profound alternative, not, however, on the precise point of the spirituality of the soul, but on the utility of philosophy as such, which our authors address as little as possible and which raises quite emphatic reservations in their eyes.

It is true that if we keep strictly to explicit texts, we rarely find a condemnation of philosophy in principle. Sidonius, who is as much a friend of Faustus as of his adversary Claudianus, generously bestows the title of philosopher on Faustus and even goes so far as to celebrate the bishop's mystic marriage with philosophy in terms, incidentally, which are ill suited to a bishop's gravity (but perhaps we have an image of this gravity which is not that of the fifth century):

> An artist then endowed with all these intellectual and literary excellences, you have joined to yourself a beautiful woman, but who married you in the ritual prescribed by *Deuteronomy*, my Lord Bishop. You had seen her, while still in your youth, among the hordes of the enemy, and there in the midst of the hostile ranks you fell in love with her and, defying the attempts of the opposing warriors to drive you back, you carried her off with the conquering arm of desire. Her name was Philosophy; rescued by force from the crowd of blasphemous sciences, she shaved off the locks that betokened false religion, shaved off the disdainful eyebrows of worldly knowledge, cut away the folds of her old former raiment – and by folds I mean the twists and turns of sinister dialectic screening wrong and unlawful

king the same point, which he attributes to Academica II, XI, 35, where I cannot find it – p. 512 in Loeb]

> behavior: and then, when cleansed in every part, she united herself with you in a mystic embrace.[71]

Henceforth, fully subdued, this companion will leave her new master neither in his labors, nor in his solitude. He does not wear a beard nor don the mantle, traditional emblems of the philosophical vocation, but he no longer seeks to extract vanity from this simplicity, any more than he exhibits his scorn for the world by an untidy gown in the manner of the Cynics.[72]

It would be pointless to deny the role of literature in the passage quoted, which develops the well known theme of the captive maiden of *Deuteronomy* with a certain ingeniousness.[73] Still, let us acknowledge the

71 Sidonius, *Letters*, vol. II, Book IX, 9,12, (p. 541, Loeb Library).

72 Sidonius, *Letters*, vol. II, Book IX, 9, 14, (pp. 542–544, Loeb Library).

73 Jewish legislation allowed an Israelite to marry a foreign woman captured from the enemy, but after a delay of a month and after having obliged her to shave her hair, cut her nails, change garments, etc. cf.. *Deuteronomy*, 21, 10 ff. St. Jerome uses the same theme in *Letter 70* to Magnus (*Nicene and Post-Nicene Fathers*, vol. I, *St. Jerome: Letters and Select Works*, ed. Philip Schaff and Henry Wace, Grand Rapids, Michigan: William Eerdmans, reprinted 1983, p. 149): "[St. Paul] had read in *Deuteronomy* the command given by the voice of the Lord that when a captive woman had had her head shaved, her eyebrows and all her hair cut off, and her nails pared, she might then be taken to wife. Is it surprising that I too, admiring the fairness of her form and the grace of her eloquence, desire to make that secular wisdom which is my captive and my handmaid, a matron of the true Israel? Or that shaving off and cutting away all in her that is dead whether this be idolatry, pleasure, error, or lust, I take her to myself clean and pure and beget by her servants for the Lord of Sabaoth: My efforts promote the advantage of Christ's family, my so-called defilement with an alien increases the number of my fellow-servants." André Labhardt has commented on this text with great insight, "Sur une page de saint Jérôme," in *Hommage et reconnaissance, recueil de travaux publiés à la occasion du soixantième anniversaire de Karl Barth*, Neuchâtel and Paris: Delachaux & Niestlé, 1946, pp. 56–62. According to Labhardt, the image is explained with the help of another analogy familiar to the Christians of the first centuries, which called *captivi* those whom the devil holds prisoners, in particular heretics and pagans. Ancient culture under the empire of Satan is similar to the captive woman . . ." It may be noted that for his part Gregory of Nazianzus wanted to make all science "captive" (αἰχμαλωτίζειν) of Christ, according to the recommendation of St. Paul, *II Corinthians*, 10, 5. Cf. *Eulogy of St. Basil*,

symptomatic character of this reproach incurred by the twists and turns of tedious dialectic. The remark here goes to the heart of the matter. What one pleases to denounce as superfluous, might well in certain cases be supremely useful and even indispensable. We already see how under the praise a more subtle criticism hides, intended or not. An examination of the ideas of Faustus and even more those of Cassian of whom Faustus is a faithful disciple, will reveal how much these observations are justified.

The pages which Faustus devotes to the nature of the soul, in effect, evince a mind unfamiliar with the employment of the technical terminology of psychology. Furthermore, we see him rise up against the "vain curiosity" condemned by St. Paul, characteristic of *animalis homo*, the curiosity demonstrated precisely by the man who acts out of completely worldly prudence instead of letting himself be guided by God, and who, yielding to a guilty inclination, "delights in philosophical studies" and in "the exploration of questions beyond our understanding."[74]

11, *Patrologia Graeca*, vol. 36, column 508 C. St. Ambrose gave this passage of *Deuteronomy* another interpretation; what is said here of the captive woman is applied to the infidel soul which must undergo the same treatment before being able to be united to God; cf. *Epistula 31* (ad Irenaeum), *Patrologia Latina*, vol. 16, column 1113–1114; *Epistula 33*, column 1117. According to Clement of Alexandria, it is the foreign woman of *Proverbs*, 5, 20, who personifies classical culture, whose utility must be recognized, but toward whom certain prudence is appropriate. Cf. André Labhardt, "Sur une page de saint Jérôme," and P. Camelot, "Les idées de Clément d'Alexandrie sur l'utilisation de la science et de la littérature profane," in *Recherches de science religieuse*, vol. 21, 1931, pp. 38 ff. In another letter of St. Jerome (*Epistula 52* ad Nepotianum, 2–3, p. 414 16 ff Hilberg (*Corpus Scriptorum Ecclesiasticorum Latinorum*, vol. 54), Christian wisdom now appears disguised under the appearance of a woman . . . that mysterious Sunamite, at the same time virgin and spouse, who came to warm the cold limbs of the aged King David, *III Kings*, 1, 1 ff. – On the personifications of philosophy and the apocalyptic character of this literary genre in the fifth and sixth centuries, see Pierre-Paul Courcelle, *Les lettres grecques en Occident*, p. 279. The most famous example, of course, is that of Boethius, *De Consolatione Philosophiae* 1 (prose), p. 2, 5 ff, Weinberger (*Corpus Scriptorum Ecclesiasticorum Latinorum*, vol. 67).

74 Faustus of Riez, *Epistula 5*, p. 191, 22 Engelbrecht: "At vero animalis efficitur [homo], quando adhuc parum Deum cogitans secundum animam saeculari prudentia ad aliquarum rerum providentiam permovetur, quando aut investi-

Remarks of this kind, which are very frequent, especially in Cassian, invite us to ask what difference it makes when philosophy is treated so harshly. What is this curiosity, presented as so reprehensible, that we are led to believe is a sort of original sin? We might think that it concerns a simple caution, in name of the one thing only that is necessary, as distinct from any occupation foreign to monastic life capable of being considered a waste of time for a monk. Does not Scripture say that we will have to render account even of vain words?[75] It is easy to conceive that in an environment consecrated to asceticism, faults of this sort take on special importance. Still the fuss that is made about curiosity and the insistence with which it is denounced let us understand that the dreaded evil is more serious. In the last analysis, it reduces to two principal forms: on the one hand it is what has been called the religion of culture – St. Augustine said: the religion that takes for its object the perfection and wisdom of the reasonable soul[76] – and on the other hand the danger of heresy.

Is not entrusting oneself to philosophy to rely on one's own powers, to want to delve into the reasons of things on one's own rather than to recur to scripture and the teaching of the saints as every monk and every good Christian ought to do?[77] Such a move only leads ultimately to alienate the soul from God and to incite it to seek its point of support in itself. Nothing is more likely to engender pride, that wound nurtured by philosophers, which by seeking to surpass others, makes us presume upon our strength and rush to damnation.[78]

gandis pro curiosa vanitate rerum latentium causis aut philosophicis studiis delectatur. . . ."

75 *Matthew*, 12, 36.

76 St. Augustine, *De Vera Religione*, LV, 110: "Non sit nobis religio vel ipsa perfecta et sapiens anima rationalis . . ."

77 Faustus, *Epistula 7,* 200, 18 ff. Cassian, *Conlationes*, II, 24, 2, p. 63, 8 ff Petschenig, and *passim*. This constant appeal to the tradition of the Fathers and example of the ancients is characteristic of the authors who belong to the Lérins group.

78 Cassian, *Conlationes*, II, 24, 2, p. 63, 8 ff: "Qui obstinatione et pertinacia mentis suae definitionibus potius propriis quam seniorum traditionibus adquiescens quali fine suum propositum terminarit, procul dubio meministis, siquidem relicta heremo rursus ad inanem philosophiam mundi huius ac vanitatem saeculi devolutus praedictam sententiam seniorum sui casus signet exemplo ruinaque

Let us grasp the profound reversal of values implied in this position. Philosophy is no longer, as it was, the means by which the soul is ordered and relates itself in the first place to eternal things.[79] On the contrary, it is the source of disorder and confusion. Instead of teaching us about the only really important truths and thereby purifying the soul of its passions, philosophy turns us from wisdom and from our true good. From eminent instrument of perfection, it has become an obstacle and a snare of the devil: *diaboli quidem perniciosa inlusio*.[80] Thus it is proper to distrust in the highest degree the philosophers who reintroduce "the vain noises of the world"[81] into the life of the monk and snatch him from his solitude to precipitate him again into the "folly of the world and inanity of human doctrines."[82]

Philosophers dispose of superlatively powerful means for this. So great is the impact of their word, of their Ciceronian eloquence, *tulliana facundia*, cultivated with so much art, which seduces us; so great is their dialectical prowess, their skill in disputing and constructing syllogisms which sway us.[83] Let us note in passing the reference to the two essential components

sua cunctos doceat neminem definitionibus suis vel proprio iudicio confidentem perfectionis culmen aliquando posse conscendere, sed ne diaboli quidem perniciosa inlusione non decipi." Cf. *Conlationes*, I, 20, 2, p. 30, 2 ff.

79 Without going back to Plato, simply see the praise of philosophy in Cicero, *Tusculan Disputations*, V, II (J.E. King translation, Cambridge, Mass.: Harvard University Press, 1927, 2001), p. 429: "O philosophy, thou guide of life, o thou explorer of virtue and expeller of vice! Without thee what could have become not only of me but of the life of man altogether . . . thou hast been the teacher of morality and order . . ."

80 Cassian, *Conlationes*, II, 24, 2, p. 63, 16

81 Cassian, *Conlationes*, I, 20, 3, p. 30, 11: "Quo genere illi quoque decepti sunt, qui post professionem monachi nitore sermonis et quibusdam sunt philosophorum dogmatibus inlecti, quae prima fronte piis quibusdam sensibus ac religioni consonis audientes velut auri fulgore fallentia, quos semel superficie inlexerant, velut nomismatibus aereis falsisque deceptos perpetuo nudos ac miseros reddiderunt, vel ad saeculi eos strepitum revocantes vel ad haereticos errores ac praesumptiones tumidas pertrahentes."

82 Cassian, *Conlationes*, II, 24, 2, p. 63, 11.

83 Cassian, *De Institutis Coenobiorum*, XII, 19, p. 220, 3 ff Petschenig (*Corpus Scriptorum Ecclesiasticorum Latinorum*, vol. 17): "Haec est proprie humilitas erga Deum, haec est antiquissimorum patrum sincera fides, quae penes successores ipsorum mera nunc usque perdurat. Cui fidei virtutes apostolicae, quae saepe

of ancient culture, rhetoric and dialectic,[84] but let us note above all the wholesale condemnation of this subtlety beloved of the philosophers and to which Mamertus, as we have seen, so firmly adhered.

It is not necessary to see in these reiterated warnings a mere posture of disparagement. The work of Franz Cumont and Henri-Irenée Marrou[85] use archeological data to reveal all the attraction which an already imperiled

numero per eos manifestatae sunt, non solum apud nos, sed etiam apud infideles et incredulos indubitatum testimonium reddunt. Qui simplicem piscatorum fidem corde simplici retinentes non eam *syllogismis dialecticis* et *Tulliana facundia* spiritu concepere mundano, sed experimento vitae sinceris actuque purissimo, correctione quoque vitiorum, et ut verius dixerim in ipsa perfectionis inesse naturam oculatis indiciis deprehenderunt, sine qua nec pietas in Deum nec vitiorum purgatio nec emendatio morum nec virtutum consummatio poterit adprehendi." Cf. *Contra Nestorium*, III, 15, 2, p. 280, 22 (*Corpus Scriptorum Ecclesiasticorum Latinorum*, vol. 17): "Sed subtilitatem hanc discretionis tuae apostolus Dei forte non norat et elegantiam iudicii tui ac differentiam non habebat, homo videlicet rusticus et imperitus, dialecticae artis nescius, philosophicae disputationis ignarus, cui scilicet institutio Domini sui abunde sufficiebat et qui nihil omnino sciebat nisi hoc quod Domino docente cognoverat."

84 The two headings of the accusation, dialectical skill and the art of speaking well, habitually go together; cf. Tertullian, *De Carnis Resurrectione*, 5, p. 31, 10 Kroyman (*Corpus Scriptorum Ecclesiasticorum Latinorum*, vol. 47): *rhetoricari, philosophari*; Origen, *Contra Celsum*, I, 62, p. 113, 28 Koetschau (*Die griechischen christlichen Schriftsteller*, vol. 2); Arnobius, *Adversus Nationes* II, 11, p. 77, 22 Marchesi: "nam et verbis eos luculentissimis scimus loqui et compositionibus fluere levigatis, concludere acutissime syllogismos, ordinare sequaciter inductiones, suas reddere definitionibus formulas . . ." Lactantius, *De Opificio Dei*, 20, 3, p. 63, 17 Brandt (*Corpus Scriptorum Ecclesiasticorum Latinorum*, vol. 27): "Incredibilis enim vis eloquentiae et argumentandi disserendique subtilitas quemvis facile deceperit;" Lactantius, *De Opificio Dei*, 20, 5, p. 64, 5: "fallax copiosaque facundia;" Jerome, *Adversus Helvidium*, 2 *Patrologia Latina*, vol. 23, column 185 A: "campum rhetorici eloquii dialectorum tendiculas;" *Commentarium in Evangelium Matthei*, ch. 13, *Patrologia Latina*, vol. 26, column 90 B: "dogmata philosophorum splendor eloquentiae et compositio sermonum," etc.

85 Franz Cumont, *Recherches sur le symbolisme funéraire des romains* (Paris: Geuthner,1942); Henri-Irenée Marrou, Μουσικὸς ἀνήρ, *Étude sur les scènes de la vie intellectuelle figurant sur les monuments funéraires romains* (Grenoble: Didier et Richard, 1938).

ancient culture could exercise on literate individuals of the late period, a culture which only assumed greater value in the eyes of its adherents. We are in the presence of one of the deepest reasons for the resistance to Christianity in intellectual circles. The rivals of the true God were no longer the divinities of the Greek or Roman pantheon. It had been ages since one argued about Jupiter's existence; one did not ask whether a story was true or false![86] But in

86 If the gods of paganism really were dead, how do we explain the passion of the fifth and sixth century apologists (Arnobius, St. Augustine) to combat them? Franz Cumont, *Oriental Religons in Roman Paganism* (New York: Dover Publications, 1911, 1956, trans. Grant Showerman), pp. 14–15 and 202–205, has posed the problem with great lucidity and solved it rather paradoxically, to generalize a little. If we accept Cumont's thesis, we must admit that Christian apologetic would not have succeeded in following the evolution of pagan doctrines and "fought especially the beliefs of the ancient Grecian and Italian religions that had been abolished or were dying out, while they neglected the living beliefs of the contemporary world" (p. 15). Even the best minds would have lost any sense of their reality and their efforts only succeeded in embracing a shadow. Thus, "By a peculiar irony of fate those controversies are today in many instances our only aid in reviving the idolatry they attempted to destroy" (p. 15). That a great part of the pagan erudition of *The City of God* originates directly in Varro, as Cumont remarks (p. 202), is disputed by no one. Still, it seems difficult to settle this question globally without distinguishing between the people, to whom the first five books of the work are devoted, and cultured circles with which the following books deal; cf. St. Augustine *Retractationes*, II, 43, 1. We know the tenacity with which the populace clings to ancient traditions, and consequently, the difficulties we encounter when it is a matter of determining to what extent this popular religion had survived, even if it finds scant echo in literary texts and the epigraphy of a period. As for the elite, by testimony of St. Augustine himself, its disaffection from pagan gods was not new. All the same it tended to maintain their cult, deemed useful for the mass of the illiterate. Among ancient thinkers, only Epicureans and some Cynics dared to deny the existence of the gods openly, something explained easily by the asocial character of their philosophy. It must not be forgotten that only starting with Hobbes will political philosophy judge itself capable of assuring a valid social order without basing itself on belief in the divinity.

Much remains to be said on the survival of pagan gods and their degree of reality at the end of antiquity. The same problem reappears at the time of the Renaissance, where it has been studied by Jean Seznec, *The Survival of the Pagan Gods. The Mythological Tradition and Its Place in Renaissance Humanism*, trans. Barbara Sessions (New York: Pantheon Books, 1953).

their place another, more formidable, idol had arisen; the culture which had inspired the most beautiful pages of antiquity, which was expressed in the graceful images amid which educated people grew up, and whose finesse and elegance violently contrasted with the sometimes barbarous exterior of the new religion.[87] Had not Plato proclaimed in a passage which should be imitated even by Christians, that for man culture was the first of all goods, πρῶτον τῶν καλλίστων τοῖς ἀπίστοις ἀνδράσιν?[88] Elevated to be an absolute, the object of an authentic cult, it became a greater obstacle to the conversion of the elite,[89] and it posed a sometimes painful problem of conscience for the Christian who had necessarily to confront it because of his intellectual formation. Nothing further was necessary to discredit it irremediably in ascetic circles.

This discredit is accentuated if it is admitted that pagan thought makes the purity of the faith undergo grave danger. Many Christians had learned to see philosophy as the source on which heresies feed.[90] According to

87 Arnobius, *Adversus Nationes*, II, 66, p. 143, 21 Marchesi: "Nam quod nobis obiectare consuestis, novellam esse religionem nostram et ante dies natam propemodum paucos neque nos oportuisse antiquam et patriam linquere et in barbaros ritus peregrinosque traduci, ratione istud intenditur nulla." Cf. Lactantius *Divinae Institutiones*, V, 1, 15, p. 401, 5 ff Brandt (*Corpus Scriptorum Ecclesiasticorum Latinorum*, vol. 19). Young Augustine had felt the same reaction reading the Bible for the first time, *Confessions*, III, 5, 9 (p. 39 Sheed translation): "When I first read those Scriptures, . . . they seemed to me unworthy to be compared with the majesty of Cicero."

88 Plato, *Laws* I, 644 a 8. The idea is taken up in the same terms by Clement of Alexandria, *Pedagogue*, I, 5, 16, 1, p. 99 18 Stählin (*Die griechischen christlichen Schriftsteller*, vol. 12) and by Gregory of Nazianzen, *Eulogy of St. Basil*, 11, 1, *Patrologia Graeca*, vol. 36, column 508 B: Οἶμαι δέ πᾶσιν ἀνωμολογῆσθαι τὸν νοῦν ἐχόντων, παίδευσιν τῶν παρ᾽ ἡμῖν ἀγαθῶν εἶναι τὸ πρῶτον. Cf. Plutarch, *De Liberis Educandis*, 8 E; Libanius, *Orationes*, 52, 13.

89 To these reasons of a philosophical and aesthetic order, in certain cases, concerns of a religious and mystical order are added, like this belief in divinization by the culture born from Pythagorianism, which became generalized in this period; cf. Henri-Irenée Marrou, Μουσικὸς ἀνέρ, p. 231 ff; Pierre Boyancé, *La culte des muses chez les philosophes grecs* (Paris: E. de Boccard, 1936), p. 233 ff; Franz Cumont, *Recherches sur le symbolisme funéraire des romains*, pp. 262 ff and *passim*.

90 About heresy (on the occurrence of Gnosticism) as "secularization or acute

Cassian, Nestorius's subtlety of distinctions and pretended elegance of judgments were what led him to collapse into error. How superior the simplicity of the apostle St. Thomas, who knows no dialectic, who understands nothing of philosophers' discussions, but whose doctrine is only the more heavenly and exempt from corruption for that. One word suffices him: *Dominus meus et Deus meus*, to refute what this heretic put so much art and effort into establishing.[91] Likewise, it is by recourse to dialectic, *arte dialectica*, that another heretic strives to shake the faith of Abbot Macarius, to catch him in a trap of "Aristotelian thorns." He desists, finding himself confounded by the saint's reply, as brief as it is pertinent: "Not in words consists the kingdom of God, but in virtue."[92]

Therefore, what an aberration it is to want to appropriate that "false coin" for ourselves! Far from enriching us, it despoils us of our true wealth and leaves us miserable and naked.[93] The example of Achan, who for having stolen a golden bar in the spoils of Hai deserved to be stoned, ought to put us on guard forever against such a temptation.[94] No! Despite their pretensions, philosophers do not know true virtue, which consists not in words but in acts.

Hellenization" of Christianity, cf. Adolf von Harnack, *Lehrbuch der Dogmengeschichte*, fifth edition, vol. I (Tübingen: C. B. Mohr, 1931), pp. 250 ff.

91 Cassian, *Contra Nestorium*, III, 15, 2, p. 281, 6 ff (*Corpus Scriptorum Ecclesiasticorum Latinorum*, vol.17): "Itaque ille ut tu forsitan putas rusticus et imperitus brevi te nunc responsione concludit, paucis sermonibus suis conterit. Quid ergo apostolus Thomas tetigit, cum ad palpandum Deum accessisset? Christum utique absque dubio. Quid autem exclamavit? Dominus, inquit, meus et Deus meus."

92 Cassian, *Conlationes*, XV, 3, 1–2, p. 428, 24 ff (*Corpus Scriptorum Ecclesiasticorum Latinorum*, vol. 13): "Nam cum haereticus quidam, qui Eunomii perfidiam sectabatur, sinceritatem catholicae fidei arte dialectica subvertere conaretur magnamque iam hominum multitudinem decepisset, rogatus a catholicis viris, qui ruina tantae subversionis gravissime movebantur, beatus Macarius, ut simplicitatem totius Aegypti ab infidelitatis naufragio liberaret, advenit. Quem cum haereticus arte dialectica fuisset adgressus et ad Aristotelicas ignorantem spinas vellet abducere, beatus Macarius apostolica multiloquium eius brevitate concludens, 'non est,' inquit, 'in verbo regnum Dei, sed in virtute.'"

93 Cassian, *Conlationes*, I, 20, 3, p. 30, 13; see note 81 above.

94 Cassian, *Conlationes*, I, 20, 3, p. 30, 13. The episode is described in *Joshua*, 7, 19 ff.

In this criticism, the old opposition between *res* and *verba* reappears, but internalized and adapted to the demands of Christian morality. Virtue does not only rule our external behavior. It ought to rectify even the dispositions of the soul. Socrates had only the externals of that virtue. He himself recognizes he was a pederast, although he never gave in to his inclination: εἰμι γάρ, ἐπέχω δέ.[95] Now it is precisely this inclination that must be corrected. In short, if we want to reach perfection, it is not from the delirious imagination of philosophers that we must seek the means to do so but from those who have attained it themselves and have an experiential knowledge of it.[96]

Is it necessary to recall that this indictment is not without precedent? In the West, Tertullian always exploited the vein with brio. He had fixed the vocabulary and method.[97] We know celebrated passages of his which make philosophers out to be "the patriarchs of heretics"[98] denouncing their

95 Cassian, *Conlationes*, XIII, 5, 3–4, p. 366, 6 ff (*Corpus Scriptorum Ecclesiasticorum Latinorum*, vol. 13). On the accusation of pederasty brought against Socrates by ecclesiastical authors starting with Tertullian, cf. Waszink, *Tertulliani De Anima*, pp. 94–95.

96 Cassian, *Institutiones*, XII, 15, p. 215, 19 (*Corpus Scriptorum Ecclesiasticorum Latinorum*, vol. 17): "Ideoque si ad verum consummationem virtutum volumus effectu et opere pervenire, illis debemus adquiescere magistris ac ducibus, qui hanc non vaniloqua disputatione somniantes, sed re atque experimentis adprehendentes nos quoque docere atque ad eam dirigere similiter possunt et viam, quemadmodum perveniamus ad eam, certissimo tramite demonstrare, quique ad hanc fide se potius pervenisse quam laborum merito testabantur." By contrast, in conformity with his principles, Pelagius found men of eminent virtue among pagan philosophers. Cf. *Ad Demetriadem*, *Patrologia Latina*, vol. 30, column 18: "Quam multos enim philosophorum et audivimus et legimus, et ipsi vidimus castos, patientes, modestos, liberales, abstinentes, benignos, et honores mundi simul, et delicias respuentes, et amatores justitiae non minus quam scientiae."

97 On Tertullian's attitude toward profane culture, see lastly the excellent article by André Labhardt, "Tertullien et la philosophie ou la recherche d'une 'position pure'," in *Museum Helveticum*, vol. 7, 1950, pp. 150 ff.

98 Tertullian, *De Anima*, 3 (*The Ante-Nicene Fathers*. Vol. III, *Latin Christianity: Its Founder Tertullian. I Apologetic; II. Anti-Marcion; III. Ethical*, Grand Rapids, Michigan: William B. Eerdmans , 1983 reprint of Edinburgh edition, p.183); *Adversus Hermogenem*, 8 (*The Ante-Nicene Fathers*. Vol. III, p. 482), quoted by

"extravagant and idle" curiosity[99] and taking to task dialectic, that subtle instrument of thought.[100] He likewise marshaled all the texts of Scripture capable of being interpreted in this sense.[101]

Jerome, *Epistula 133*, 2, p. 243, 1 Hilberg (*Corpus Scriptorum Ecclesiasticorum Latinorum*, vol. 56); *De Praesciptione. Haereticorum,* 7, p. 9, 6 Kroymann (*Corpus Scriptorum Ecclesiasticorum Latinorum*, vol. 70): "Ipsae denique haereses a philosophia subornantur. . . . Eadem materia apud haereticos et philosophos volutatur." *Apologetics*, 47, 9, etc.; cf. Waszink, *Tertulliani De Anima*, pp. 114–115. The idea reappears frequently in Christian apologetics of the first centuries, e.g., Gregory of Nyssa, *Contra Eunomium*, I, *Patrologia Graeca*, vol. 45, column 265 B; the impiety of the Arian Aetius originates in Aristotle (ἡ ῾Αριστοτέλους κακοτεχνία); Jerome, *Tractatus in Psalmum 143*, p. 63, 25–26 Morin (*Anecdota Maredsolana*, III, 2): "omnes vero haeretici Aristotelici et Platonici sunt." Cf. Jerome, *Tractatus in Psalmum 143*, p. 267, 20 ff., p. 285, 23.

99 Tertullian, *De Anima*, 58 (*A Treatise on the Soul*, *The Ante-Nicene Fathers*. Vol. III, p. 235); cf. *Adversus Marcionem*, 1, 2, p. 292, 23 Kroymann (*Corpus Scriptorum Ecclesiasticorum Latinorum*, vol. 47). But, at the risk of seeming to contradict himself, Tertullian himself had to make certain concession to profane culture; Cf. *De Idolatria*, 10, p. 40, 12 ff. Reifferscheid (*Corpus Scriptorum Ecclesiasticorum Latinorum*, vol. 20): ". . . quomodo quis institueretur ad prudentiam interim humanam vel ad quemcumque sensum vel actum, cum instrumentum sit ad omnem vitam litteratura? Quomodo repudiamus saecularia studia, sine quibus divina non possunt? Videamus igitur necessitatem litteratoriae eruditionis." Cf. *De Corona*, 7, p. 168, 8 Kroymann (*Corpus Scriptorum Ecclesiasticorum Latinorum*, vol. 70); *De Anima*, 2 and *passim*.

100 Tertullian is one of the few ecclesiastical writers to scorn dialectic; cf. André Labhardt, , "Tertullien et la philosophie ou la recherche d'une 'position pure'," p. 180.

101 In part the difficulty arises because the term "philosophy" has a pejorative sense in the New Testament, e.g., *Colossians*, 2, 8: "See to it that no one deceives you by philosophy and vain deceit. . . ." St. Augustine never awarded himself the title of philosopher; cf. Marrou, *Saint Augustin et la fin de la culture antique*, p. 166, note 5. Even the authors who resort to the philosophers most easily, ordinarily surround themselves with precautions. Mamertus pretends to do so only because his adversary has pronounced their name, *De Statu Animae*, p. 104, 19: "Neque mihi profecto cordi foret mutuum ex his carpere quippiam, nisi iste corporis amicus sola philosophici nominis mentione terriculamenta quaedam nobis scientiae profundioris ostentavisset." Certainly, from the beginning Christians insisted a great deal on the intellectual, doctrinal character of their religion, and the word *philosophy* is often found in their

Accordingly, what is striking in our fifth century authors is less the originality of the views expressed than their persistence. After several centuries of confrontation and struggle, the contest was far from being definitively won in favor of culture. Everything indicates that the attitude of average minds and ascetic circles had varied little on this point. Instead of assisting in the elaboration of a compromise or, to put it better, a more viable notion of the relations between Christian thought and culture, rather, we keep finding the obsession with a "pure position," the conviction that any nuances introduced in these matters are cowardice or concessions, and finally, the sentiment that the greatness of Christianity is never better assured than when it shelters itself from any contact with alien elements.

Unfortunately, in throwing away the kernel with the husk, we lose the only means of which the mind disposes to penetrate further into certain truths of the natural order. We are also exposed to an even more serious danger which consists in interrogating Scripture on a question that Scripture does not at all try to answer. When we trace the history of this anti-pagan polemic, we should never lose sight of the idea that every discussion supposes a previous agreement between the two opposed parties. The discussion demands that they understand each other at least about the nature of the problem being debated and the terms in which it is posed. Involving the struggle against the pagans in the treatment of the human soul, having to sustain diametrically opposed theses, was by that very fact to situate oneself in a terrain which was not necessarily that of the Bible. The Bible is

works; cf. Marrou, Μουσικὸς ἀνήρ, pp. 273–283. However, it is no less true that the term often takes on a peculiar sense in their writing, very different from the one it had in the pagans. Thus St. John Chysostom will speak of the "philosophy of St. Matthew" (*Homilia in Mattheum*, 57, *Patrologia Graeca*, vol. 58, column 549), and when he recommends "the true philosophy" to a young student, he quite simply understands he is exhorting him to the practice of Christian virtues (*Epistula 61*, *Patrologia Graeca*, vol. 52 column 642). Cassian himself will employ the expression *philosophia Christiana*, but to apply it to the Fathers of the Desert; cf. *Conlationes*, IV, 1, 1, p. 97, 15 (*Corpus Scriptorum Ecclesiasticorum Latinorum*, vol. 13): "Inter ceteros Christianae philosophiae viros abbatem quoque vidiumus Danihelem, aequalem quidem in omni virtutum genere his qui in heremo Sciti conmanebant, sed pecularius gratia humilitatis ornatur." Cf. *Contra Nestorium*, VII, 27, 1, p. 385, 13 (*Corpus Scriptorum Ecclesiasticorum Latinorum*, vol. 17).

turned into the guarantor of a doctrine which as such is outside of the Bible's concerns and which is, even in the last analysis, contrary to certain of the Bible's basic presuppositions. Faith itself becomes indirectly compromised, and in this sense Mamertus is not mistaken in reproaching his adversary with ultimately not following either reason or authority.[102] It turns out that the true defenders of the Christian faith were precisely those who are accused of making a pact with the devil.

In this regard, it is interesting to compare the position of the Marseilles authors with what Heraclides and his colleagues, the bishops of the province of Arabia, defended around 245, two centuries earlier, in the course of an episcopal conference which Origen had been invited to preside and whose minutes he wrote.[103] Thanks to this curious document, we can take stock of the confusion of certain Christians, zealous about orthodoxy and fidelity to the letter of Scripture, who still took blood to be the human soul, according to a remark in *Deuteronomy*.[104] Despite the precautions with which

102 *De Statu Animae*, p. 22, 1; p. 37, 19: "Et quia ipse, quantum loquitur, non tam probatae rationi aut intemerandae auctoritati, sed humanae magis opinioni concessit, id inpenso opere nititur, ut spreta auctoritate divina, omissa quoque ratione perspicua, clausis ut aiunt oculis sibimet adsentiamur."

103 Jean Scherer, *Entretien d' Origène avec Héraclide et les évêques ses collègues sur le Père, le Fils et l'âme* (Cairo: Publications of the Fuad I Society of Papyrology, vol. 9, 1949).

104 *Deuteronomy*, 12, 23: "Only beware of this, that thou eat not the blood, for the blood is for the soul: and therefore thou must not eat the soul with the flesh." Cf. *Genesis*, 9, 4; *Leviticus*, 17, 11. Blood was considered the seat of life because, when an animal loses its blood, it dies. Like life, which comes from God, blood, therefore, deserved the greatest respect from men. In fact, this idea has a whole history; notably medical literature gave it currency, and from there it had entered the broad stream of ancient culture. Cf. Hippocrates, *De Natura Hominis*, 6; Galen, *De Dogmate Hippocratis et Platonis*, 2, 8, p. 248 Müller; Tertullian, *De Anima*, 5; Alexander of Aphrodisias, *De Anima Liber cum Mantissa*, (*Praeter Commentaria Scripta Minora*. *Supplementum Aristotelicum*, vol. 2, pars 1, Berlin: G. Reimer, 1887–1892), p. 118, 4 Bruns; Clement of Alexandria, *Pedagogue*, I, 39, 2, p. 113 14 Stählin (*Die griechischen christlichen Schriftsteller*, vol. 12); Hyppolytus, *Philosophoumena*, 22, 5 (Cf. Diels, *Doxographi Graeci*, p. 572, 14–16); Lactantius, *De Opificio Dei*, 17, p. 55, 12–18 Brandt (*Corpus Scriptorum Ecclesiasticorum Latinorum*, vol. 27, 1); Plotinus, *Enneads* IV, 7, 8 (pp. 360–365 in *Plotinus IV*, ed. and trans. by A. N. Armstrong, Cambridge, Mass.: Harvard

he cloaks himself and despite his efforts to treat the subject "according to Holy Scripture" and not "according to the Greeks,"[105] Origen did not manage to calm all spirits, so much so that one of the bishops, Demetrius, could not keep from remarking: "Behold our brother Origen, who teaches that the soul is immortal!"[106] To resolve the apparently contradictory affirmations of the Bible on this question would have required an intellectual preparation far beyond that of the companions of Heraclides. The bishops of Arabia had not yet discovered philosophy; the monks of Lérins had forgotten it . . .

That the attitude of Cassian, Faustus of Riez, and their disciples was not the only one possible in this time, is what the example of Claudianus Mamertus demonstrates dazzlingly, as we are going to see.

University Press, 1984); Nemesius, *De Natura Hominis*, *Patrologia Graeca*, vol. 40, column 541 B-C; Macrobius, *Commentarium in Somnium Scipionis* I, 14, 20; Ambrose, *De Isaac et Anima*, 2, 3, p. 644, 23 Schenkl (*Corpus Scriptorum Ecclesiasticorum Latinorum*, vol. 32, 1); *De Noe*, 25, 92, (*Corpus Scriptorum Ecclesiasticorum Latinorum*, vol. 32, pp. 478 6 ff; *Epistula* 34, *Patrologia Latina*, vol. 16, column 1119 C; Chalcidius, *In Timotheum*, ch. 220, p. 255, 6 Wrobel; ch. 221, p. 257, 4 ff. On this question, cf. Franz Rüsche, *Blut, Leben und Seele*, Paderborn, 1930, reprinted New York: Johnson Reprint Corp, 1968.

105 Jean Scherer, *Entretien d'Origène avec Héraclide*, p. 168, 2.

106 Jean Scherer, *Entretien d'Origène avec Héraclide*, p. 166, 24.

Chapter Three
Claudianus Mamertus and the Neo-Platonic Concept of the Soul

> Et nos quidem in nobis, tametsi non aequalem, immo valde longeque distantem, neque coaeternam et, quo brevius totum dicitur, non eiusdem substantiae cuius Deus est, tamen qua Deo nihil sit in rebus ab eo factis natura propinquius, imaginem Dei, hoc est illius summae Trinitatis, agnoscimus ad hoc reformatione perficiendam, ut sit etiam similitudine proxima.
> St. Augustine, *De Civitate Dei*, XI, 26

In a thesis devoted to Claudianus Mamertus,[1] René Marie de la Broise managed to discover no less than seventeen proofs of the incorporeality of the soul scattered throughout *De Statu Animae*, which he duly proceeded to isolate and submit to a more or less rigorous critique. The exact number is unimportant. What is debatable is the method employed. It hardly permits us to grasp the author's thought as it burst forth. The approach ends by giving us an excessively fragmented, completely static, frozen vision of the work, one ultimately without great interest. Others, like Schulze[2] and Zimmermann,[3] make the effort to analyze *De Statu Animae* minutely, book by book, chapter by chapter, closely following the author's thought, but for

1 René Marie de la Broise, *Mamerti Claudiani Vita Eiusque Doctrina de Anima Hominis*, Paris: Retaux-Bray, 1890.

2 M. Schulze, *Die Schrift des Claudianus Mamertus, Presbyter zu Venne, über das Wesen der Seele*, Dresden: Rammingsche Buchdruckerei, (Dissertation, Leipzig), 1883.

3 F. Zimmermann, "Des Claudianus Mamertus Schrift *De Statu Animae Libri Tres*," in *Divus Thomas* (Fribourg), vol. 1, 1914, pp. 238–256, 332–368, 470–495.

that very reason they forbid themselves to step back, renouncing the effort to grasp the thought and give real explanations.

Despite the diversity of points of view, in both cases the failure is primarily due to having taken no account at all of the form in which *De Statu Animae* was put forward. What should have been stressed from the start is that we find an occasional work of controversy, not a systematic treatise like so many others in the period. From that comes the apparent disorder of ideas, the absence of a connecting thread indicated by the author himself and, consequently, our difficulty in grasping the internal development of his thought. It goes without saying that a work of this type obeys very different laws from those which govern classical treatises and that the same criteria can hardly be applied to both. Nobody will be surprised that the virtues we have a right to expect from a methodic exposition – logical rigor, relentless linkage of ideas – are often missing in a work which owes its rhythm to the demands of polemic and to objections raised by the adversary. It would be churlish to hold against an author the neglect of certain traits which he did not have to cultivate in the same degree as others and which might have positively hindered attainment of the goal he had set himself.

Is this to say that rigor is totally absent? As long as a work emanates from a thinker, whatever his originality, under whatever contingent form circumstances have imposed, we ought to be able to find the deep intellectual life that drives that author, the fundamental ideas which let him respond to an opponent's challenges, ideas which he has the merit of expounding in function of the needs of the moment. This was precisely the task which faced us.

To discover Claudianus's doctrine, the first step is to determine as exactly as possible what was taught about the human soul at the end of antiquity. An attentive examination of the treatises which have come down to us, reveals the existence of a well defined tradition, to which reference is generally made and which serves different authors as their point of departure. Two issues immediately stand out here. The incorporeality of the soul can be denied because of a rejection of the notion of a spiritual soul, whose intrinsic possibility is not acknowledged and whose very existence seems contradictory – this is the case of those who reduce all that is real to the corporeal, whom St. Augustine reproaches for being unable to go beyond the limits of sense knowledge.[4] Or the objections may concern the union of soul and body or, as it will be called later, the problem of communication of substances, which for a long time constituted the greatest obstacle with which the defenders of the spirituality of the soul collided.

We have been able to show that these questions in fact are what most of the treatises on the soul take up one after the other; two of their chapters are regularly titled Περὶ ψυχῆς and Περὶ ἑνώσεως τῆς καὶ τοῦ σώματος. This is confirmed by a detailed comparison of these treatises whose first chapter conforms to an established framework where the questions are studied in succession about the existence of the soul, its substantial character, its incorporeality, and its immortality. The proof of these affirmations is to be furnished elsewhere; we limit ourselves for the moment to remit the reader there. Since the considerations which appear in different places within *De Statu Animae* can be grouped quite naturally under the rubrics which have just been indicated, we could not do better than to follow this order ourselves in the exposition that we will provide. The present chapter will deal with the nature of the soul and the questions related to it; the following chapter will concern itself more particularly with the problem of its union with the body.

I

From the first lines devoted to the problem of the soul, we find in Mamertus a series of remarks that, however much mixed with Scripture, are totally linked to a philosophical tradition. We propose to speak of the cosmological proof of the existence of the soul developed in the chapters IV and V of Book One (p. 37, 25 ff). For anyone slightly initiated in ancient philosophy, the ideas expressed run the risk of seeming trivial; it will be necessary to remember that they are rather infrequent in Christian authors of the period in the West.

4 St. Augustine, *De Civitate Dei*, XI, 10, 58 (*Corpus Christianorum*, vol. 48, p. 331): "Neque hoc ita dixerim, quasi aer sit anima, quod putaverunt quidam qui non potuerunt incorpoream cogitare naturam." Cf. *De Genesi ad Litteram*, X, 24, p. 327, 20 Zycha (*Corpus Scriptorum Ecclesiasticorum Latinorum*, vol. 28, 1).

In its simplest form, the proof in question may be articulated as follows: without the presence of an incorporeal being, the universe would be incomplete, truncated, and consequently unworthy of an infinitely good and all powerful God. Thus, it must be admitted that this being exists; it is precisely the human soul.

The force of the argument rests in the first place on the principle, accepted as evident, according to which the perfection of the universe demands that all beings should be represented, from the highest to the lowest. The totality which results from it is not a simple heap of heterogeneous individuals without relation one to another, but a hierarchically organized totality where each being is not only distinct from those who surround it, but situated in relation to them according to its degree of perfection. The incorporeal creature prevails over the corporeal in dignity, the living over the non-living.[5] This order is reflected even in the elements, among which fire occupies the first place, followed by air, water, and earth.[6] Ontological hierarchy then, but also hierarchy in regard to action, for only what is higher is able to act upon what is lower, and not vice versa.[7] If even a rose were lacking in the rank list of creation, the beauty of the totality would be compromised. By an even stronger reason, it would be compromised if the most perfect creature, the incorporeal being, were not found.[8] The cosmos would be uncrowned; even more, it would not contain any creature who would be in the likeness of the creator, because only that which is incorporeal truly reflects the perfection of the incorporeal being par excellence.[9] Following

5 *De Statu Animae*, p. 38, 20.

6 *De Statu Animae*, p. 48, 16 ff.

7 *De Statu Animae*, p. 49, 4.

8 *De Statu Animae*, p. 38, 5: "Mirum autem videtur subplemento rerum defore aliquid, si rosae flosculus non existeret, et non defore si incorporea substantia non esset creata. Ne ergo non minimum aliquid, sed vel potissimum deforet creaturae plenitudini, debuit incorporea quoque substantia creari."

9 *De Statu Animae*, p. 38, 9: "Sed ad creatoris forte referatur iniuriam, si incorporeum aliquid ac sibi simile condidisse dicatur, quia simile Deo nihil invenitur in corpore. Sed ab ipso Deo similitudo Dei anima dicitur humana, in corpore autem nulla esse potest similitudo divina." Cf. p. 40, 22: "Si imago Dei est humana anima, incorporei videlicit imago est, si incorporei imago est, incorporea utique ipsa est. At si incorporea non est, incorporei prorsus imago non est."

the profoundly spiritualist tendency of the Platonic current, Mamertus straightaway and categorically rejects any idea of a divine likeness in bodies. Scripture rightly says that man has been created in the image of God, but by man we must understand true man, that is to say, the human soul.[10]

In the second place, the demonstration supposes that the world is the work of an infinitely good and all-powerful God, creator *omnipotentissimus idemque benignissimus*.[11] A Christian could hardly subscribe to the absolute dualism of Gnostic systems, nor even to the mitigated dualism in which certain forms of neo-Platonism tended to consider the world as a product of a defective demiurgery, a sort of runt to which an intermediate power, limited in its activity, had not managed to give a suitable form. All creatures owe their existence to divine goodness. The body itself is a good, although inferior. What is more, this divine goodness has to manifest itself by creation, for the essence of divine goodness is precisely to diffuse itself and to communicate itself to others. God is not an egotist turned in upon his own well-being, an envious being who haggles with creatures over the gift of being that he makes. His characteristic is to wish to create and, on the other hand, his power is such that it executes all that this goodness dictates to him without difficulty.[12]

10 *De Statu Animae*, p. 40, 8: "De vero homine, hoc est de hominis anima quaerimus." Cf. p. 85, 15; p. 98, 14; p. 40, 14: "sicut rei corporeae nulla imago esse potest nisi corpus ita nequaquam imago incorporei invenitur in corpore."

11 *De Statu Animae*, p. 38, 22

12 *De Statu Animae*, p. 38, 22 ff.: "Enim vero creator omnipotentissimus idemque benignissimus substantiam omni corpore potiorem sibique similem si non creavit, quam creari debuisse iam constitit, aut noluit aut certe non potuit. Si voluit et non potuit, omnipotentia caruit. Si potuit et noluit, quod etiam cogitatu est nefas, invidit. Non autem potest vel omnipotentia non posse vel bonitas invidere. Creare ergo incorporeum et potuit et voluit, igitur et creavit. Nisi forte dicas fieri non debuisse, quod ille potuit velle, qui non potuit velle, nisi quod debuit facere. Quid mihi nunc creatum non esse contendas, quod creari debuisse non dubitas? Creari certe debuissse, quia cum creator incorporeus maximum bonum sit, et creatum incorporeum magnum bonum sit, et creatum corpus, quod nisi creatum non est, aliquod bonum sit, a summo Deo qui est maximum bonum, sicut creatum est corpus aliquod bonum, ita creari debuit incorporeum magnum bonum, quia non conveniret omnipotenti bono, qui fecit omnia bona valde, perfectionem plenitudinis rerum vel in minimis

The thinly disguised influence of a certain number of ideas dear to the Platonic tradition is recognizable in this whole development. The notion of the perfection of the cosmos, of the creative good which communicates itself to other beings by a sort of necessity in its nature, or even the absence of any envy in that supremely perfect being, are all considerations which, despite evident alterations, ultimately proceed from the *Timaeus*'s myth of the demiurge,[13] whatever the way by which the author may have come to know it.

This consideration is not at all implausible in itself. Of all the Platonic dialogues, the *Timaeus* is, with the *Phaedo*, perhaps the one that was most read up to the end of antiquity. We know that there were at least nineteen complete commentaries on the *Timaeus*, without counting numerous partial commentaries and others about which we are unsure.[14] It is said that Proclus went so far as to affirm that if necessary the *Timaeus* would replace all the rest for him and that, personally, he had no objection to the master's other works being suppressed.[15] Furthermore, we find in *De Statu Animae* an echo of this special esteem for the *Timaeus*, considered the masterpiece of the

truncam facere, non dicam potissima non creare." Cf. St. Augustine, *De Genesi ad Litteram*, IV, 16, p.113, 10 Zycha (*Corpus Scriptorum Ecclesiasticorum Latinorum*, vol. 28, 1): "Sed bona facere si non posset, nulla esset potentia; si autem posset nec faceret, magna esset invidentia;" John Chrysostom, *Treatise on Virginity*, *Patrologia Graeca*, vol. 48, column 538. On the absence of envy in God, cf. Plato, *Timaeus*, 29 e, to which the pages of *De Statu Animae* which we comment here ultimately go back; *Phaedrus* 247 a, and the famous passage of *The Laws*, 713 d on the subject of divine philanthropy. The doctrine was well known by the neo-Platonists; see the references gathered by René Roques, *L'univers dionysien*, Paris: Aubier, 1954, p. 316, note 1.

13 Plato, Timaeus, 29 d ff. On the different neo-Platonic interpretations of this myth, cf. André-Jean Festugière, *La Révélation d'Hermès Trismégiste*, vol. 3, *Les doctrines de l'âme*, Paris: Lecoffre,1953, pp. 63 ff.

14 Cf. Hans Krause, *Studia Neoplatonica*, Leipzig: Oswald Schmidt, 1904, pp. 46 ff.

15 To it he added the Chaldean Oracles, cf. Marinus, *Vita Procli*, p. 30 Boissonade, Leipzig: Weigelii, 1814. For Iamblicus, the two absolutely indispensable Platonic works are the *Parmenides* for what concerns the intelligible world (περὶ τῶν ὄντως ὄντων) and the *Timaeus* for what concerns the things of this world (περὶ . . . ἐγκοσμίων); cf. Proclus, *In Timaeum*, vol. 1, p. 13, 15 ff. Diehl.

greatest philosopher, as the peak and culmination of philosophy in a way, *arx quaedam et quidam vertex philosophiae*.[16] The allusion is all the more interesting because it is placed in a passage inspired by Porphyry's *De Regressu*, which must have contained, as has been shown,[17] long extracts taken from different works by Plato. In the Platonic school, the *Timaeus* serves as the basis for discussions on the soul, this dialogue being the only one where Plato expounded upon the question somewhat systematically. When he prepares himself to go into this problem in depth, Plotinus affirms he has to follow what he calls "a new way."[18] Henceforth he is going to refer above all to the *Timaeus*. It is while speaking about the *Timaeus* that Proclus gave us his great dissertation on the nature of the soul,[19] and likewise that Chalcidius developed his own ideas on the subject.[20]

But then, if the ideas of the *Timaeus* were so accessible in a variety of forms, it might seem astonishing that other Christian authors did not favorably receive the doctrine developed by Claudianus. Certainly, many of them, and particularly Ambrose and Augustine, applied the *Genesis* passages about man being created in the divine likeness to the human soul.[21] Furthermore, we find allusions in Augustine to the notion that the universe derives its perfection from the presence of all beings and especially from the best among them, namely, spiritual beings; but, when developed attentively, these allusions seem rather to indicate a certain aversion toward what an instant ago we called the cosmological proof for the existence of the soul.[22] To our

16 Claudianus Mamertus, *De Statu Animae*, p. 128, 1.

17 Pierre-Paul Courcelle, *Les lettres grecques en Occident*, second edition, Paris, 1948, p. 228.

18 Plotinus, *Enneads* IV, 2, 1, (pp. 2–3, *Plotinus IV*, Loeb Classical Library, trans. A. H. Armstrong, Cambridge, Mass.: Harvard University Press, 1984).

19 Proclus, *In Timaeum*, 170 D ff., vol. 2, p. 102 Diehl.

20 Chalcidius, *Platonis Timaeus*, ch. 217 ff, p. 253 18 Wrobel (Leipzig, 1876).

21 On this subject see Pierre-Paul Courcelle, *Recherches sur les Confessions de Saint Augustin*, Paris: E. Brocard, 1950, p. 97.

22 St. Augustine, *De Libero Arbitrio*, III, 9. 26: "Quod autem ipsae non desunt animae, quas vel peccantes sequitur miseria, vel recte facientes beatitudo, semper naturis omnibus universitas plena atque perfecta est." Cf. *De Libero Arbitrio* III, 11, 32. To tell the truth, the author seems more concerned with situating himself in the perspective of those to whom he is speaking, than with developing this notion for its own sake.

knowledge only Arnobius attaches any importance to the notion, and he still considers it unacceptable to a Christian and only mentions it to refute it.[23]

It is certainly legitimate to see the cause of this relative silence in the mystic tendency which at this time turned men away from the sciences of nature and pushed them to seek a more direct way of union with God.[24] Rather than in the cosmic religion which had assumed such a scope in the Hellenistic period, the best minds preferred to search for contact with the divine in their own interior. In different philosophical systems, the soul continues to play the cosmic role that the *Timaeus* attributed to it; it is always the masterpiece in the totality whose harmony it assures. But at the same time, growing attraction is felt for the *Phaedo*'s eschatological Platonism, and the tenth book of the *Republic*, so rich in ideas better suited to the spiritual needs of the period, grows more attractive.

As a salvation religion, Christianity could only favor this tendency. Also considerations περὶ κόσμου generally hold an unimportant place in ecclesiastical authors. God is at the summit of beings and at the peak of creation is the human soul, the closest thing to God.[25] There, in the intimacy of hearts, God is revealed. Therefore, every other concern becomes secondary and even harmful in the measure in which it turns us away from what is essential.

Although cogent up to a certain point, these historical reasons would probably not have been decisive if a doctrinal motive had not reinforced them. We do not refer to elements of Platonic doctrine which are manifestly contrary to Biblical teaching such as the pre-existence of soul, but which it is relatively easy to set right or eliminate. More subtly, even the concept of

23 Arnobius, *Adversus Nationes*, II, 37, p. 109, 13 Marchesi: "Et quid homines prosunt mundo aut ob rei cuius sunt necessarii causam, ut non frustra debuisse credantur parte in hac agere et terreni esse corporis inquilini? Ad consummandam molis huius integritatem partem aliquam conferunt, et nisi fuerint additi, inperfecta et clauda est universitatis haec summa?"

24 On this subject one might read the remarks of Fr. Festugière, *La Révélation d'Hermès Trismégiste*, vol. 3: *Les doctrines de l'âme*, pp. 25–26.

25 St. Augustine, *Enarratio in Psalmum 145*, 4, 40 (*Corpus Christianorum*, vol. 40, p. 2107): "Natura animae praestantior est quam natura corporis, excellit multum; res spiritalis est, res incorporea est, vicina est substantiae Dei." See below in this chapter for a detailed treatment of this question.

a philanthropic God, fundamentally generous and only aspiring to communicate his goodness to creatures, as attractive as it may be at first sight, must at last seem murky to a Christian. One can hardly improve upon its explanation of the creation of the world, but, on the other hand, does it not undermine divine transcendence? Once we adopt the axiom that good is self-diffusive, it can no longer be seen how God remains independent in regard to the universe, free to create or to not create according to his pleasure. The *aporia* was not easy to resolve and, subsequently, it would give a great deal of trouble to theologians of the Platonic tendency. Without doubt it is against this teaching, inadmissible as such, that Augustine intended to react when he proclaimed the absolute liberty of God and he insisted that the creative act was gratuitous, although eminently in accordance with the divine nature.[26]

On this point Mamertus did not show the reserve of the best among his predecessors and seems to have ventured beyond the limits imposed by a more strict interpretation of dogma. At least, if we take certain expressions literally, it seems difficult not to reproach him with having made creation necessary.[27] Furthermore, this is a quite significant error, if it is an error, because it reveals to what extent Mamertus was open to pagan philosophical thought.

* * *

Such a general proof, resting only on common principles, teaches us very little about the intimate nature of the soul, or more precisely about the incorporeal being whose presence is judged indispensable for the perfection

26 St. Augustine, *Enarratio in Psalmum 113*, *Sermo* 1, 14, 3 (*Corpus Christianorum*, vol. 40, p. 1640): "Nec sic est in caelo Deus noster, quasi subtracto caelo ruinam sine sede formidet . . . Nec indiget operibus suis, tamquam in eis collocetur, ut maneat . . . Ergo in quibus est ipse, tamquam indigentia continet, non ab eis tamquam indigens continetur." Cf. *Confessiones* XIII, 38, 53; *De Civitate Dei*, VII, 30, 34 (*Corpus Christianorum* vol. 47, p. 212), etc.

27 E.g., *De Statu Animae*, p. 39, 9: "Quid mihi nunc creatum non esse contendas, quod creari debuisse non dubitas? Creari certe debuisse . . ." *De Statu Animae*, p. 40, 1: "Oportuit igitur a summo bono fieri magnum bonum, et potuit omnipotens facere, quod debuit bonus velle."

of the universe. After establishing its necessity, it remains for us to define its essence. So, what is the soul, and what are its properties? If the neo-Platonists do not always give a rigorous definition by proximate genus and specific difference, they nonetheless are in agreement on certain points which confer originality on their doctrine and set it plainly in opposition to rival doctrines. Our goal is not to totally summarize *De Statu Animae*'s teaching on this score once again, a work of doxography, necessary or not, which has already been done by others, but to highlight the fundamental ideas which serve as the author's criteria and on the basis of which he reasons.

From the outset it must be emphasized once and for all that this doctrine's most constant trait is acknowledgement of the soul as a *complete substance*, independent of the body and fully self-sufficient. Hence it is not a quality, as the Pythagorean notion of soul-harmony supposes, nor is it the Aristotelian concept of the soul as entelechy of the body, which the most widespread opinion of the time took to be a sort of variant of the first position.[28] Nor is it a substantial principle *quo*, as a no doubt more authentic interpretation of Aristotle's thought would have it, but rather a *res substantiva*,[29] fully constituted in itself, exercising its own activities without the help of any extrinsic element. Platonic doctrine remained faithful to its original inspiration in this, even if on other points it seemed to approximate that of Aristotle, to the point of deceiving certain modern critics. The marked hostility of the neo-Platonists toward the Stagirite, however, ought to put us on guard against the excessively Aristotelizing approach of certain of the Christian disciples and St. Augustine in particular. Any attempt at explanation which tries to define the soul as act of the body in a strictly Aristotelian sense and to present its relations with the body according to the matter-form scheme would rather distort our perspectives and embroil a question already quite complicated on its own.

28 Plotinus, *Enneads* IV, 7, 8^4 and 8^5 (pp. 370–379 in *Plotinus IV*, Loeb Classical Library, A. H. Armstrong trans., Cambridge, Mass.: Harvard University Press, 1984); Nemesius, *De Natura Hominis*, *Patrologia Graeca*, vol. 40, column 537 A, etc. The whole difficulty came from the fact that in presenting the soul as the act of the body (*De Anima*, II, 1, 412 b 5) Aristotle seemed to make it an accident of the body. For an explanation of this way of defining the soul, see for example St. Thomas, *In Aristotelis De Anima*, II, lectio 1, number 123 ff.

29 *De Statu Animae*, p. 104, 5.

What must be firmly maintained is that the soul is a separated substance, χωριστή, as the neo-Platonists repeat *ad nauseam*.[30] The proof is furnished by the soul's operations, some of which are apparently exercised without any involvement of the body. If the soul is the body's entelechy, Plotinus said,[31] its "withdrawal into sleep ought not to exist, since an entelechy must adhere to the being whose entelechy it is." The occurrence of dreams appeared to be a manifestation of this independent and furthermore uninterrupted life of the soul.[32] The ease with which the soul abstracts itself often, so that it becomes completely alien to what is done or said around it, even when the body is in the state of wakefulness, is another indication of the same truth.[33] It only remains to say that in these moments when the soul lives its own life, when it attends to its primary function of contemplating the Ideas, what is involved in administering the body is at least secondary, if not accessory. Let us note[34] here the special value assigned by neo-Platonism to this fact of experience which long held the attention of philosophers. While in Stoicism it appeared linked to discussions about the seat of thought in the body – chest, brain, or whatever[35] – here it means

30 E.g., Plotinus, *Enneads* I, 1, 10 (pp. 114–117, *Plotinus I*, Loeb Classical Library, A. H. Armstrong trans., Cambridge, Mass.: Harvard University Press, 1989); Porphyry, *Sententiae*, XX, etc.

31 Plotinus, *Enneads* IV, 7, 8^5, (pp. 360–365, *Plotinus IV*, Loeb Classical Library).

32 Claudianus Mamertus, *De Statu Animae*, p. 86, 2: "Quid autem illud est quod somniare dicimus, nisi quod ne defesso quidem corpore in somnosque resoluto animae vis a cogitationibus vacat?" Nemesius, *De Natura Hominis*, *Patrologia Graeca*, vol. 40, column 579 A; Priscian, *Solutiones ad Chosroen*, p. 46, 12 Bywater (*Supplementum Aristotelicum*, vol. 1, 2).

33 Claudianus Mamertus, *De Statu Animae*, p. 82, 24: "Hinc est quod etiam dum corpus administrat atque sentificat, si quando in summa eademque semper adtollitur, ita quodam modo corporeos deserit sensus ab hisdemque inlocaliter abscedit, ut coram posita non videat, ut iuxta sonantia non audiat, ut percursam legendo paginam non intellegat." Cf. St. Augustine, *De Genesi ad Litteram*, VII, 20, p. 216, 18 and ff Zycha (*Corpus Scriptorum Ecclesiasticorum Latinorum*, vol. 28, 1).; Lactantius, *De Opificio Dei*, 16, 7, p. 52, 22 Brandt (*Corpus Scriptorum Latinorum Ecclesiasticorum*, vol. 27, 1); Plotinus, *Enneads* IV, 4, 25 (pp. 204–207 Plotinus IV, Loeb Classical Library), etc.

34 See what Theophrastus, *De Sensibus*, 42, had already said on this.

35 Cf. Max Pohlenz, *Die Stoa, Geschichte einer geistigen Bewegung*, Göttingen: Vandenhoeck & Ruprecht, 1948, p. 62.

that thought is "elsewhere," that it has withdrawn entirely from the body with which it no longer has anything in common.

To say this is not enough. The soul is not only a substance separated from the body, it is positively contrary to it,[36] opposed to it in the measure in which the body can become an obstacle to its highest activity and an occasion of degradation. Far from being necessary to its perfection, the body is often only a hindrance without which the soul behaves better.[37] At each instant, life here below assumes the character of a trial that the soul must overcome if it wants to fulfill itself completely.

Here we connect with the great Platonic tradition, so sensitive to the fleeting beauties of this world, but at the same time resolved to only see in them the reflection of a higher beauty, free of limits and of the seductions of material things. Because the soul is a perfect substance in itself, it aspires to a better life; it tends toward the invisible world to which its nature is related, which "no corporeal light illuminates with its splendor."[38] Aristotle was greatly reproached precisely for having linked the soul's perfection to the presence of a material element, for having made the exercise of its higher faculties depend on the senses and on touch, the crudest of them.[39] Moreover, Aristotle failed to explain the fate of the soul after death. Once the soul is deprived of its body its situation is obviously inferior, and it must then lead a diminished life. In short, all the elements which give Platonism its strength and confer on it the high moral and human value so admired by Christians, are absent. Thus the neo-Platonists' unyielding opposition to a whole flank of Aristotelian theory is understandable, as well as the special insistence with which they always proclaim the substantial character of the soul.

The soul is a substance intrinsically and extrinsically independent of the body, an incorporeal substance, it must be added. This idea was adumbrated in the preceding remarks, but it is necessary to deal with it separately

36 Claudianus Mamertus, *De Statu Animae*, p. 103, 12: "Intellexit quoque propter inmutabilem vim contrariorum sicut tenebras luci, sicut essentiae nihilum, ita incorporeo corpus esse contrarium." Cf. *De Statu Animae*, p. 78, 20 ff; p. 130, 8, etc.

37 *De Statu Animae*, p. 158, 7.

38 *De Statu Animae*, p. 76, 15 ff.

39 Aristotle, *De Anima*, II, 9, 421 a, 19–26

and show how another polemic arose around it, directed not only against Aristotle, who was regarded as having taught that the soul was material, but above all against the Stoics. Like the neo-Platonists, the latter maintained that the soul is a substance, but a material or quasi-material substance, spread throughout the body and intimately mixed with each of its parts. Perhaps the new adversary was less formidable than the first, but it was better represented, since under the Empire, Stoicism knew much greater success than Aristotle. Consequently, here the struggle was even harsher.

As its name indicates, incorporeality is the quality of what is not corporeal. Therefore, if we want to form a precise idea of incorporeality, it is necessary to say first what a body is. Now the body is defined by quantity. According to the commonly received definition, amply confirmed in earlier doxographic literature, corporeal is what is extended in length, width, and depth.[40] Inversely, however small it is, every body possesses each of these three dimensions and occupies a place in space from which it excludes every other body by that very fact.[41] This detail may seem superfluous. Stoic doctrine made it necessary by claiming for the πνεῦμα a subtlety such that its presence did not in any way increase the volume or weight of the body with which it was deemed to be mixed.[42] Similarly, each body, by reason of its three dimensions, is composed of various parts exterior to each other,

40 Claudianus Mamertus, *De Statu Animae*, p. 60, 2; p. 67, 6; p. 88, 15; p. 116, 1; p. 187, 2, and *passim*; St. Augustine, *De Genesi ad Litteram*, VII, 21, p. 217, 19 Zycha (*Corpus Scriptorum Ecclesiasticorum Latinorum*, vol. 28, 1); *Epistula* 166, 4, p. 551, 3 Goldbacher (*Corpus Scriptorum Ecclesiasticorum Latinorum*, vol. 44); *De Natura et Origine Animae*, IV, 21, 35, p. 413, 20 Urba-Zycha (*Corpus Scriptorum Ecclesiasticorum Latinorum*, vol. 60). Cf. Aulus Gellius, *Noctes Atticae*, V, 15, 5 (p. 428, *The Attic Nights of Aulus Gellius I*, with English trans. by John Rolfe, Cambridge, Mass.: Harvard University Press, Loeb Classical Library, 1927, 1984): "Alio quoque modo corpus esse Graeci dicunt τὸ τριχῇ διάστατον." See the evidence assembled by F. Boemer, "Der lateinische Neuplatonismus," p. 118 and Jan Hendrik Waszink, *Tertulliani De Anima*, p. 165.

41 *De Statu Animae*, p. 63, 20; p. 67, 6; p. 114, 14, and *passim*.

42 Cf. Plotinus, *Enneads* IV, 7, 8^2, pp. 366–369 (*Plotinus IV*, Loeb Classical Library).

43 *De Statu Animae*, p. 60, 1; p. 67, 13.

44 *De Statu Animae*, p. 63, 22; p. 66, 18.

situated to the right or left, before or beyond, above or below each other.[43] So it is divisible and even divisible to infinity, each part conserving the properties inherent in all bodies.[44]

In contrast to the body thus defined, what characterizes the soul and all incorporeal beings is to lack length, breadth, and depth, any quantitative size: *spiritus quantitatem non habet*.[45] Nor does the soul have any other parts properly speaking, because its faculties – memory, judgment, will – although distinct, are inseparable from each other, and the indissoluble link that exists among them imitates the three divine Persons' unity, incomparably superior to that of bodies.[46]

We can still talk about greatness of soul, but in a completely different sense. In this case we refer to spiritual greatness, not greatness of mass.[47] For, though all of the same nature, human souls are not equal among themselves. Some happen to be superior to others in science or virtue. They are not thereby quantitative any more than the science thanks to which they are distinguished.[48] To confirm this, we have only to compare "the immense soul" which, in Virgil's term, the bee's "narrow chest" shelters, to the soul of certain much greater animals like the camel.[49] Will we still say that the greatness of a soul is measured by the dimensions of the body it animates? Or to speak more philosophically, are we simply considering the completely relative notion of corporeal greatness? A thing is only large or small by

45 *De Statu Animae*, p. 194, 17.

46 *De Statu Animae*, p. 95, 17 ff.

47 *De Statu Animae*, p. 70. 12; p. 60, 15; p. 69, 9.

48 *De Statu Animae*, p. 60, 18: "Nam et animam anima praestantiorem saepe et experimur et didicimus, nec tamen eandem, quam secundum potentiam praestantiorem didicimus, secundum molem, quae nulla illi est, credimus esse maiorem. Illud etiam nec te arbitror diffiteri quamlibet multas animas perfecte sapientes non plus sapere idem una anima perfecte sapiente, nec quod una omnimodis volet anima, multas id omnimodis volendo plus velle, nec quod quaecumque optime meminerit, multas melius memoriae tenacitate meminisse."

49 *De Statu Animae*, p. 107, 13 - p. 109, 18. Cf. St. Augustine, *De Quanitate Animae*, XIV, 24 (p. 67 *De Quanitate Animae/On the Measure of the Soul*, trans. Francis Tourscher, Philadelphia: Peter Reilly, 1933): ". . . a little bee knows more than an ass: to compare the sizes of which [the ass and the bee]is surely worse than asinine."

comparison to another, and the same thing will be declared now great, now small, according to the different objects to which it is compared. Thus there exists an *idea* of greatness independent of material beings, an "incommensurable measure"[50] to which intelligence refers when it pronounces upon the greatness or smallness of any object, one which subsists even in the absence of any material object. That is to say, not all greatness is corporeal, and without this notion of intelligible greatness, it will even be impossible to speak of the greatness of material beings.

These notions, developed by the author with a great deal of satisfaction and often at greater length than they seem to merit, must not hide the real problem that they aim to resolve and to which the label *de quantitate animae* is rather suitable. The question to answer is how the soul can animate a body that has three dimensions in all its parts, since the soul has none. The Stoics had long emphasized the difficulty.[51] The simplicity with which they posed it no doubt made its solution more difficult, and the fact that it was often discussed by late authors lets us understand that it continued to seem decisive to many minds.

De Statu Animae made the term *inlocalitas* fashionable to refer to this problem. F. Boemer showed[52] that the expression, which Mamertus employed for the first time, did not, as Theiler held, correspond to the Greek ἄτοπος, which has the sense Mamertus assigns to *inlocalitas* only rarely and in very specific cases. Rather, it corresponds to ἀδιάστατος, and it primarily designates the non-extended, non-spatial character of the soul. Still, the notion has a relation to the localization of the soul, because the fact of occupying a determined place in space stems immediately from the quantitative nature of a being. What is characteristic of the soul is thus to be in a body, though not like water in a vase or in the manner in which a body would be present, but in the mode of spiritual beings, that is to say, without being commensurable to it. It is at the same time everywhere and nowhere,

50 *De Statu Animae*, p. 113, 8.

51 Plotinus studies the problem at length, particularly in *Enneads* VI, 4 (pp. 126–279, *Plotinus IV*, Loeb Classical Library).

52 F. Boemer, "Der lateinische Neuplatonismus," pp. 111–126. The conclusions drawn from the abundant material gathered in these pages should, however, be viewed with some reservations. See the review by R. Beutler in *Gnomon*, vol. 13, 1937, pp. 552–558.

and complete in each part of the body.[53] Since it is never possible for a body to be in contact with another body by each part of itself at the same time, the soul is not less in the smallest part of the body than in another larger one or in the whole body.[54]

The same thing follows from an analysis of sensation. Indeed, it is impossible to admit with the Stoics that sensation occurs by transmission, each part of the πνεῦμα a communicating the impression felt at an extremity of the body to a neighboring part until it arrives at the principal part, that is to say the heart, and finally becomes conscious. Because then there would be as many sensations as distinct parts of the πνεῦμα. The soul would not experience pain where it takes place, and it would even be incapable of knowing whether it is the foot, the hand, or some other part of the body which suffers. On the contrary, it is the whole soul which experiences the least sensation in the exact place of the body where it is produced; this shows clearly that the soul exists simultaneously and without division in the whole body.[55]

This said, we can explain in what the divine likeness, already claimed for the soul, consists. Formally, it is as a spiritual being that it has been created in the likeness of God. Just as God fills the whole universe with his simultaneous, undivided presence, the soul by reason of its incorporeal nature is entirely present in the body it vivifies without thereby being measured by it.[56]

However, our definition will be adequate only in so far as it permits us to distinguish the human soul from that of animals or from the vital principle that animates plants and that is also incorporeal, although in general our authors deny it the title of soul.[57] A last essential characteristic, rationality, should be added to the traits already noted. The human soul is not only an incorporeal substance, it is a thinking, *reasoning* substance. By reason, indeed, man is separated from and superior to the brutes. Were there nothing more noble than sensitive life in him, that is to say what he shares

53 *De Statu Animae*, p. 155, 12; p. 185, 18, and *passim*.

54 *De Statu Animae*, p. 63, 3.

55 *De Statu Animae*, p. 67, 23 ff.; cf. Plotinus, *Enneads* IV, 7, 7 (pp. 356–361 Plotinus IV, Loeb Classical Library).

56 *De Statu Animae*, p. 155, 8 ff.

57 *De Statu Animae*, p. 73, 18: "animadvertas licet defore fixis viventibus animam, sed non defore incorpoream vitam;" cf. p. 81, 20 and below in the next chapter.

with the other animals, it would be necessary to confess that the other animals often win over him in perfection. How many of them enjoy keener sight, more refined senses than ours![58]

Evidently one need not be a neo-Platonic to teach that the soul is rational. However, the doctrine that thought is not an accident but the very substance of the soul is accepted as a characteristic feature.[59] The soul in itself is all thought, *tota cogitatio est*, as well as all love, *tota dilectio est*,[60] the two notions being inseparable. What is accidental is not the fact of thinking, it is thinking about some particular thing, that the soul attends to different objects successively.[61] This activity is so essential that, as we have seen, it continues even during sleep.[62]

58 *De Statu Animae*, p. 49, 8.

59 *De Statu Animae*, p. 186, 2: "Substantialiter inest animae rationcinari."

60 *De Statu Animae*, p. 86, 9; p. 87, 1. See an analogous identification of substance and powers in the Trinity, in whose image the soul is created, Marius Victorinus, *Adversus Arium*, I, 37, *Patrologia Latina*, vol. 8, column 1069 A: "ibi enim potentia, substantia; non enim *aliud potentia, aliud substantia*," and op. cit., III, 10, column 1106 C: ". . . quia et *ipsa voluntas substantia est*." Cf. Claudianus Mamertus, *De Statu Animae*, p. 86, 5: "Verum tu idcirco vel maxime de animae statu falleris, quia *aliud animam, aliud esse animae potentias* credis. Quod enim cogitat acccidens eius est, substantia vero qua cogitat. Hoc equidem de voluntate opportet agnoscas. Nam sicut tota anima cogitatio est, ita anima tota voluntas est et quae perfecte vult tota vult, et ut supra dictum est, quaecumque illi velle accidentia est, *ipsum vero velle substantia est*." As Fr. Henry noted, *Plotin et l'Occident*, p. 59, these texts of Victorinus seem to reproduce almost word for word Plotinus, *Enneads* VI, 8, 13 (p. 268, *Plotinus VII*, Loeb Classical Library, A. H. Armstrong trans., Cambridge, Mass.: Harvard University Press, 1988): αἱ δὲ ἐνέργειαι ἡ οἷον οὐσία αὐτοῦ, ἡ βούλησις αὐτοῦ καὶ ἡ ουὐσία ταὐτὸν ἔσται. Reacting against Plotinism, the Greek commentators – see section 2 of the present chapter – later reestablished the distinction between the soul's essence and its operations; e.g., Simplicius, *In Aristotelis De Anima*, p. 240, 33 Hayduck: "Accordingly, although the highest essence of the soul remains absolutely identical, its activity, which does not remain identical, cannot be confused with the essence, if it is true that sometimes it thinks, sometimes it does not think."

61 *De Statu Animae*, p. 86, 1: "anima nempe variare cogitata potest, non cogitare non potest."

62 See note 32 in this chapter.

Still, it must also be added that the very reason which raises humans above the animals can be clouded by the effect of passion and that, if humans do not make an effort to live according to their true selves, they effectively become like brutes, like them slaves to imagination and the senses.[63] The neo-Platonists had a strong a sense of spiritual values and of the gap that very often exists between man as he is in fact and as he ought to be; too strong to believe that human dignity is separable from the right exercise of the most noble faculties or from the effort that human dignity imposes on us to tear ourselves away from lower goods.

By this rational character the soul is in contact with the Ideas, proportioned to the intelligible world, and of its same nature. These Ideas are its food, just as material elements are the body's nourishment.[64] The Platonic school went further and attached this doctrine to the theory of remembering. Since it happens that when a person is interrogated on subjects he has never studied, he answers correctly, these Ideas are familiar to him, he knows them already by nature, or he has acquired them previously. As is known, Augustine reproached himself for having adhered to this position rashly in his first works.[65] But if Augustine rejects as incompatible with Christian faith the notions of prior existence of the soul in another world and of the remembering with which the prior existence is linked, nevertheless, he recognizes that intelligible and immutable things are within the reach of the soul, that it is suited of itself to understand them, and that one can say in this sense that the soul is connected to them. Of course, these ideas are not subsistent realities, as they were for Plato. They only have existence in God, and he created all things by them.[66] Around the same time,

63 *De Statu Animae*, p. 85, 16.

64 *De Statu Animae*, p. 131, 8. On the soul's food, a commonplace in antiquity, cf. Soranus, apud Tertullian, *De Anima*, 6, 6; Nemesius, *De Natura Hominis*, *Patrologia Graeca*, vol. 40, column 541 A; Pseudo Maximus, *De Anima*, *Patrologia Graeca*, vol. 91, column 357 A; earlier Plato, *Protagoras*, 313 c, 314 b; *Phaedrus*, 247 c-d, 248 b-c, *Phaedo*, 84 a etc.

65 St. Augustine, *Retractationes*, I, 4, 4; I, 8, 2; cf. *De Quantitate Animae*, XX, 34 (pp. 92–95 Latin text and English trans. Francis Tourscher, Philadelphia: Peter Reilly, 1933); *De Trinitate*, XII, 15, 24.

66 *De Statu Animae*, p. 178, 12: "Non enim ex rerum notitia est creatoris scientia, sed existentia rerum ex notitia creatoris." Cf. *De Statu Animae*, p. 51, 10; St.

however, Victorinus, who evidently remained more faithful to the Platonic tradition, still expressed himself as if the ideas were creatures of God themselves.[67]

Because of its historical interest, let us note the definition of the ideas that Mamertus offers in this regard. The definition is identical or almost identical to what we find in Victorinus and St. Augustine:

Marius Victorinus, *Adversus Arium*, IV, 5, *Patrologia Latina*, vol. 8 col. 1116 C:	St. Augustine, *De Diversis Quaestionibus 83*, Quaestio 46, 2:	Claudianus Mamertus, *De Statu Animae*, p. 112, 6:
Deus, inquam, primo universalium existentias substantiasque progenuit, *has Plato ideas vocat*, cunctarum inexistentibus specierum *species principales* . . .	Sunt namquae ideae *principales formae* quaedam . . . atque has rerum *rationes principales appellat ideas Plato*.	Sic et in *his principalibus formis* ratio par est, *quas Plato ideas nominat*.

That the three texts attributed the definition to Plato naturally does not mean that it was taken from him directly. Furthermore, the likelihood that St. Augustine depends on Victorinus or that Mamertus depends on Augustine or Victorinus seems to be precluded by the verbal differences

Augustine, *De Civitate Dei*, XI, 10, 74 (*Corpus Christianorum*, vol. 48, p. 332): "Neque enim multae, sed una sapientia est, in qua sunt infiniti quidam eique finiti thesauri rerum intelligibilium, in quibus sunt omnes invisibiles atque incommutabiles rationes rerum etiam visibilium et mutabilium, quae per ipsam factae sunt. Quoniam Deus non aliquid nesciens fecit, quod nec de quolibet homine artifice recte dici potest; porro si sciens fecit omnia, ea utique fecit quae noverat. Ex quo occurit animo quiddam mirum, sed tamen verum, quod iste mundus nobis notus esse non posset, nisi esset; Deo autem nisi notus esset, esse non posset." Cf. *Confessiones*, XIII, 38.

67 Marius Victorinus, *Adversus Arium*, IV, 5; *Patrologia Latina*, vol. 8, column 1116 C.

that we can observe.[68] Since this is one of the best known doctrines of the Academy, and since the definition is abundantly represented in the earlier doxographic tradition, we would be inclined to believe that it goes back to an ordinary handbook of philosophy. Such handbooks existed and were still used in Gaul as well as in Africa in the fifth century.[69] Mamertus himself informs us, in terms somewhat reminiscent of St. Augustine's, that he has drawn from two different sources: one the text he had before him while composing his treatise, the other certain philosophical readings from an earlier period of his life, whose substance he retained.[70] We can legitimately

68 In the same passage St. Augustine elaborates upon the usage of the synonyms *formae* and *species*, which exactly translate the Greek ἰδέαι, and their relation to *rationes*, which corresponds literally to λόγοι but does not substantially differ from the other two in meaning. See Étienne Gilson's remarks, *The Christian Philosophy of Saint Augustine* (trans. L.E.M. Lynch, New York: Random House, 1960), pp. 198–199. Cf. St. Augustine, *De Civitate Dei*, VII, 28, 18 (*Corpus Christianorum*, vol. 47, p. 210): "Dicit enim [Varro] se sibi multis indiciis collegisse in simulacris aliud significare caelum, aliud terram, aliud exempla rerum, quas Plato appellat ideas." Tertullian, *De Anima*, 18, 3 (and Jan Hendrik Waszink's commentary, p. 258): "Vult enim Plato esse quasdam substantias invisibiles incorporales supermundiales, divinas et aeternas, quas appellat ideas, id est formas, exempla et causas naturalium istorum manifestorum et subiacentium corporalibus sensibus, et illas quidem esse veritates, haec autem imagines earum." A. Solignac's excellent article, "Analyse et sources de la Question *De ideis*," *Augustinus Magister*, vol. I, Paris, 1954, pp. 311–315, offers numerous references to doxographic collections or to handbooks where our definition of the ideas appears in one form or another.

69 Regarding these handbooks, cf. Pierre-Paul Courcelle, *Les lettres grecques en Occident*, pp. 122–123, 179–181, 241, and *passim*, and A. Solignac, "Doxographies et manuels dans la formation philosophique de saint Augustin," in *Recherches Augustiniennes*, vol. 1, Paris, 1958, pp. 113–148.

70 *De Statu Animae*, p. 191, 6: "Hinc accidit quod libellorum a me transmissorum editio, quos philosophicae artis subtilissima disputatione disposui, me fecit cautum atque sollicitum, ut eorundem intellegentiam iudicio non committerem meo, sed ad potioris peritiam desinarem, *et non tantum ea, quae nunc ex eorum [philosophorum] lectione percepi, verum etiam quae unde iam pridem memoriae reservanda mandavi* iudicio tuo probanda transmisi." In reading this text we keep in mind the remarks by A. Engelbrecht, *Corpus Scriptorum Ecclesiasticorum Latinorum*, vol. 11, p. xlvi. Claudianus's words can be compared to those of St. Augustine, *Confessiones*, V, 3, 3: "*multa philosophorum legeram memoriaeque mandata retinebam*."

suppose that in the first case he refers at least to Porphyry's *De Regressu*, from which we now know that he took several quotations.[71] Indeed, in view of the number and length of these texts – the one from the *Phaedo* occupies nearly two pages – it is not plausible that they were quoted from memory. By contrast, in the second case, it may very well be that we are dealing with one of the handbooks in use at the time, summing up in condensed and easily graspable form the philosophers' chief doctrines.[72] The absence of

71 Cf. Pierre-Paul Courcelle, *Les lettres grecques en Occident*, pp. 225–235.

72 Again, it is tempting to attribute to this sort of handbook or some treatise of liberal arts several elements whose source is only indicated vaguely, traces of which are found in other authors. Thus we find:

Claudianus Mamertus, *De Statu Animae*, p. 63, 11:	St. Augustine, *De Genesi ad Litteram*, VII, 13, p. 212, 7 Zycha (*Corpus Scriptorum Ecclesiasticorum Latinorum*, vol. 28, 1):
Nam et cum flamus et reflamus, particulas eius [sc. aeris] haurimus et reddimus, quas in pastum totius corporis **venae** illae capiunt, **quas** ἀρτηρίας Graeci **vocant**, per quas idem **aer** in temperamentum trium elementorum **pulmonum** quoque indefessa agitatione *dispergitur* . . . p. 45, 4: Hinc est quod etiam in corpore humano principalem prae omnibus sensibus locum visus accepit. Ab interno scilicet *calore* cordis ac **iecoris igniculi** quidem indefessim *scintillantes in cameram capitis* **quasi in caelum nostri corporis subvolant. Ex quibus radii per oculorum media** profusi ac lumini extero commixti corporum quae inciderint repercussu retroversim cedentes eorundem colores ac formas hariunt . . .	Deinde si non est contemnendum, quod medici non tantum dicunt, verum etiam probare se adfirmant, quammvis omnis caro terrenam soliditatem in promptu gerat, habet tamen in se et **aeris** aliquid, quod et **pulmonibus** continetur et a corde **per venas, quas arterias vocant**, *diffunditur*; et **ignis** non solum *fervidam qualitatem*, cuius sedes in **iecore** est, verum etiam luculentam, quam velut eliquari ac **subvolare** ostendunt in *excelsum cerebri locum*, **tamquam in caelum corporis nostri. Unde et radii** *emicant* **oculorum et de cuius medio** velut centro quodam non solum ad oculos, sed etiam ad sensus caeteros tenues fistuale deducuntur, ad aures videlicet, ad nares, ad palatum, proper audiendum, olfaciendum atque gustandum . . .

direct references to the authors and content of these handbooks for the time being unfortunately keeps us from determining precisely the role they played. But there is no doubt that that role was considerable and that the study of certain puzzling features of the period would be greatly facilitated if that role were better known.

The second passage from Claudianus may be contrasted with Apuleus, *Apologia*, 15, p. 18, 9 Helm: ". . . an, ut alii philosophi disputant, **radii** nostri seu **mediis oculis** *proliquati* **et lumen extrario mixti** atque ita uniti, ut Plato arbitratur, seu . . ." Engelbrecht, who already noted this parallel (*Untersuchungen über die Sprache des Claudianus Mamertus*, p. 439 ff), concluded that Claudianus depended on Apuleus. Since the points of contact between Claudianus and St. Augustine are more frequent, the former derivation seems unlikely. At most we can imagine a more remote common source.

It still seems that certain reflections on geometry found in *De Statu Animae* go back to some handbook: e.g., p. 88, 9: "Linea est, ut doctissimi atque excellentes viri non dixere solum, sed ratiocinando probavere, longitudo simplex, quae in corpore prorsus nequeat inveniri," and p. 89, 4: "Haec ergo de qua loqui institueram longitudo cum fuerit puncto inchoata punctoque finita, a Graecis γραμμή, a nostris linea dicitur." Cf. Aulus Gelleus, *Noctes Atticae*, I, 20 7(p. 92, *The Attic Nights of Aulus Gellius I*, Loeb Classical Library): "'Linea' autem a nostris dicitur, quam γραμμή Graeci nominant. Eam M. Varro ita definit [frag. 350 Bipont]: 'Linea est,' inquit, l'ongitudo quaedam sine latitudine et altitudine.'" In regard to one Hermophiles who taught geometry without a stick and so without drawing figures in the sand, whose name is known only through *De Statu Animae*, p. 174, 4, his method makes us recall the *figurarum positae sine pulvere formae* of which Licentius's poem speaks according to Varro (in Augustine, *Epistula* 26, *Corpus Scriptorum Ecclesiasticorum Latinorum*, vol. 34, 1, p. 89, 11). Furthermore, part of the doctrine that Varro expounded in his mathematical treatises seems to have been faithfully summarized by Claudianus, *De Statu Animae*, p. 130, 2:

"Marcus Varro, sui saeculi peritissimus et teste Tullio omnium sine dubitatione doctissimus, quid in musicis, quid in arithmeticis, quid in geometricis, quid in philosophoumenon libris divina quadam disputatione contendit, nisi ut a visibilibus ad invisibilia, a localibus ad inlocalia, a corporeis ad incorporea miris aeternae artis modis abstrahat animum et in corpora, hoc est in adversa sibi dilapsum sui compotem faciat?" Regarding this quote, see lastly A. Solignac, "Doxographies et manuels dans la formation philosophique de saint Augustin," in *Recherches*, vol. I, Paris, 1958, p. 122 and note 26.

II

If we add immortality[73] to the properties just enumerated – substantial character, incorporeality, rationality – we have all the principal elements by which the neo-Platonists defined the human soul, and which in many cases constitute the skeleton of the treatises they have left us. In general we can say that these essential traits represent the achievements of struggles against rival schools carried on during several centuries. It may be that the majority of the late authors do not demonstrate much originality in the discovery of ideas. However, even when they do not go beyond scholastic teaching, their remarks allow us to understand how neo-Platonic doctrine, previously elaborated by a few great minds, imposed itself little by little and obtained wide diffusion especially due to the work of popularization carried out by disciples. Just on this score they deserve to be valued.

But there is something more important. By condensing what they considered to be the kernel of their doctrine into a simplified pattern that was easy to remember, the neo-Platonists attract our attention to a second question closely linked to the first, which poses an equally sensitive problem for Christians, namely the *divinity of the soul*. Would not defining the soul as an incorporeal, intelligent, simple, and immortal substance thereby make it a divine being? "The soul is of divine and eternal stock," is the conclusion which forced itself on Plotinus at once, after expounding on the nature of the soul according to the same pattern sketched above.[74] Thus in one of his treatises, the second to be precise, we find what is perhaps the clearest and most emphatic affirmation of the theory of the soul's divinity, which can be said to constitute a turning point in the history of thought.[75]

It is not that neo-Platonism created this doctrine from nothing. We know the importance that the notion of the soul's filiation with the divine had in Plato.[76] Despite its particular modalities, neo-Platonism claimed to be the development of the master's thought and often based itself upon his own words. Many passages from the Dialogues were literally reproduced

73 *De Statu Animae*, p. 76, 8; p. 179, 11 and *passim*.
74 Plotinus, *Enneads* IV, 7, 10 (pp. 380–385, *Plotinus IV*, Loeb Classical Library).
75 Werner Jaeger, *The Theology of the Early Greek Philosophers*, Oxford: Clarendon Press, 1947, p. 88.
76 Plato, *Phaedo*, 80 a-b; *Republic*, X, 611 e; *Laws*, X, 899 d, etc.

by later writers, who in their turn proclaimed that our soul "raises us – seeing that we are not an earthly but a heavenly plant – up from earth toward our kindred in the heaven,"[77] or again, "Of all a man's own belongings, the most divine is his soul, since it is most his own."[78]

By the period we are studying, the idea had long ceased to belong exclusively to the Platonic or Pythagorean currents. Indeed, there were few schools that did not affirm the soul's divinity in one way or another, from Stoicism to diverse Gnostic systems and even Epicureanism, which, however, denied its immortality. Divinization obtained through culture or by a kind of priestly, initiated knowledge, or simply by the momentary identification of the soul contemplating divinity, is no longer the achievement of heroes and emperors, but is accessible to everyone, even children.[79] Few ideas have caught fire like the ancient concept of the soul. From this viewpoint, the Incarnation, conceived as man's divinization, had nothing which could offend pagan sensibilities. What was unacceptable was the idea of a humiliated God, ridiculed and ignominiously put to death, as, for example, Celsus's criticism make us see.[80] A God could only be beautiful; it pertained

77 Plato, *Timaeus*, 90 a, (p. 245 trans. R. G. Bury, *Timaeus, Critias, Cleitophon, Menexenus, Epistles*, Cambridge, Mass.: Harvard University Press, Loeb Library 1961); Clement of Alexandria, *Protrepticus*, X, p. 72, 28 Stählin (*Die griechischen christlichen Schriftsteller*, vol. 12): οὐράνιον φυτόν. Nemesius, *De Natura Hominis*, *Patrologia Graeca*, vol. 40, column 533 B.

78 Plato, *Laws*, V, 726 a 3 (p. 323, R. G. Bury trans. *Laws* I, Cambridge, Mass.: Loeb Library, Harvard University Press, 1961; cf. Iamblicus, *Protrepticus*, 5, p. 29 15 Pistelli (Leipzig, 1888): τῶν ἡμετέρων κτημάτων μετὰ θεοὺς ψυχὴ θειότατον οἰκειότατόν τέ ἐστι.

79 Cf. Henri-Irenée Marrou, Μουσικὸς ἀνήρ (Grenoble: Didier et Richard, 1938), p. 231 ff.

80 Cf. Origen, *Contra Celsum*, VI, 75, p. 145, 1 ff. Koetschau (*Die griechischen christlichen Schriftsteller*, vol. 3). Inspiring themselves in the celebrated texts of Isaiah, Christians were led to develop the theme of the ugliness of Christ; cf. Tertullian, *De Carne Christi*, 9, 29, p. 216 Kroymann (*Corpus Scriptorum Ecclesiasticorum Latinorum*, vol. 70); *De Idolatria* 18, p. 52, 17 Reifferscheid (*Corpus Scriptorum Ecclesiasticorum Latinorum*, vol. 20); Clement of Alexandria, *Pedagogue*, III, I, p. 237, 18 Stählin (*Die griechischen christlichen Schriftsteller*, vol. 12), etc. On the demands of the ancients about the "beautiful order," see the still interesting remarks of Lessing, *Laocoon*, 2.

to him to never abandon the beautiful order, εὐσχημοσύνη, so dear to the Greek ideal.

Nevertheless, it is still true and pertinent for our purposes, that, as familiar as it was to the majority of ancient writers, this doctrine assumed a vigor and philosophical significance in neo-Platonism and particularly in Plotinus that it had never possessed previously and would not achieve again. It can be stated without exaggeration that the divinity of the soul was not affirmed more absolutely and more categorically at any other point in the history of ancient thought. The soul is no longer simply the "divine being," related to the gods of whom the *Sophist* spoke; it is "a god."[81]

> To know the nature of a thing we must observe it in its unalloyed state, since any addition obscures the reality. Clear, then look: or, rather, let a man first purify himself and then observe: he will not doubt his immortality when he sees himself thus entered into the pure, the Intellectual. For, what he sees is an Intellectual-Principle looking on nothing of sense, nothing of this mortality, but by its own eternity having intellection of the eternal: he will see all things in this Intellectual substance, himself having become an Intellectual Cosmos and all lightsome, illuminated by the truth streaming from the Good, which radiates truth upon all that stands within that realm of the divine.
>
> Thus he will often feel the beauty of that word, 'Farewell: I am to you an immortal God,' [Empedocles *apud* Diogenes Laertius, VIII, 62], for he has ascended to the Supreme, and is all one strain to enter into likeness with it. (*Enneads* IV, 7, 10, pp. 380-385, *Plotinus IV*, Loeb Classical Library)

The same notion is even more clearly emphasized in the last part of Macrobius's *Commentary on the Dream of Scipio*. As much as the author pretends to only want to explain Cicero's secret thought, it is obvious that the ideas he attributes to Cicero with more generosity than historical accuracy

81 Plato, *Sophist*, 216 b (*Theaetetus, Sophist*, Cambridge, Mass.: Loeb Classical Library, Harvard University Press, 1977, p. 266), "And though I do not think he is a god at all, I certainly do think he is divine . . . "

were developed in a neo-Platonic context and with the aid of neo-Platonic concepts, as the explicit reference to the *Enneads* bears witness.[82] After setting forth a doctrine which often coincides with Plotinus word for word, he comes to the great truth in which the whole world finds its completion, namely, that "the soul is not only immortal, but it is a god."[83]

We are all the more entitled to conclude that this doctrine takes on a new resonance here, for Plotinus himself signaled his desire to depart from the traditional teaching by completely disengaging the higher part of the soul from the sensible world where it is submerged.[84] Proclus, who is fully aware of the originality of this position and who reacts in the opposite direction, notes that its goal is to link the soul as closely as possible to the νοητά and assure the continuity of one hypostasis with another.[85]

However, let us keep from giving this theory a simplistic or naively idealist interpretation, which the superficial reading of certain passages of the *Enneads* might suggest. It is not that we are to represent man as we see him, with his manifest imperfections, as a pure marvel and still less take him for a god. In the text of the *Commentary* to which we have just alluded, Macrobius already warns against this pitfall. In effect, he says it would be dangerous to want to teach man that he is a god without first making him understand his true nature. We would risk convincing him that the feeble and perishable in us is also divine.[86] What is properly divine is the soul considered in itself, in "its immutable and eternal essence."

82 Macrobius, *Commentarium in Somnium Scipionis*, II, 12, 7: "Et quia Tullio mos est profundum rerum scientiam sub brevitate tegere verborum, nunc quoque miro compendio tantum includit arcanum quod Plotinus magis quam quisquam verborum parcus libro integro disseruit, cuius inscriptio est *quid animal quid homo*." He refers to the first treatise of the *Enneads* I, What is an Animal? What is Man?

83 Macrobius, *Commentarium in Somnium Scipionis*, II, 12, 5, p. 264, 23 Eyssenhardt: "Et haec sit praesentis operis consummatio, ut animam non solum inmmortalem sed deum esse clarescat."

84 Plotinus, *Enneads* IV, 8, 8, (p. 421 *Plotinus IV*, Loeb Classical Library): "And, if one ought to dare to express one's own view more clearly, contradicting the opinion of others, even our soul does not altogether come down, but there is always something of it in the intelligible . . ."

85 Proclus, *In Parmenidem*, p. 948, 18.

86 Macrobius, *Commentarium in Somnium Scipionis*, II, 12, 6.

The impact of this affirmation becomes clear if we go back to the first treatise of the first *Ennead* to which Macrobius refers us in the same passage of the *Commentary*. We learn that the faults we commit, which again are not to be denied, far from being imputable to the soul, are due to its absence. They come precisely from the soul's not having intervened to rectify the vicious dispositions of the inferior part of the being. Man is not defined only by his soul, as might be believed from certain formulas taken from Plato. He is a mixture of contrary elements intimately associated despite their heterogeneity. Every fault is caused when the worse part of the "couplement" that is man achieves a victory over him.[87] This fault is only possible because he has not been touched by the Intelligence at the precise moment. Since the Intelligence is alien to what is produced in spite of it, something in which it takes no part, it bears no responsibility. It necessarily remains untouched. Faults committed do not belong to it. By definition they fall into the category of acts belonging to the composite and only affects the lower part of man. The soul remains beautiful and even "at peace and always within itself."[88]

Analogous observations must be made about another equally important problem which bears some relation to the first, namely of time in the soul. Taken in itself time does not inhere in the soul any more than change. Only in relation to the body and sensations, which are temporal by nature, is the soul in time.

In this context we must give particular importance to the seventh treatise of *Ennead* III, entitled "Time and Eternity," and not, as is frequently done by those who are interested in Plotinian psychology, exclusively to *Ennead* IV, which is entirely devoted to problems about the soul.[89] Being

87 Plotinus, *Enneads* I, 1, 9 (pp. 112–115 *Plotinus I*, Loeb Classical Library).

88 Plotinus, *Enneads* I, 1, 9 (p. 113, *Plotinus I*, Loeb Classical Library): "The nature of that higher soul of ours will be free from all responsibility for the evils that man does and suffers; these concern the living being, the joint entity, as has been said."

89 On time in Plotinus, cf. John F. Callahan, *Four Views of Time in Ancient Philosophy* (Cambridge Mass.: Harvard University Press, 1948; reprinted Westport, Conn.: Greenwood Press, 1979), pp. 88–148. The author does not seem to have brought out the point upon which we insist here, although he recognizes the importance of the treatise on eternity.

eternal, the soul is prior to time and is situated outside of it: "It is because the things which it generates are not eternal, but encompassed by time; since even the [individual] souls are not in time, but such affections as they have, and the things they make [are encompassed by time]. For the souls are eternal, and time is posterior to them . . ."[90] Just as the simple, indivisible soul somehow acquires extension through the requirements of the body it vivifies, although exempt from time, so also, Plotinus says, the soul is "temporalized" to impress its image on what is corporeal.[91] Time is born from this "fall" of the soul, which thus appears as a kind of fragmentation or "continual progress" of its own life.[92]

The last in the hierarchy of divinities, the soul is the first of the intelligible beings to enter time, which it engenders and possesses with its own acts.[93] Inversely, exactly as time owes its existence to the initiative of the soul, time is annihilated when the part of the soul that is immersed in the sensible returns to the tranquility of intelligible being.[94] The qualities acquired because of the role the soul is called to play in the sensible world are all accidental determinations, which are provisionally added to its essence without altering its purity and of which it is to be again despoiled at the moment of rejoining the world of ideas to which the soul belongs.[95]

The moral corollary of this doctrine must be an exhortation to live according to our nature, "neglecting nothing which the soul may contain of the divine."[96] All the philosopher's efforts should converge on a single goal, "to bring back the god in us to the divine which is in the All," according to the well known *logion* reported by Porphyry.[97] The Socratic γνῶθι σεαυτόν

90 Plotinus, *Enneads* IV, 4, 15 (p. 175, *Plotinus IV*, Loeb Classical Library).
91 Plotinus, *Enneads* III, 7, 11 (pp. 336–343, *Plotinus III*, Loeb Classical Library, A. H. Armstrong trans., Cambridge, Mass.: Harvard University Press, 1980).
92 Plotinus, *Enneads* III, 7, 12 (p. 341, *Plotinus III*, Loeb Classical Library).
93 Plotinus *Enneads* III, 7, 13 (pp. 352–353, *Plotinus III*, Loeb Classical Library).
94 Plotinus, *Enneads* III, 7, 12 (pp. 342–349, *Plotinus III*, Loeb Classical Library).
95 Cf. Plotinus, *Enneads* I, 6, 6, (pp. 246–253, *Plotinus I*, Loeb Classical Library).
96 Plotinus, *Enneads* VI, 9, 32, p. 188 Bréhier edition (Plotinus, *Ennéades*, Paris: Les Belles Lettres, 1924–1938, re-published, 1954–1960). [Translator's note: I have been unable to locate the text in Armstrong's translation of the *Enneads* in the Loeb Classical Library.]
97 Porphyry, *Vita Plotini*, 2, line 25 (pp. 6–7, *Plotinus I*, Loeb Classical Library).

is no longer what it was in the classical Greek period, an appeal to moderation, a formula expressing the ideal of being measured above all. It is an invitation to become aware of one's own divinity. Libanius in his turn will say that the only goal of philosophy is to know oneself and to thus assimilate oneself to the gods.[98] It is no more and no less than becoming what we already are by nature, what we have never ceased to be despite momentary forgetfulness. "We become god, or rather, we are already god!"[99]

* * *

The divine character of the soul had never been stressed so obstinately, so much so that Plotinus's own disciples would refuse to follow the master in this matter. This significant fact sheds retrospective light on the novelty of Plotinus's move. If we can believe Iamblichus, Porphyry already had his doubts on the subject, now adhering to the solution of the illustrious head of the school, now vehemently departing from it.[100]

Doubts give way to certainty. Divergence flowers when we reach Iamblicus, Proclus, and their successors. One after the other, they reproach Plotinus for having abandoned the school's doctrine, for having exaggerated the soul's perfection, for not having sufficiently distinguished the soul from the intellect; in reaction, they will be themselves led to insist on its nature as an inferior being. The soul's supposed perfection is incompatible with the state of sin and weakness in which we see it. We can not respond to this objection by simply saying with Plotinus that the soul is immutable and impeccable in its essence, because the soul is responsible for the

98 Libanius, *Orationes*, 18, 18 ff, vol. II, p. 244, 10 Foerster (Leipzig, 1904).

99 Plotinus *Enneads* VI, 9, 9, (pp. 334–339 in *Plotinus VII*, Loeb Classical Library). On this point see Maurice de Gandillac, *La sagesse de Plotin* (Paris: Hachette, 1952), especially p. 184 ff.

100 *Apud* Iamblichus, *De Anima*, p. 365, 17 Wachsmuth (from Festugière's translation in *La révélation d'Hermès Trimégiste*, vol. III, p. 184): "Porphyry himself is in doubt on this matter; sometimes he abandons it with vehemence; sometimes he adheres to it as to a doctrine transmitted from the beginning. According to this opinion, therefore, the Soul in no way differs from the Intellect, the gods, and the higher kinds, at least in what concerns the total substance of the Soul."

choices man faces and, in the event, is what yields to evil and irrationality:

> What then is that in us which sins when under the impulse of irrationality we pay attention to a lascivious image? Is it not the decision of the will? And how would it not be this decision? Because thanks to it we struggle against the reckless products of imagination. But if our decision sins, how will the soul be without sin?[101]

From a different point of view, but also for the purpose of reducing our idea of the soul to more modest proportions, Proclus situates time above the soul and will deny that the soul is prior to time, that the soul could be freed of it, and even that the soul is always actually thinking.[102]

The new doctrine, which goes back before Plotinism to the earlier Platonic tradition, readily considers the soul to be an "intermediate substance," a kind of intermediary between "the corporeal, divisible kinds and the indivisible, incorporeal kinds," whose function is to link the former to the latter. In this capacity, it participates "both of the higher and the lower, it is neither permanent nor entirely mutable."[103] Simplicius, who was not

101 Iamblichus apud Proclus, *In Timaeum*, 341 E, vol. III, p. 334, 4 ff. Dieh!l (Festugière. *La Révélation d'Hermès Trismégiste*, vol. 3, *Les doctrines de l'âme*, p. 252).

102 Proclus, *In Timaeum*, 241 F ff, vol. III, p. 12, 5 Diel; Proclus, *In Timaeum*, p. 333, 28 (Festugière, *La Révélation d'Hermès Trismégiste*, vol. 3: *Les doctrines de l'âme*, p. 252 "Starting from these reflections, we rise up against Plotinus and the great Theodore [of Asina] who maintain that there is something out of reach in us which is impassible and always thinking in act. For Plato only admitted two circles in the composition of the soul. Now, of these two circles, according to him, one is bound, the other shaken, and both the former which is bound, and the latter which is shaken, can no longer exercise intellectual liberty. Also, the divine Iamblichus quite rightly attacked those who thought in this way."

103 Iamblichus, *De Anima*, p. 365, 28 Wachsmuth (Festugière, p. 185); Simplicius *In Aristotelis De Anima*, p. 240, 33, Hayduck (Festugière, p. 253): "But, since the soul's supreme essence itself does not remain without mixture in the course of its inclination towards objects of the second rank, so that in this way this essence also is intermediate, as Iamblicus notes in his *Treatise on the Soul*, not

afraid to manifest his opposition to Plotinus and who openly adopted Iamblichus's point of view, expresses the same notion in equivalent terms: "It is why we admit neither, as Plotinus wants, that there is something in the soul which always remains equally identical, nor that its procession is complete in the fall toward generation."[104] The essence of this new tendency might well be summed up in an expression of Priscian which may originate in the same source: "It is not only according to its modes of being that [the soul] changes, but in a certain fashion also in its essence."[105]

* * *

This doctrine of the divinity of the soul, already vigorously criticized by pagans, naturally must have seemed unacceptable to Christians and must have provoked even sharper opposition among them. One of the most constant characteristics of their treatises is the concern to describe in the clearest possible manner the distance which separates the soul from God. Precisely from fear of having to make the soul equal to God, Maximus the Confessor will note later[106] that many Christians tried to undermine the very foundations of the pagan theory by denying the incorporeality of the soul.

Perhaps when Maximus wrote, such concerns would have seemed vain. But that had not always been the case. We have examined Faustus of Riez

only between the divisible and indivisible, but also between the generated and ungenerated, the perishable and imperishable, and in this way, for this very reason, whether it thinks or does not think . . . it is certainly plausible or rather necessary that not only the soul's activity but its very essence, and this essence at its highest level (I mean of our own soul), is enfeebled in some way, slackens, and sinks so to speak in the course of its inclination toward objects of the second rank, not that it entirely goes out of itself (because in that case it would no longer remain a soul), but it no longer conserves its purity, so that it remains both the same and not the same . . . and thus, as it has been divided in some fashion by the change, and has not remained what it was, it also allows its activity to be separated from its essence, so that it also comes about that it does not act." Cf. Simplicius, *op. cit.*, p. 89, 22 Hayduck (Festugière, p. 254)

104 Simplicius, *op. cit.*, p. 5, 38 ff.

105 Priscian, *Metaphrasis in Theophophrastum*, p. 32, 13 Bywater (Festugière, p. 257).

106 Maximus the Confessor, *Epistula* 6, *Patrologia Graeca*, vol. 91, column 428.

at length. The enormous prestige of authors like Ambrose and Augustine had not been able to reassure him on this point. We must mention here the still more striking example of Arnobius, a contemporary of Porphyry, whose *Adversus Nationes* roughly coincides with the apogee of neo-Platonism, and undoubtedly represents the most violent and extreme attack known against the theses of the soul's spirituality and divinity. We propose to return elsewhere to some of the problems posed by the work's second book which is largely devoted to the question of the human soul. It suffices here to underline some words of particular interest. Even Tertullian, the relentless adversary of philosophy in any form, did not go so far in his negations. Not only do incorporeality and the simplicity of the soul seem inadmissible to this rhetorician converted to Christianity late in life, but also immortality, the soul's substantial nature, even rationality, in a word, all the attributes with which the neo-Platonists were accustomed to characterize it.[107] By the end of the diatribe, where the author's personal thought can not always be clearly discerned, man does not appear in any way to be superior to brutes; he is lowered to the rank of brute; and there is no longer any distinction from them.[108] No doubt, a considerable dose of rhetoric is included in these obviously exaggerated remarks, but the rhetoric only heightens the essential point of the whole polemic, namely the categorical refusal to accept a doctrine which had become extremely dangerous by its currency and the quality of its defenders.

When the Fathers admit the thesis of the soul's spirituality, as they most often do, they find themselves all the more obliged to dissipate any ambiguity by multiplying clarifications regarding the manner in which the soul is distinguished from the divine essence. We have only to go through Gregory of Nyssa's *De Anima et Resurrectione* or Maximus the Confessor's *Letter* 6 to observe how strongly they feel the need to draw a clear, hard boundary between God and the human soul. Since the soul is not a perfect image (εἰκών) of God like the Word but has merely been created in the image of God (κατ' εἰκόνα), the soul necessarily falls short of the supreme

107 Arnobius, *Adversus Nationes*, II, 26, p. 97, 18 Marchesi and II, 30, p. 101, 21 (immortality); II, 17, p. 85, 21 ff Marchesi (rationality); II, 26, p. 97, 7 ff. Marchesi (substantial nature), etc.

108 Arnobius, *Adversus Nationes*, II, 17, p. 86, 2.

being's perfection. Its character of created being keeps it in a state of dependence and inferiority such that strict identification with the divine nature becomes unthinkable.[109]

Cassiodorus's *De Anima* is obviously less profound and more of a textbook than the two works just cited and in a sense illustrates better the desire to rectify, because the author follows the outline of pagan treatises step by step and admits their conclusions in the measure of the possible. But at the appropriate moment he does not fail to introduce the corrections which keep the reader from the temptation to imagine the soul as divine substance. Despite its dignity, the soul is capable of deviation, *convertibilis*, subject to error and failure, and consequently still quite far from divine perfection.[110]

* * *

What has been said so far lets us understand better the manner in which Mamertus and before him St. Augustine, intended to resolve this problem in their own way. We can affirm without paradox that neo-Platonic teaching was both the closest to Christianity and the farthest away, because of its insistence on the soul's divinity. Consequently, the task was to carefully salvage the elements of truth that neo-Platonism carried without thereby adhering to the extreme conclusions into which its principal representatives fell.

There are few Christians who have developed such a nuanced and profound idea of the closeness of the soul to God as Augustine. The soul is not a divine substance. However, its perfection is such that it is impossible to conceive a being which comes closer to God: *Deo nihil in rebus ab eo factis natura propinquius*,[111] so that if, as a mere hypothesis, the soul were material,

109 Gregory of Nyssa, *De Anima et Resurrectione*, *Patrologia Graeca*, vol. 46, column 41 C; Maximus the Confessor, *Epistula* 6, *Patrologia Graeca* vol. 91, column 429 B. Maximus follows his predecessor's text step by step here.

110 Cassiodorus, *De Anima*, *Patrologia Latina*, vol. 70, column 1287 A.

111 St. Augustine, *De Civitate Dei,* XI, 26 ff. (*Corpus Christianorum*, vol. 48, p 345.) Cf. *De Quanitate Animae*, 34, 77: "Audisti quanta vis sit animae ac potentia: quod ut breviter colligam, quemadmodum fatendum est, animam humanam non esse quod Deus est; ita praesumendum, nihil inter omnia quae creavit,

it would logically be necessary to conclude that God was also.[112] Far above corporeal nature the soul has in itself more reality than the whole changing world ranged in space. Invisible, incorporeal, it orders its thoughts, takes in an infinite number of images representing all beings; it directs its body, and without being able to pretend to be divine it is, however, close to the substance of God: *vicina est substantiae Dei*.[113]

If the bishop of Hippo could let himself go so far, he must have disposed of an infallible criterion thanks to which anything tending to make the soul equal to God had been surely and deliberately dismissed. This criterion is the essential mutability of all created beings. Thus, we understand he returned quite often to the question of change in the soul. *To be* in the full sense is to be immutable, immutable being a kind of measure of reality.[114] In this sense, God alone among all beings possesses the fullness of being, because he truly "is." Every created being, whatever its dignity, by the mere fact of being subject to change, attests to its own imperfection. It acquires qualities that it did not yet have or loses those it already possessed. Thus it is composed of being and non-being and does not reach the simplicity of the absolute being. In this perspective how meaningful is the beautiful phrase of *Contra Maximinum Haereticum*, where it is affirmed that to change is to die in some manner: *in omni enim mutabili natura, nonnulla*

Deo esse propinquius;" *De Beata Vita*, I, 4: "Animadverti enim et saepe in sacedotis nostri [sc. Ambrosii], et aliquando in sermonibus tuis, cum de Deo cogitaretur, nihil omnino corporis esse cogitandum, neque cum de anima; nam id est unum in rebus proximum Deo."

112 St. Augustine, *De Genesi ad Litteram*, X, 24, p. 327, 10 Zycha (*Corpus Scriptorum Ecclesiasticorum Latinorum*, vol. 28, 1): "Nulla enim proprior natura est, qua diligenter inspecta possit etiam Deus, qui supra omnem creaturam suam incommutabilis permanet, incorporaliter cogitari, quam ea quae ad ipsius imaginem facta est, et nihil vicinius at fortasse nihil tam consequens, quam ut credito, quod anima corpus sit, etiam Deus corpus esse credatur."

113 St. Augustine, *Enarratio in Psalmum 145*, 4, 40 (*Corpus Christianorum*, vol. 40, p. 2107).

114 St. Augustine, *Tractatus in Johannis Evangelium*, 38, 10,19 (*Corpus Christianorum*, vol. 36, p. 343): "Res enim quaelibet prorsus qualicumque excellentia, si mutabilis est, non vere est; non enim est ibi verum esse, ubi est et non esse. Quidquid enim mutari potest, mutatum non est quod erat; si non est quod erat, mors quaedam ibi facta est; peremtum est aliquid ibi quod erat, et non est."

mors est ipsa mutatio.[115] Thereby the *aporia* about immortality of the First Epistle to Timothy is resolved most skillfully.[116] It is true to say with St. Paul that only God is immortal, because only he is simple and immutable. As to the soul, even if it is to exist always, it cannot possess all its being at the same time. The mutations to which it is subject makes it die ceaselessly in some part of itself. There is always a sense in which it can be said that it is not. An impassable chasm separates it from "he who is" by his essence.

Mamertus is going to develop his own thought on this subject in an analogous context, often following St. Augustine. After defending the soul's spirituality against attacks by Faustus of Riez, as we have seen, it remained for Claudianus to orient his demonstration to avert what constitutes the most serious objection to his thesis in his adversary's eyes and to show how, in spite of everything, the soul in itself is not a divine being. Mamertus will do this first by underlying the soul's created and therefore finite character. As incorporeal being, it resembles God; as creature, it is inferior to him.[117] Indeed, one thing is the Truth and another thing the image of this Truth: *aliud namque est veritas, aliud imago veritatis*.[118] The image is distinguished from the original by definition, it carries an element of otherness, it supposes a certain remoteness and degradation, and this moves closer to pure mutability and non-being.

This inferiority is manifested in the soul's being subject to quality. The fact that it is not quantitative does not imply, as Faustus held, that it is God. It means at most that it is distinct from the body and superior to it. By contrast, it does not escape quality, and nothing else is necessary to show that it is not divine: *si, ut quantitatis, ita etiam qualitatis expers esset, profecto enim Deus esset, identidemque si, ut qualitati, ita etiam quantitati cederet, corpus*

115 St. Augustine, *Contra Maximinum Haereticum*, II, 12, *Patrologia Latina*, vol. 42, column 768.

116 *In Timothei*, 6, 16; Cf. above ch. II, note 38. Cf. St. Augustine, *De Genesi ad Litteram*, VII, 28, p. 228 Zycha.

117 *De Statu Anima*, p. 40, 8: "De vero homine, hoc est de hominis anima quaerimus. Non est haec aequalis Deo, sed similis: similis utique quantum incorporea incorporeo, inferior quantum creata creatori, similis quantum intellectualis lux luci intellegibili: quantum mutabilis creatura inmutabili creatori dissimilis."

118 *De Statu Animae*, p. 40, 13.

esset.[119] None of the ten Aristotelian categories corresponds to God; only some are applied to the soul. Every one of them may be attributed to the body.[120]

To be subject to quality means that the soul knows the vicissitudes of temporal mutations; it means to move if not in space like body, at least in time, to pass from pride to humility, from ignorance to science, from anger to calm.[121] Our author could find in St. Augustine's *De Genesi ad Litteram* some considerations that he gives us here, as can be seen by the following comparisons:

De Genesi ad Litteram p. 259, 8 Zycha	*De Statu Animae*, p. 65, 6
Exempli etiam gratia *per tempus* movetur animus vel *reminiscendo*, quod oblitus erat, vel discendo, quod nesciebat, vel volendo quod nolebat . . . Ac per hoc sicut *per tempus et locum movet corpus ipse tantum per tempus motus conditus spiritus*, ita per tempus movet conditum spiritum ipse nec per tempus nec per locum motus conditor spiritus . . .	*Temporale* est autem, quod paulo ante superba, nunc humilis, prius laeta, nunc tristis, dilexit ante, nunc odit, prius *aliquid oblita*, nunc *meminit*. Huius modi autem motibus animae non communicat corpus, quibus inmoto nihilominus corpore movetur, unde datur intellegi *animam per tempus inlocaliter moveri* atque ab eadem *corpus et temporaliter et localiter moveri* . . .

119 *De Statu Animae*, p. 182, 24.

120 *De Statu Animae*, p. 69, 4: "Ex illis Aristotelicis categoriis nulli prorsus subiacet essentia divina, rursus anima humana non omnibus subiacet, porro corpus quodlibet subiacet omnibus. Nam de Deo non dicimus qualis est, quia non potest comparari quasi ad aliud, ut dicatur: talis est. Nec dicimus quantus est, quia non mole magnus est, nec quid habet, quia nihil non habet, nec quo modo est, quia ipse modus est, nec habitum eius inquirimus, quia continet omnia, nec locum, quia non nisi corpus in loco est, nec tempus, quia sempiternitas est, nec actum, quoniam quietus agit, nec passionem, quia non patitur. Iam decima immo prima est ipsa substantia, de qua haec praedicamenta texuntur." Cf. St Augustine, *De Trinitate*, V, 1, 2, *Patrologia Latina*, vol. 42, column 912. According to F. Boemer, "Der lateinische Neuplatonismus," pp. 87–96, Ma-

This intrinsic mutability does not keep the soul from being immobile in relation to the body which it moves in space, and this stability is yet another sign of its superiority in regard to the body:

De Genesi ad Litteram, VIII, 21 p. 260, 10 Zycha	*De Statu Animae*, p. 64, 24:
Quae si posset diligenter inspicere . . . inveniet ea, quae, per spatia locorum moventur, nisi ab eis, quae loco fixa sunt, non moveri. Non enim *movetur* solus *digitus*, *nisi* manus fixa sit, a cuius articulo, velut inmoto cardine, moveatur. Sic tota palma ab articulo cubiti, sic cubitus ab articulo *humeri*, humerus ab scapula cum movetur *stantibus* utique cardinibus, quibus motio nitatur, it per loci spatium, quod movetur . . . Denique nec *in ambulando pes* lavatur, nisi *alius fixus* totum corpus ferat . . .	Hic oportet accipias nihil moveri posse nisi ab innoto, atque ut id docaemus exemplo, *digitum* certe *nisi stante manu movere* non possumus, motus autem brachii ab *humeri* stabilitate est. Et ut non diutius inmoremur, *in gradiendo* utique *pes* unus *figendus est*, ut *alter* promoveri queat.

Again the soul appears as an intermediary between God and the corporeal world of which it is in charge. Since it is impossible for us to know positively what God is, it is at least necessary to know that thanks to this gradation of beings we are capable of raising ourselves to Him.[122] So the

mertus followed Marius Victorinus rather than St. Augustine here. On this point, which remains unclear, see lastly W. Schmid, "Claudianus Mamertus," in *Reallexion für Antike und Christentum*, vol. 3, columns 174–175.

121 *De Statu Animae*, p. 69, 22, Cf. Plato, *Laws*, 897 a 1.

122 *De Statu Animae*, p. 193, 10: "Sic enim volumus inspirante domino et auxiliante, ut non tantum creaturam ipsius scrutemur, verum etiam ascendentes ad creatricem substantiam per ea, quae facta sunt, intellectu conspiciamus et, quamvis non perveniamus ad id, ut eius substantiam intellegere valeamus et quid sit sciamus, saltem id, quod non sit, evidentissime teneamus." Cf. *De Statu Ani-*

notion of intermediary, *medioximum* – the word is as expressive as rare in the Christian Latin world[123] – best defines the soul's status[124] and sums

mae, 102, 23; St. Augustine, *Enarratio in Psalmum 85*, 12, 23 (*Corpus Christianorum*, vol. 39, p.1186): "Deus ineffabilis est; facilius dicimus quid non sit, quam quid sit." *De Trinitate*, VIII, 2,3 (*Patrologia Latina*, vol. 42, column 948): "Non enim parvae notitiae pars est, cum de profundo isto in illam summitatem respiramus, si antequam scire possimus quid sit Deus, possumus iam scire quid non sit."

123 *De Statu Animae*, p. 183, 3: "Nunc vero medioximum quiddam naturae incorporeae, sed creatae sortita [anima] nec Deus est, quoniam qualitatem habet, nec corpus, quia non habet quantitatem." Arnobius employs the expressions *medietas* or *media qualitas* in a similar if not identical sense; cf. *Adversus Nationes*, II, 31, p.103, 11 Marchesi, and II, 14, p. 82, 10. In pagan authors the word *medioximum* is used to designate demons, those intermediate beings between gods and men, or else sea gods in contrast to those above and below; cf. Apuleus, *De Platone et eius Dogmate*, I, 11, p. 45, 12 Thomas: "Tertium habent [deorum genus] quos *medioximos* Romani veteres appellant, quod et sui ratione et loco et potestate diis summis sunt minores, hominum natura profecto maiores." Martianus Capella, II, 154: "Hos omnes Graeci δαίμονας dicunt ἀπὸ τῶν δαήμονας εἶναι; Latini *medioximos* vocitarunt." Plautus, *Cistellaria*, 512: Ita me di deaeque superi atque inferi et *medioxumi* . . ." Servius, *Vergilii Aeneida*, III, 134: "Quidam aras superiorum deorum volunt esse, *medioxumorum*, idest marinorum, ſocos, inferorum mundos." Cf. Georg Wissowa, *Religion und Kultus der Römer*, second edition, Munich: C.H. Beck, 1912, p. 38, note 4. Among Christians, the only one to use the word *medioximum* besides Claudianus seems to be Apollinaris Sidonius, although he gives it a quite different meaning; cf. *Letters*, vol. II, Book IX, 3, 5 (p. 514, Loeb Library).

124 After Tertullian the word *status*, whose French equivalent is *condition*, is generally employed to express either the soul's essence or inner nature, or his present or future state. In the first sense, cf. Tertullian, De *Anima*, 4, 1, where *status* is contrasted with *census animae* (origin of the soul), and again II, 1, where it is opposed to *actus* (acts or operations of the soul). On *status* in Tertullian, cf. V. Naumann, "Das Problem des Bösen in Tertullians zweitem Buch gegen Marcion," in *Zeitschrift für Katholische Theologie*, vol. 58, 1934, p. 339, note 11. In the second sense, cf. *De Statu Animae*, p. 85, 12: "Illa [anima] namque si in status pristini sublimitate mansisset, a quo sponte dilapsa est, numquam contra spiritum caro, nec contra carnem spiritus concupisset." Cf. *De Statu Animae*, p. 97, 3 and p. 171 10 (*indemutabilis status*). In his memoir on Claudianus Mamertus (*De Veris Inlustribus*, 83), Gennadius explains *status* as *substantia*. Claudianus seems to have been inspired by the title of Faustus of

up the essence of the teaching which *De Statu Animae* tries to develop in its various facets. By developing it judiciously, our author can set forth the soul's spiritual character without fear of slighting God's unique perfection.

* * *

To complete this outline, we must examine how the relationships between God and the world came to be formulated on the basis of these notions. Among the terms which *De Statu Animae* employs in this context, one expression, *stabilis motus*,[125] occurs repeatedly and ought to detain us because of its unusual appearance. The author wants to convey the message that God never ceases to act, without departing from his immobility, the condition and primary sign of his perfection. Here again, in writers of the low period it is possible to discern common concerns, perhaps even certain dependence, and glimpse a new intersection of Christian and pagan influences.

Riez's work, which drew a distinction between the nature of the soul (*status animae*) and its operations (*qui de anima nascitur cogitationis adfectus*), *Epistula 3*, p. 175, (*Corpus Scriptorum Ecclesiasticorum Latinorum*, vol. 21).

125 *De Statu Animae*, p. 30, 24: "Omne etenim temporaneum mobile atque mutabile inmutabilis et stans sempiternitas includit adficiens salubriter aliqua, iudicialiter aliqua adfici sinens, ipsa ab omni adfectu vel motu temporis et loci satis aliena, *praedita illo tantum motu qui stabilis dicitur*, ex qua et per quam et in qua est omne quod solo tempore et ab ipsa tantum movetur, et omne quod et per tempus et locum ab illa movetur neque solo tantum tempore. Sed istinc alias." *De Statu Animae*, p. 64, 14: "Tres ergo esse motus, stabilem, inlocalem localemque iam notum est. *Stabilis motus* Dei est, inlocalis animae, localis corporis. *Stabilis motus* est quod Deus creaturam non semper fecit, sed tamen eandem non nova voluntate tunc creare voluit cum creavit, quia semper tunc voluit creare cum fecit. Tunc temporis significatio est, semper non ad tempus pertinet. Tunc ergo istud ad principium temporis pertinet, non ad tempus, quia temporaneum motum stabilitas sempiternae voluntatis includit, ac per hoc semper tunc velle *stabilis motus* est." Cf. *De Statu Animae*, p. 65, 5 and p. 82, 2: "Administrat inrationalis anima corpus animale in salutem scilicet eius, et administrat animam rationalem intellectus rationis capax in salutem videlicet animae rationalis operante atque administrante Deo principali potestate et *stabili motione* atque ininitiato substantiarum cardine . . ."

At first sight and prescinding from the context, we might be tempted to believe that *stabilis motus* simply designated regular or periodic movement, in contrast to disordered movement like the φορὰ ἄτκακτος mentioned in the *Timaeus*, which Chalcidius indeed translates by *motus instabilis*.[126] This is not or is no longer the precise sense which the texts we consider confer on it. F. Boemer correctly saw that in the former case we had an oxymoron, seeming to unite in one formula and conciliate two apparently contradictory notions.[127] But we believe he was mistaken in holding that the expression and its variants belong to the *Corpus Hermeticum*,[128] and in concluding thereby that hermetic thought influenced Claudianus's thought. There is ample room to think that the word and especially the doctrine played a much larger role than contemporary theological discussions like to admit and that neo-Platonism itself contributed more than any other school to their diffusion.

A passage of Favonius Eulogius gives a preliminary indication of the path to follow. In it the formula *stabilis motus* seems to be utilized in the precise and somewhat technical sense and that we have just encountered. We read in the *Disputatio de Somnio Scipionis* (p. 3, 32 ff Holder): *Dyas vero* **ut theologi asserunt**, *secundus est motus. Primus enim* **motus** *in monade* **stabilis et consistens**, *in dyade velut foras egreditur; primumque conubium poetae fabulose dixerunt sororis et coniugis, quod videlicet unius generis numero coeunte copuletur; et Iunonem vocant, uni scilicet Iovi accessione alterius inhaerentem. Ab hoc numero mundus apparuit mente ac materia, quae Grece dicitur* ὕλη, *constructus*.

126 Chalcidius, *In Platonis Timaeum*, ch. 31, p. 95, 24 Wrobel. Cf. Plato, *Timaeus*, 30 a; Plotinus, *Enneads* I, 8, 4, 3 (pp. 286–287, *Plotinus I*, Loeb Classical Library). Hermogenes apud Hippolytus, *Elenchus*, VIII, 4, 17 etc.

127 F. Boemer, "Der lateinische Neuplatonismus," pp. 169 ff.

128 E.g., Asclepius, 31, p. 339, 10 Nock-Festugière: "Itaque, quamvis sit aeternitas stabilis, inmobilis atque fixa, tamen quoniam temporis, quod mobile est, in aeternitatem semper revocatur agitatio eaque mobilitas ratione temporis vertitur, efficitur, ut et ipsa aeternitas inmobilis quidem sola per tempus, in quo ipsa est et est in eo omnis agitatio videatur agitari. Sic efficitur ut et aeternitatis stabilitas moveatur et temporis mobilitas stabilis fiat fixa lege currendi. Sic et deum agitari credibile est in se ipsum eadem inmobilitate. Stabilitas etenim ipsius in magnitudine est inmobilis agitatio; ipsius enim magnitutidinis inmobilis lex est. Hoc ergo, quod est tale, quod non subicitur sensibus, indefinitum, inconprehensibile, inaestimabile est; nec sustineri etenim nec ferri nec indagari postest. Ubi enim et quo et unde aut quomodo aut quale sit, in-

Although the passage's allusion to "theologians" is too vague to show exactly whose authority Favonius invokes, it still can orient our research in a fairly well determined direction. These *theologi* are clearly not the poet-theologians, as in the beginning, because the context distinguishes them from the *poetae* who had expressed the same doctrine in mythical form. Beyond doubt they are philosophers, perhaps even neo-Platonists to whom the term is often applied in the period.[129]

As much or more than in Hermetism, it is in the neo-Platonists, Christian and pagan, where we find the notions of *mobilitas* and *stabilitas* characteristically linked. Emerging from the *Parmenides*,[130] often reshuffled in the course of an already several-centuries-old tradition, they end by constituting a clearly defined theme, as we can infer from two passages of Marius Victorinus and Claudianus Mamertus where our formula occurs, still as an anonymous reference:

Marius Victorinus, *Adversus Arium* IV, 8, *Patrologia Latina*, vol. 8, column 1119 A	Claudianus *Mamertus, De Statu Animae*, p. 30, 24,
Cum enim se ut existat operatur, recte et intus motus, et *cessans motus est nominatus*.	Omne etenim temporaneum mobile atque mutabile inmutabilis et stans sempiternitas includit . . . , praedita *illo* tantum *motu qui stabilis dicitur* . . .

From the passage of *Adversus Arium* we must likewise contrast the expressions *motio requiescens* and *motus quiescens*,[131] as well as certain passages

certum est. Fertur enim, in summa stabilitate, et in ipso stabilitas sua, sive deus sive aeternitas sive uterque sive alter in altero sive uterque in utroque sunt."

129 Cf. L. Ziehen, "Θεολόγος," in P.W., *R.E.*, vol. V, A, 2, column 2031.

130 In this regard see E. R. Dodds, "The *Parmenides* of Plato and the Origin of the Neo-Platonic One," in *Classical Quarterly*, vol. 22, 1928, pp. 129–142. Similarly, Christians could appeal to the *Book of Wisdom*, 7, 22 ff, where the description of Wisdom sets immobility and activity side by side without them canceling each other out. Cf. Gregory the Great, *Homiliae in Ezechielem*, I, 50, 10, *Patrologia Latina*, vol. 76, column 824 C: "Omnipotens spiritus . . . simul et mobilis et stabilis dicitur."

131 Marius Victorinus, *Adversus Arium*, columns 1073 A and 1133 D.

which take up and make explicit the idea of rest which is at the same time movement: *quamquam dicatur quies, movetur autem intus motu unde vivit sibi,*[132] or again: *ibi motio est, et non simpliciter motio, sed prima motio, quae genus sit et ipsa status, et idcirco ipsa substantia. Sed ista et longioris et alterius quaestionis.*[133]

Father Henry, whose attention had been drawn to this series of texts, observes that in the last passage Victorinus opens up a perspective which he is reluctant to fully articulate. Victorinus gives us a glimpse of the existence of a doctrine already well known and capable of further development. Henry detects a possible influence of Plotinus and in the absence of more exact parallels, suggests comparison with *Ennead* VI, 8, 16, 14, where the expression ἐνέργεια μένουσα recalls our *cessans motus* and its variations.[134] From this angle we will re-encounter the neo-Platonic source to which the text already cited from Favonius Eulogius would seem to direct us.

Whereas Victorinus primarily saw this doctrine as a way of deepening his understanding of the Trinity, Augustine who knew the doctrine equally well, set it forth in detail in function of the problem of creation. On the issue he poses a sensitive question for Christians, one familiar to theologians and philosophers. How can we reconcile the immutability of the divine will, inseparable from its perfection, with the notion of creation in time? If the world has not always been and if it owes its existence to God, at a precise moment in the eternal duration there was a new decision. By that very fact it became impossible to hold that divine thought was

132 Marius Victorinus, *Adversus Arium*, column 1125 A.

133 Marius Victorinus, *Adversus Arium*, column 1063 A.

134 Cf. Plotinus, *Enneads* II, 2, 3, lines 20–22 (p. 50, *Plotinus II*, Loeb Classical Library, A.H. Armstrong trans., Cambridge, Mass.: Harvard University Press, 1990: Ὁ δὲ νοῦς . . . ἕστηκε γὰρ καὶ κένεῖται; *Enneads* VI, 7, 13, 33–34 (p. 128, 130, *Plotinus VII*, Loeb Classical Library) : Πανταχοῦ δ᾿ αὐτός [νοῦς] ἐστι. Μένουσαν οὖν ἔχει τὴν πλάνην. Cf. Numenius *apud* Eusebius, *Praeparatio Evangelica*, XI, 18, 21, vol. II, p. 48, 18 Mras (*Grieschen christlichen Schriftsteller der ersten Jahrhunderte*, Berlin: 1956): Ἀντὶ γὰρ τῆς προσούσης τῷ δευτέρῳ κινήσεως τὴν προσοῦσαν τῷ πρωτῳ στάσιν φημὶ ενῖαι κίνησιν σύμθυτον, ἀφ᾿ ἧς ἥ τε τάξις τοῦ κόσμου καὶ ἡ μονὴ ἡ ἀΐδιος καὶ ἡ σωτηρία ἀναχεῖται εἰς τὰ ὅλα. Eusebius labels Nemenius himself a "theologian," *Praeparatio Evangelica*, XI, 18, 13, vol. II, p. 42, 16 Mras.

unalterable. The Bible raises the same issue in its manner by teaching that God rested on the seventh day, all the while affirming that God never ceases to act.[135] Thence will come absolutely interminable discussions re-examining the question from every angle, Augustine tries to show that the two notions are not mutually exclusive.[136] As opposed as these notions might seem, they imply no contradiction, because God did not have to go back on his eternal pauses. Creation in time was decreed from all eternity.

Similarly, once created, the world requires that God continue to act upon it to evade nothingness. The world receives its existence at each instant from the hands of God, in a way the pivot and ground of all things. The day after the creation God the creator did not change into a do-nothing God, *Deus otiosus*. He acts always, without his rest being attenuated by that activity: *novit quiescens agere, et agens quiescere*.[137]

It is in this context that the formula *stabilis motus* appears again. Augustine is quite sensitive to its oddness and seems to want to excuse himself, but the formula is the only possible way to express a profound truth: *Satis adparet recte intuentibus hunc ipsum incomparabilem et ineffabilem, et si possit intellegi, stabilem motum suum rebus eam [sc. Sapientiam] praebere suaviter disponendis, quo utique subtracto, si ab hac operatione cessaverit, eas continuo perituras* (*De Genesi ad Litteram*, IV, 12, p.109, 6 Zycha).

Could we translate a reality which surpasses all human categories, other than by way of this paradoxical expression? Here we have one example among many others of theological affectation, constrained to combine normally incompatible notions to express or suggest a truth which has no equivalent in the realm of our own experience. For Augustine there only exists one point of comparison: this is the soul, which itself moves the body; it animates in a very mysterious fashion without moving

135 John 5, 17: "My Father *works* even until now, and I work."

136 Cf. above all, St. Augustine, *De Genesi ad Litteram*, IV, 11 ff, p. 107 10 Zycha (*Corpus Scriptorum Ecclesiasticorum Latinorum*, vol. 28, 1).

137 St. Augustine, *De Civitate Dei*, XII, 18, 38 (*Corpus Christianorum*, vol. 48, p. 374): "Non itaque in eius vacatione cogitetur ignavia desidia inertia, sicut nec in eius opere labor conatus industria. Novit quiescens agere et agens quiescere. Potest ad opus novum non novum sed sempiternum adhibere consilium." Cf. *De Genesi ad Litteram*, IV, 12, p. 109, 7 Zycha; *De Genesi ad Litteram*, IV, 13, p. 110, 24; *Confessions*, XIII, 36–38, etc.

itself, and[138] which thus imitates the perfection of the divine being from afar.

Independently of St. Augustine, with whom he shows few exact points of contact on this occasion, the author of *De Statu Animae* is able to draw support quite skillfully from this doctrine in favor of the thesis whose champion he had become. This systematic use of the expression *stabilis motus*, quite rare in the Latin world, is taken up in several places where the same idea is explained, indicating clearly that we do not find a word used by chance, but a firm principle upon which Augustine has reflected and from which he intends to draw all its consequences. Thanks to this principle, Augustine had a new way in which he could express the idea of a hierarchical universe, where the privileges of God are safeguarded at the same time as the reflection of his perfections appear in creatures. Faustus of Riez's accusation of impiety lodged against the supporters of the spirituality of the soul is henceforth baseless. The truly guilty are, on the contrary, those who deny the incorporeality of the soul and do God the injury of believing that he could not have created a being in his image.[139]

* * *

Even when we define the soul as an independent substance, it obviously has relations with the body, however we envisage these relations. If we have avoided allusion to them where possible in treating the nature of the soul, it is because the neo-Platonists themselves generally tended to separate the two questions. It will be easier now to come back to the special problems that the union of body and soul pose and to appreciate the originality of the efforts made to resolve them.

138 St. Augustine, *De Libero Arbitrio*, III, 28: "Miramur quippe animi naturam mutabilitate corporis non mutari." *De Diversis Questionibus 83, questio 8*: "Et cum anima voluntate, id est, illo motu qui localis non est, corpus suum tamen localiter movet, non ex eodem monstratur et ipsa localiter moveri. Sicut videmus a cardine moveri aliquid per magnum spatium loci, et tamen ipsum cardinem non moveri loco." Cf. Claudianus Mamertus, *De Statu Animae*, p. 65, 8: "Huiusmodi autem motibus animae non communicat corpus, quibus inmoto nihilominus corpore movetur, unde datur intellegi animam per tempus inlocaliter moveri atque ab eadem corpus et temporaliter et localiter moveri, eandem vero a corpore localiter non moveri." See above, this chapter.

139 *De Statu Animae*, p. 161, 18; cf. p. 38, 9 ff.

Chapter Four
Neo-Platonism and the Union of Soul and Body

Nec vero credi licet quorumque coniunctionem corporum unitatem Trintitatis imitari aut eidem *inconfusibiliter posse misceri*.
Claudianus Mamertus, *De Statu Animae*, p. 59, 23

I

To study the union of soul and body after neo-Platonism is to go back over a frequently debated question which, indeed, has still hardly been sorted out. If we do not hesitate to add to this already considerable dossier, it is not simply to clarify certain obscure passages of *De Statu Animae*. It is also to draw attention to a little known feature of neo-Platonic doctrine and its use by ecclesiastical authors. Because of the elliptical character of Claudianus Mamertus's remarks, they do not lend themselves to an analysis of the type that seems necessary. Hence there can be no objection to first examining the matter in St. Augustine, to immediately pick up the thread of the ideas in *De Statu Animae*, in the light of the results achieved.

Fr. C. Couturier[1] felicitously formulated the problem of the unity of the human composite according to Augustine in the following terms: The relations between body and soul, the two elements constituting man, are articulated in St. Augustine by divergent formulas. Some come out of the "scheme of accidental union" and in the last analysis go back to Plato. These define man only as soul and make the body a simple instrument of the soul, according to the well known phrase of *De Moribus Ecclesiae Catholicae*: "Man, then, as viewed by his fellow-man is a rational soul with a mortal

1 C. Couturier, "La structure métaphysique de l'homme d'après saint Augustin," in *Augustinus Magister*, volume I, Paris, 1954, pp. 543–550.

and earthly body in its service."[2] Other formulas, like that in *De Ordine*, "Man is a mortal, rational animal,"[3] suppose a closer link between soul and body, and they suggest rather a mode of substantial union in the manner of Aristotle. Did St. Augustine contradict himself or did he elaborate an original doctrine "capable of flowing into all the formulas without doing violence to any"?[4]

After research Fr. Couturier believed he should opt for the latter solution: the unity of man is "neither accidental, nor substantial, but hypostatic." In the last analysis it finds "its proper metaphysical expression . . . by analogy with the mystery of the Incarnate Word."[5]

For his part, Étienne Gilson judged Augustinian thought to be undecided on this point, and, while denying that the bishop of Hippo had been interested in this problem, affirmed that his Christianity had led him to correct the formula inherited from Plato.[6]

2 St. Augustine, *De Moribus Ecclesiae Catholicae*, ch. 27, 52 (*Of the Morals of the Catholic Church*, *The Nicene and Post-Nicene Fathers*, vol. IV, ed. Philip Schaff, Grand Rapids, Michigan: William Eerdmans, reprinted, 1983, p. 55); cf. *De Quantitate Animae*, chapter XIII, 22 (*De Quantitate Animae. The Measure of the Soul*, Latin text with English trans. and notes by Francis E. Tourscher, Philadelphia: Peter Reilly Company, 1933, p. 61): "For it appears to me that the soul is a definite substance endowed with reason fitted to rule the body."

3 St. Augustine, *De Ordine*, II, 31; *De Quantitate Animae*, XXV, 47–49 (Tourscher, pp. 122–129); for other references, see Couturier, "La structure métaphysique," p. 543. There is the same wavering in Claudianus Mamertus, who defines man both as soul alone (*De Statu Animae*, p. 40, 8: "De vero homine, hoc est de hominis anima quaerimus"; cf. p. 85, 15; p. 98, 14), but also as a being composed of soul and body (*De Statu Animae*, p. 179, 10: "Ex anima constamus et corpore"; Cf. p. 43, 6; p. 58, 12; p. 131, 20; p. 153, 8; p. 158, 9 etc.).

4 C. Couturier, "La structure métaphysique," p. 544.

5 C. Couturier, "La structure métaphysique," p. 550.

6 Étienne Gilson, *The Christian Philosophy of Saint Augustine* (trans. L.E.M. Lynch, New York: Random House, 1960), p. 45, "We are sometimes surprised that he did not discuss or even notice, the metaphysical difficulties implied in such a [Platonic] definition. The reason is simply that the abstract problem of man's metaphysical structure seeemed to him an idle one." In a note to this passage (p. 271, note 5) Gilson explains: "Thus Augustine inherited a Platonic definition of man. On the other hand, his Christianity compels him to give

We readily acknowledge with Fr. Couturier that Augustine's doctrine is not fully that of either Plato or Aristotle. Can we infer from that that Augustine elaborated a personal theory? We would first have to establish that the only choice was between these two classical theses, which does not seem to be the case. The problem was continually raised throughout antiquity[7] and had already been resolved in an original way by neo-Platonism. Indeed, we can say that there is a specifically neo-Platonic doctrine of the relations of soul and body, whose novelty and importance have not been sufficiently noted. Everything leads us to believe that Augustine utilized this doctrine in its basic outline and made it his own. The following remarks attempt to bring out the essentially neo-Platonic character of Augustinian thought on this precise point[8] and at the same time show the interest of

staunch support to the unity of the human composite made up of a soul and a body. Whence arises in him a certain indecisiveness of thought that is often perceptible in his texts, especially when he is trying to make Plato's formula express a Christian notion of man."

7 Varro, *De Philosophia*, *apud* St. Augustine, *De Civitate Dei*, XIX, chapter 3 (*A Select Library of the Nicene and Post-Nicene Fathers of the Christian Church*, edited by Philip Schaff, volume II, *St. Augustine's City of God and Christian Doctrine*, Grand Rapids, Michigan, William B. Eeerdmans, reprinted, 1983, p. 400): "[H]e thinks that, first of all, we must define man. . . . is it neither the soul alone nor the body alone, but both together, which are man, the body and soul being each a part, but the whole man being both together?" St. Augustine adds that Varro preferred this third solution. In *De Moribus Ecclesiae Catholicae*, I, 4, *Patrologia Latina*, vol. 32, column 1313, where the same problem is raised, Augustine indicates that there is a response, but he cannot stop for it because of lack of time: "Difficile est istam controversiam diiudicare; aut si ratione facile, oratione longum est." Cf. Plotinus, *Enneads* I, 1, 5, line 1 (pp. 102–103, *Plotinus I*, Loeb Classical Library, A. H. Armstrong trans., Cambridge, Mass.: Harvard University Press, 1989) and *passim*; Nemesius, *De Natura Hominis*, *Patrologia Graeca*, vol. 40., col. 593 B: "Plato does not want to admit that an animal is a being composed of soul and body, but a soul which uses a body and that the body is in some way its clothing. But that also has its difficulties."

8 The issue is not to deny profound transformations St. Augustine achieved in neo-Platonic doctrine as a whole. Our reflections merely concern the problem of the *mode of union* of soul and body which is, of course, only an aspect of this doctrine. We should similarly note that Fr. Couturier's article deliberately sets aside the question of Augustinian sources and does not in principle ex-

the solution whose applications amply transcend the boundaries of pure psychology.

Epistula 137 to Volusianus gives us the basic text. As is well known, in the letter St. Augustine reviews various traditional themes in anti-Christian polemics, a matter on which the pagan Volusianus (*Epistula 135*) and Marcellinus (*Epistula 136*) had felt the need to seek illumination: virgin birth of Christ, delay of the Incarnation, the scandal of a God-man, etc.

Among other objections to the doctrine of the Incarnation, the pagans maintained that it was impossible for God to unite himself to a human nature. In the passage we propose to examine (*Epistula 137*, 11) Augustine tries to show that this union is not implausible, and contrasts this fact, which has only occurred once, with a still more mysterious one which, however, recurs every day: the union of man in soul and body.[9] It is easier in fact, says Augustine, to conceive the union of two spiritual substances than that of a spiritual substance and a corporeal substance.[10] What happens is that we trivialize the realities to which habit has familiarized us. If we only took the trouble to examine them more closely, they would seem astonishing to us.[11]

Augustine's whole effort consists in showing that if soul and body are united in man to form a single person, with more reason we can admit the possibility of Christ's case where two incorporeal substances, the divine Word and the soul, are joined.[12] It is true that the union of soul and body is something we experience ourselves, whereas we are obliged to *believe* that a union

clude the position we defend here at all. For a more detailed exposition of the author's ideas, cf. "Structure métaphysique de l'être crée d'après saint Augustin," in *Recherches de Philosophie*, vol. I, pp. 57–84.

9 St. Augustine, *Epistula 137*, 11, p. 109, 15 Goldbacher (*Corpus Scriptorum Ecclesiasticorum Latinorum,* vol. 44): "Sic autem quidam reddi sibi rationem flagitant, quo modo Deus hominis permixtus sit, ut una fieret persona Christi, cum hoc semel fieri oportuerit, quasi rationem ipsi reddant de re, quae cotidie fit, quo modo misceatur anima corpori, ut una persona fit hominis."

10 *Epistula 137*, p. 110, 12: "Verum tamen duarum rerum incorporearum commixtio facilius credi debuit quam unius incorporeae et alterius corporeae."

11 *Epistula 137*, p. 109, 2: "Denique quam multa usitata calcantur, quae considerata stupentur."

12 *Epistula 137*, p. 110, 15: "Multo magis incorporeum est Verbum Dei ac per hoc Verbi Dei et animae credibilior debuit esse permixtio."

has been effected of the divinity and humanity of Christ.[13] But, supposing that we did not have that experiential knowledge of the human composite, would we not judge the mixture of two incorporeal substances more plausible a priori than that of an incorporeal substance and a corporeal substance?[14]

We see that the author is not trying to articulate a new theory of man on the model of the Incarnation. He simply defends the latter's possibility by making an appeal to the doctrine of the union of soul and body, which he takes to be admitted by his adversary. The whole argument becomes unintelligible if we maintain that Augustine uses a concept of the human composite which is itself inspired in Christian faith. We would have a true vicious circle in that case.

Now, what is this mode of union of soul and body to which Augustine alludes? The few lines which describe it seem highly revealing to us. They reproduce in detail an argument that we find elsewhere and whose origin we can determine rather exactly. For greater clarity, let us set the essential passages in parallel at once:

Augustine, *Epistula 137*, 11, p. 110, 3 Goldbacher (*Corpus Scriptorum Ecclesiasticorum Latinorum*, vol. 44)	Nemesius, *De Natura Hominis*, *Patrologia Graeca*, vol. 40, col. 592 B ff.	Priscian, *Solutiones*, p. 51, 4 Bywater (*Supplementum Aristotelicum*, vol. 1, 2)
"In illa ergo persona **mixtura** est **animae** et **corporis**, in hac persona **mixtura** est Dei et hominis, si tamen recedat auditor a consuetudine corporum, *quo solent duo liquores ita misceri, ut neutrum*	Ἀνάγκη γὰρ, ἢ ἡνῶσθαι τὴν ψυχὴν καὶ τὸ σῶμα . . . ἢ κεκρᾶσθαι, . . . ὁς οἶνον καὶ ὕδωρ . . . Καὶ ἡ κρᾶσις δὲ τοῦ οἴνου καὶ τοῦ ὕδατος ἀμπότερα συνδιαφθείρει. Οὔτε γὰρ ὕδωρ ἐστὶ	"Si enim **corrupta** sint unita, unam perficiunt substantiam; si vero salvari possunt, etsi fortassis nos lateat, non videtur connaturaliter in unam substantiam uniri, *sicut mixtum ex vino et aqua* . . . Incorporales enim essentiae cor-

13 *Epistula 137*, p. 110, 18: "Sed hoc in nobis ipsis experimur, illud in Christo credere iubemur."

14 *Epistula 137*, p. 111, 1: "Si autem utrumque nobis pariter inexpertum credendum praeciperetur, quid horum citius crederemus?"

servet integritatem suam, quamquam et in ipsis corporibus, **aeri lux incorrupta misceatur.** Ergo persona hominis **mixtura** est animae et corporis, persona autem Christi mixtura est Dei et hominis . . . verum tamen *duarum rerum* **incorporearum commixtio** facilius credi debuit quam *unius incorporeae* et alterius corporeae.	καθαρὸν τό κρᾶμα, οὔτε οἶνος . . . καὶ ἑνοῦται τῳ ἀέρι τὸ φῶς, ἀσυγχύτως ἅμα αὐτῷ κεχυμένον.	poribus uniuntur et manent inconfusae. . .; **lux vero unitur** quidem **aeri** sicut ea quae sunt **concorrupta**, et inconfusa manet ad eum . . .**incorporalia** igitur et **corporibus** et per eandem analogiam **incorporalibus aliis** unita et *commisceri* possunt et segregari, ac per hoc **mixtura** corporaliter non facta, sed secundum compassionem et similitudinem, ad illud inclinat."[15]

Short though it is, this passage from *Epistula 137* opens the way to a number of precise connections with the other two. First, the vocabulary present in the three texts shows resemblances which do not seem merely coincidental: *mixtura*, *misceri*, *commixtio*, *servare integritatem*, *corrupta*, *incorrupta*, just as later, *uniri quodam modo*, *coaptari*, *excepta concretione*,[16] as it happens, are true key concepts and almost technical terms.

More striking still are the two examples used: That of light and of air is repeated and is expressed by the same turn of phrase in all three cases.[17] In the example about the mixture of two liquids, Nemesius and Priscian

15 On this work of Priscian, cf. A. Wilmart, "Les réponses de Priscien le philosophe sous le nom de saint Augustin," in *Revue Bénédictine*, vol. 49, 1937, pp. 3–12. The text which has come down to us is an ancient translation of a lost Greek original.

16 *Epistula 137*, 12, p. 113, 5.

17 Cf. Plotinus, *Enneads* IV, 3, 22 (p. 103, *Plotinus IV*, Loeb Classical Library, A.H. Armstrong trans., Cambridge, Mass.: Harvard University Press, 1984): "Are we to say then that when soul is present to body it is present as fire is

make two specifications. On the one hand, they indicate the nature of the substances, water and wine and, on the other hand, after affirming that both were corrupted, they add that this corruption is only apparent. Although we cannot perceive it, the two liquids are really only juxtaposed. The proof is that they can be separated again with the help of a sponge soaked in oil.[18] Augustine leans to the commonly admitted doctrine according to which a liquid which enters into composition with another liquid loses its own nature and is transformed into a new homogeneous substance.[19] Oil seemed

present to air? For this too like soul is present without being present, and is present throughout the whole and mixed with none of it, and stays still itself while the air flows past . . ." Chalcidius, *In Timaeum*, ch. 227, p. 265, 4 Wrobel: "Proprium vero est hoc eius naturae quae est sine corpore, ut lucis, quae corpus aereum penetrat." Psellos, *De Omnifaria Doctrina*, 34 Westerink.

18 Priscian, *Solutiones*, p. 51, 5: "Si vero salvari possunt, etsi fortassis nos lateat, non videtur connaturaliter in unam substantiam uniri, sicut mixtum ex vino et aqua, siquidem olearis spongia repellit puram ex mixtura aquam, et papyrus similiter." Nemesius makes the same remark, *De Natura Hominis*, *Patrologia Graeca*, vol. 40, col. 592 C. For the distinction between true and apparent mixture, see Aristotle, *De Generatione et Corruptione*, I, 10, 327 b 33. It is in this work rather than in *De Caelo*, where the distinction only appears incidentally (cf. III, 4 and *passim*), that the most complete explanation of the Aristotelian doctrine of mixtures is found. Chapter X of Book I precisely defines mixture and distinguishes it clearly from generation, with which Aristotle's predecessors confused it; cf. 327 b 7 ff. Since mixture, like generation, is the result of a qualitative change, it is to *De Generatione et Corruptione*, whose object is alteration or movement in quality, that its consideration belongs. In *De Caelo*, on the contrary, the elements are considered as subject of movement in regard to place, which constitutes the proper object of that treatise. We cannot agree with Paul Moraux's hypothesis, "Recherches sur le *De Caelo* d'Aristote," in *Revue Thomiste*, vol. 51, 1951, p. 188, according to which the study of the elements in *De Generatione* derives from that of *De Caelo* and would only be its complement. This interpretation totally neglects the formal point of view in which Aristotle situates himself in each of the works.

19 The two liquids example is already found in Alexander of Aphrodisias, *De Anima*, p. 116, 5 Bruns: "Furthermore, if the soul spreads entirely through the whole body and mixes itself with it, the animal will have neither soul nor body, but will be something else, a composite of the two substances, corrupted or transformed like hydromel (μελίκρατον)." See Alexander, *ibid.*, on the case of wine and honey (οἰνόμελι), which form a perfectly homogeneous mixture.

to be an exception to the rule.[20] Furthermore, these differences are quite unimportant. The example is shared, and the same conclusions are always drawn from it.

In general the doctrine is not only analogous but strictly identical. It originates as a polemic against Stoicism, as Nemesius explicitly says,[21] and

Cf. Plotinus, *Enneads* IV, 7 , 8² (pp. 367, 369, *Plotinus IV*, Loeb Classical Library): "But if the mixture of bodies allows none of the bodies which are mixed to exit in actuality, the soul would not be actually present in bodies either, but only potentially, and would lose its existence as soul, just as, if sweet and bitter are mixed, the sweet does not exist; we shall not then have a soul." Porphyry *apud* Proclus, *In Timaeum*, 218 C, vol. II, p. 253, 26, Diehl: Ο μὲν Πορφύριος ἐπὶ τὰ αἰσθητὰ φερόμενος καὶ ἐπὶ τὰς μιξεις τὰς ἐνύλους τὸ μελίκατον καὶ τὸ οἰνόμελι ἄνω καὶ κάτω θρυλεῖ πᾶν μὲν ὁμοιομερὲς ὂν, ἄλλοις δὲ ἄλλο πάθος ἐμποιοῦν. Τοὺς μὲν γὰρ ἡ οἰνωδεία μᾶλλον, τοὺς δὲ ἡ γλυκύτης διατίθσιν. Chalcidius, *In Timaeum*, ch. 227, p. 265, 4 Wrobel: "Proprium vero est hoc eius naturae, quae sine corpore est . . . ut dulcedinis quae pervadit melleum corpus." Psellos, *De Omnifaria Doctrina*, 90 Westerink. Boethius, who follows Aristotle here, notes that when two substances are mixed in unequal proportions, what is produced is not a mixture, but real corruption of the weaker substance, *Contra Eutychen*, 6, p. 108 Stewart-Rand-Tester: "Potest enim aquae qualitas a vini qualitate aliquid pati. Atque idcirco si multum quidem fuerit aquae, vini vero paululum, non dicuntur immixta, sed alterum alterius qualitate corrumpitur. . . . Si vero sint mediocres sibique aequales vel paulo inaequales naturae quae a se facere et pati possunt, illae miscentur et mediocribus inter se qualitatibus temperantur." Cf. Aristotle, *De Generatione et Corruptione*, I, 10, 328, a 25. Supplementary information may be found on the question of mixtures in Harry Austryn Wolfson, *The Philosophy of the Church Fathers*, volume I, Cambridge, Mass.: Harvard University Press, 1956, pp. 374 ff. The example of the mixture of wines came from daily experience. Drinking pure wine was a barbarous act. Sea water was added to certain Greek wines.

20 E.g., Arnobius, *Adversus Nationes* II, 7, p. 73, 8 Marchesi: "Quid sit quod humores universi unum corpus efficiant mixtione, solum oleum respuat immersionem in se pati, sed in suam naturam impenetrabile semper perspicue collegatur." Cf.Aristotle, *De Generatione Animalium*, II, 2, 735 b 26; *De Plantis*, II, 2, 823 a 30; *Meteorologica*, IV, 7, 383 b 20 ff; the same remark on viscous substances is made in *De Generatione et Corruptione*, I, 10, 328 b 5.

21 Nemesius, *De Natura Hominis*, *Patrologia Graeca*, vol. 40, col. 545 A ff. Cf. Plotinus, *Enneads* IV, 7, 8² (pp. 366–369 in *Plotinus IV*, Loeb Classical Library).

as the very terms of the debate indicate: κρᾶσις, παράθεσις, ἀλλοίωσις, etc. In support of the corporeality of the soul, the Stoics insisted that no relation was possible between a corporeal and an incorporeal substance.[22] Now we must recognize that there is certain communication between soul and body. Experience shows us that they act upon each other. The soul vivifies the body. When it undergoes the feeling of shame or when it is afraid, the body reddens or pales, as the case may be. Inversely, the soul suffers the repercussion of corporeal passions like pain.[23] If we consider the body as simple apparel or as an instrument of the soul, as Plato invites us to do, it is difficult to explain that mutual influence. The cloak and what it covers do not form a single being,[24] or as Plotinus remarks: "From the Soul using the body as an instrument, it does not follow that the Soul must share the body's experiences: a man does not himself feel all the experiences of the tools with which he is working."[25]

The hypothesis of a simple juxtaposition (παράθεσις) must be excluded. The possibility of mixture (κρᾶσις) remains. But every genuine mixture, as we have seen,[26] implies the transformation of substances into a

22 Cleanthes *apud* Tertullian, *De Anima*, 5, 5: "Corporalium et incorporalium passiones inter se non communicare." Alexander de Aphrodisias, *De Anima*, p. 117, 9 Bruns: ἀλλά καὶ ὁ λόγος ψευδὴς ὁ λέγων ἀσώματον σώματι μὴ συμπάσχει ὥστε εἶναι ἀσώματον τὴν ψυχήν. Severus *apud* Eusebius, *Praeparatio Evangelica*, XIII, 17, 5, vol. II, p. 240, 8 Mras. Plotinus, *Enneads* I, 1, 3 (p. 98, *Plotinus I*, trans. A. H. Armstrong, Cambridge, Mass.: Harvard University Press, Loeb Library, 1966, 1989: Σῶμα μὲν γὰρ σώματι ἄλλῳ μεταδώσει τῶν ἑαυτοῦ, σῶμα δὲ ψυχῇ πῶς Nemesius, *De Natura Hominis*, *Patrologia Graeca*, vol. 40, col. 548 A: Οὐδὲν ἀσώματον συμπάσχει σώματι, οὐδὲ ἀσωμάτῳ σῶμα, ἀλλὰ σῶμα σώματι. Aulus Gellius, *Noctes Atticae*, V, 15, 3 (pp. 426, 428, *The Attic Nights of Aulust Gellius I*, with English trans. by John Rolfe, Cambridge Mass.: Harvard University Press, 1927, 1984) "Corpus autem est quod aut efficiens est aut patiens; id Graece definitur: τὸ ἔτοι ποιοῦν ἢ πάσχον. Quam definitionem significare volens Lucretius poeta ita scripsit [*De Rerum Natura*, I, 304]: Tangere enim aut tangi, nisi corpus, nulla potest res."

23 Nemesius, *De Natura Hominis*, col. 548 A. Cf. Plotinus, *Enneads* I, 1, 5 (pp. 102–107, *Plotinus I*, Loeb Classical Library).

24 Nemesius, *De Natura Hominis*, col. 593 B.

25 Plotinus, I, 1, 3 (pp. 98–101, *Plotinus I*, Loeb Classical Library).

26 See above notes 18 and 19.

new substance, different from the first two, and thereby, the disappearance of them and their properties. In that case, there would no longer be soul nor body, but a third substance, a result of the fusion of the two.

To successfully confront these objections, the Stoic enumeration of modes of union must be shown to be incomplete. It is not true that every ἕνωσις must involve an ἀλλοίωσις.[27] Between juxtaposition and mixture properly speaking there is room for a new type of union,[28] namely a union without confusion (ἄμικτος, ἀσυγχυτος, ἕνωσις),[29] which allows each substance to subsist in its integrity. There we have union in the full sense of the world, a kind of intermediary between the other two, which has in common with κρᾶσις the intimate approximation of two substance to the point of making them a single being, but which like παράθεσις, does not imply their annihilation. This is what permits Plotinus to affirm without contradicting himself that *we* (τὸ ἡμεῖς) designates both the soul and the composite.[30] While recognizing the soul's primacy and defining "true man"[31] as the soul, he recognizes that the "animal" or what he still calls "the whole essence of man"[32] is a mixture (μικτόν) of higher and lower elements,

27 Nemesius, *De Natura Hominis*, col. 596 A: ἐπὶ δὲ τῶν νοητῶν ἕνωσις μὲν γίνεται, ἀλλοίωσις δὲ οὐ παρακολουθεῖ . . . Καὶ ἥνωται τοίνυν καὶ ἀσυγχύτως ἥνωται τῷ σώματι ἡ ψυχή. Furthermore, see the detailed critique of the Stoic doctrine of "complete transfusion" in Plotinus, *Enneads* II, 7 (pp. 194–205, *Plotinus II*, Loeb Classical Library, Cambridge, Mass.: Harvard University Press, 1990).

28 Nemesius, *De Natura Hominis*, col. 601 B: καινότερος οτος ὁ τρόπος τῆς κράσεως ἢ ἑνώσεως.

29 Σύγχυσις, κρᾶσις, and μίξις are frequently interchangeable, especially in late texts Σύγχυσις is never used by Aristotle and seems to owe its popularity to Stoicism; Cf. Chrysippus, *Stoicorum Veterum Fragmenta* 2, 153 In Aristotle μιξις is the generic term which serves to designate both the mixture of two liquids which unite to form a homogeneous total, like water and wine (κρᾶσις) or the mixture of two solids which remain distinct, like grains (σύνθεσις); cf. *Topics*, IV, 2, 122 b 26 ff; *De Generatione et Corruptione*, I, 10, 328 a 6 ff.

30 Plotinus *Enneads* I, 1, 10 (pp. 108–109, *Plotinus I*, Loeb Classical Library).

31 Plotinus *Enneads* I, 1, 7 (p. 109, *Plotinus I*, Loeb Classical Library); *Enneads* I, 1, 10 (pp. 114–115, *Plotinus I*, Loeb Classical Library).

32 Plotinus *Enneads* I, 1, 7 (p. 109, *Plotinus I*, Loeb Classical Library).

closely united so that when the body experiences, we can say that it is *we* who experience.[33]

This original mode of union is characteristic precisely of spiritual substances,[34] whether they are united among themselves or whether they are joined to bodies.[35] To understand it, we must abstract from what the senses reveal to us,[36] but it is not completely without an analogy in the corporeal realm, as is shown by the example of the light and the air, which are united without being corrupted. That is why the term *illumination* is particularly apt to designate this presence of the soul to the body. We must not view it as a merely gnoseological reality. We find it again in contexts which in themselves have nothing to do with the problem of knowledge.[37] However, since this action of the soul has the effect of impressing its reflection in bodies and thus rendering matter intelligible in different degrees, it is not without relation to intellectual illumination.

That, in brief, is the doctrine to which *Epistula 137* alludes. Can we identify its immediate origin?

Happily, Nemesius and Priscian, who unquestionably derive from a

33 Plotinus *Enneads* I, 1, 10 (pp. 114–115, *Plotinus I*, Loeb Classical Library). Cf. Aexander of Aphrodisias, *De Anima*, p. 117, 11 Bruns: The incorporeal element of man does not experience as we say that two friends sympathize. What experiences is the composite, the animate formed of a soul and a body. St. Augustine, *De Genesi ad Litteram*, III, 16, p. 82, 17 Zycha (*Corpus Scriptorum Ecclesiasticorum Latinorum*, vol. 28, 1): "Nam et ipse corporis dolor in quolibet animante magna et mirabilis animae vis est, quae illam conpagem ineffabili permixtione vitaliter continet et in quandam sui moduli redigit unitatem, cum eam non indifferenter, sed, ut ita dicam, indignanter patitur corrumpi atque dissolvi." Cf. *De Civitate Dei*, XIX, 12, 103 (*Corpus Christianorum*, vol. 48, p. 678).

34 Nemesius, *De Natura Hominis*, col. 593 B: Ἔλεγε γὰρ [i.e. Ammonius] τὰ νοητὰ τοιαύτην ἔχειν φύσιν. Chalcidius, *In Timaeum*, ch. 227, p. 265, 5 Wrobel: "Proprium vero est hoc eius naturae quae est sine corpore." Priscian, *Solutiones*, p. 51, 11 Bywater: "Natura ista incorporalium . . ."

35 Priscian, *Solutiones*, p. 52, 16: "Incorporalia igitur et corporibus et per eandem analogian incorporalibus aliis unita et commisceri possunt et segregari . . ."

36 St. Augustine, *Epistula 137*, 11, p. 110, 5: " . . . si tamen recedat auditor a consuetudine corporum."

37 Plotinus, *Enneads* I, 1, 10 (pp. 114–117, *Plotinus I*, Loeb Classical Library; I, 1, 12 (pp. 116–121 *Plotinus I*, Loeb Classical Library

common source,[38] took care to indicate the work which inspired them, namely, Porphyry's *Quaestiones Commixtae*. Nemesius says so explicitly in the course of his exposition,[39] and that the same title figures among those from Priscian's introduction to the *Solutiones* tells us from where he drew his doctrine. We should recall that the question of the relations of soul and body strongly interested Porphyry. He recounts that he discussed it with Plotinus for three days, to the desperation of his fellow disciple Thaumasius, who would have preferred an uninterrupted exposition from the master.[40]

Similarly, it should be noted that this is at least in part the doctrine attributed by Nemesius to Plotinus's teacher Ammonius Saccas.[41] Von Arnim proved that the bishop of Emesa obtained the cited quotation from Porphyry.[42]

The passage in *Epistula 137* which immediately follows the one we have just analyzed confirms the hypothesis of a loan from pagan philosophy. Augustine alludes to philosophers who said true and useful things, although often mixed with error, and who, hungry for divinity, mistakenly searched for God with pride instead of humility, as the Incarnation taught us to do.[43] It is possible that these many truths (*multa vera*) attributed to the pagans

38 Cf. Hans Friedrich August von Arnim, "Quelle der Ueberlieferung über Ammonius Sakkas," in *Rheinisches Museum*, vol. 42 (1887), pp. 278–285.

39 Nemesius, *De Natura Hominis*, col. 601 b.

40 Porphyry, *Vita Plotini*, 13, line 10 (pp. 38–39, *Plotinus I*, Loeb Classical Library). At least this is the sense that we give to Porphyry's question: πῶς ἡ ψυχὴ σύνεστι τῷ σώματι. Still, the problem discussed may have been that of the soul's fall – How does the soul come to be united with the body? – and not that of the mode of union. Cf. André-Jean Festugière, *La révelation d'Hermés Trismégiste*, vol. 3*: Les doctrines de l'âme*, Paris: Lecoffre, 1953, p. 66 and note 4.

41 Nemesius, *De Natura Hominis*, col. 601 b.

42 H. von Arnim, "Quelle," pp. 278–285.

43 St. Augustine, *Epistula 137*, 12 , p. 112, 6: "Magisterium quidem, ut ea, quae hic ante dicta sunt utiliter vera non solum a Prophetis sanctis, qui omnia vera dixerunt, verum etiam a philosophis atque ipsis poetis et cuiusce modi auctoribus litterarum (quos multa vera falsis miscuisse quis ambigat?), illius etiam in carne praesentata confirmaret auctoritas propter eos, qui illa non possent in ipsa intima veritate cernere atque discernere, quae Veritas, et antequam hominem adsumeret, ipsa erat omnibus, qui eius participes esse potuerunt,

may remit us precisely to the doctrine of the soul he has just expounded. Thus we have the advantage of connecting these texts with a passage from *The City of God*,[44] where the ideas of *Epistula 137* are revisited, often in the same terms. This time, Augustine mentions Porphyry by name.

maxime vero suae incarnationis exemplo id salubriter persuasit, ut, quoniam homines plerique divinitatis avidi per potestates caelestes, quas deos putarent, ritusque varios inlicitorum non sacrorum sed sacrilegiorum ambiendum sibi arbitrarentur ad Deum magis superbe quam pie, qua in re pro angelis sanctis eis se daemones superbiae cognatione supponunt, scirent homines tam proximum esse Deum pietati hominum . . ., ut hominem suscipere dignaretur . . ."

44 St. Augustine, *De Civitate Dei*, X, 29 34 ff (*Corpus Christianorum*, vol. 47, p. 305): "Sed huic veritati ut possetis adquiescere, humilitate opus erat, quae cervici vestrae difficillime perusaderi potest. Quid enim incredibile dicitur, praesertim vobis qui talis sapitis, quibus ad hoc credendum vos ipsos admonere debeatis; quid, inquam, vobis incredibile dicitur, cum Deus dicitur adsumpsisse humanam animam et corpus? Vos certe tantum tribuitis animae intellectuali, quae anima utique humana est, ut eam consubstantialem paternae illi menti, quem Dei filium confitemini, fieri posse dicatis. Quid ergo incredibile est, si aliqua una intellectualis anima modo quodam ineffabili et singulari pro multorum salute suscepta est? Corpus vero animae cohaerere, ut homo totus et plenus sit, natura ipsa nostra teste cognoscimus. Quod nisi usitatissimum esset, hoc profecto esset incredibilius; facilius quippe in fidem recipiendum est, etsi humanum divino, etsi mutabile incommutabili, tamen spiritum spiritui, aut ut verbis utar, quae in usu habetis, incorporeum incorporeo quam corpus incorporeo cohaerere." On the consubstantiality of the intellectual soul and of divinity, as neo-Platonism understood it, to which Augustine alludes here, see above, Chapter 3, beginning of section 2. In *De Fide et Symbolo*, IV, 10, p. 13, 15 ff Zycha (*Corpus Scriptorum Ecclesiasticorum Latinorum*, vol. 41), Augustine already responded similarly to Manichaean criticism of the dogma of the Incarnation: "Nec nobis fidem istam minuat cogitatio muliebrium viscerum, ut propterea recusanda videatur talis domini nostri generatio, quod eam sordidi sordidam putant . . . Debent igitur intueri, quo hoc putant, solis huius radios . . . per cloacarum fetores et quaeque horribilia usquequaque diffundi et in his operari secundum naturam suam nec tamen inde aliqua contaminatione sordescere, cum visibilis lux visibilibus sordibus sit natura coniunctior: quanto minus igitur poterat pollui Verbum Dei non corporeum neque visibile de femineo corpore, ubi humanam carnem suscepit cum anima et spiritu, quibus intervenientibus habitat maiestas Verbi ab humani corporis fragilitate secretius! Unde manifestum est nullo modo potuisse Verbum Dei maculari humano corpore, quo nec ipsa anima humana maculata est."

In the last analysis, as far as we can tell, the doctrine in question goes back to the third century AD[45] It is marked by several features not found in Plato and constitutes one of the clearest constituents of the specifically neo-Platonic theory of the soul. In particular, the unity of the human composite is affirmed with a vigor foreign to the dialogues. Certainly, body and soul are always presented as two complete substances, and consequently, the neo-Platonists are resolutely opposed to the Aristotelian doctrine of substantial co-principles. But it cannot be claimed that their union is merely accidental. The way the doctrine is explained is definitely subtle; the least that can be said is that it testifies to a genuine, original attempt to resolve one of the thorniest problems of psychology.

If these remarks are valid they throw new light on the impact of the argument in *Epistula 137*. It is more ingenious than seems at first sight. Augustine does not limit himself to combating philosophical reasoning directed against the dogma of the Incarnation by further philosophical reasoning of his own confection. He seizes the adversary's own argument to turn it against him. This new David intends to decapitate his enemy with the sword he has just snatched from him.[46] He shows not only that the Incarnation does not really offend reason but that it is what best conforms to the very doctrine in whose name it is attacked, because it presents the union of two incorporeal substances in the manner that the neo-Platonists themselves preach with particular insistence.

Without doubt this is why Augustine insists on the fact that the divine Word is united to another spiritual substance, the human soul. Indeed, the Word is united to a complete human nature, that is, composed of soul and body, as Augustine himself will acknowledge further on.[47] But first he did not shrink from the bit of help which gave his argument greater force.

45 What leads us to this conclusion, beside the traces we have emphasized in authors of this period, is the fact that Plotinus gave it systematic exposition in one of his first treatises, *Enneads* IV, 7, 8² (pp. 362–369 *Plotinus IV*, Loeb Classical Library). Plausibly, he only sums up a doctrine already accepted in the school, probably belonging to his master Ammonius, to whom it is attributed by Nemesius; see above.

46 Cf. St. Jerome, *Epistula 70* (*Ad Magnum*), 2, 4, p. 702, 3 Hilberg (*Corpus Scriptorum Ecclesiasticorum Latinorum*, vol. 54).

47 St. Augustine, *Epistula 137*, 12, p. 113, 5: . . . ut [Deo] sic cooptaretur *homo*

This way of responding to an adversary by reasoning from his own principles is familiar. Augustine recurs to the same procedure in regard to the resurrection of the flesh, which especially repelled pagan philosophers. Each time he posed the question, Augustine did not fail to recall that they themselves taught astral immortality, that is, an immortality in which the body also had a part.[48] We have here a typical example of the patristic commonplace that Christians ought to cultivate philosophy to be able to fight the enemies of the faith with equal weapons, that is with their own weapons.

But then, where is St. Augustine's originality? Is it simply in the astuteness he shows here as a skilled polemicist? Must we conclude, in opposition to Gilson, that his theory of the soul owes nothing to his concept of the Incarnation? This would be to ignore a powerful feature of Augustinian thought. The truth is that the two ideas give each other mutual support.

It does not seem, at least as regards the passages studied, that Augustine essentially modified the doctrine which he borrowed from the enemies of Christianity and which he used to confound them. Certainly the expression *una persona*, already used by Tertullian,[49] and which Augustine recovers two centuries later, is good Latin, but it only states in more precise terms what the Greek terminology already affirmed in its fashion. It does not follow at all that the dogma of the Incarnation was of no help to Augustine. Of course, Augustine rises from the unity of the human composite to the unity of the two natures in the person of Christ. But once the ascent finishes, we benefit by a new clarification. The light of what is higher falls on what is lower. Thanks to this reference to the *analogum princeps*, the doctrine of the union of soul and body attains a dignity and degree of certainty in

totus." Cf. *De Fide et Symbolo*, IV, 8, 12, 1 Zycha (*Corpus Scriptorum Ecclesiasticorum Latinorum*, vol. 41) where, this time against the Apollinarists, Augustine insists on the fact that the Word has equally assumed the human spirit, that is to say the higher part of the soul: ". . . ut totum hominem credat a verbo Dei esse susceptum, id est corpus, animam, spiritum."

48 St. Augustine, *De Civitate Dei*, X, 29, 58, ff (*Corpus Christianorum*, vol. 47, p. 305); *De Civitate Dei*, XIII, 16, 52 (vol. 48, p. 398), etc.

49 Tertullian, *Adversus Praxean* , 27, p. 281, 287 Kroymann (*Corpus Scriptorum Ecclesiasticorum Latinorum*, vol. 47). On the use of *una persona* in St. Augustine, cf. Tarcisus J. van Bavel, *Recherches sur la christologie de saint Augustin*, Fribourg: Éditions Universitaires, 1954, pp. 13 f.

Augustine's eyes that it did not previously possess. Such is divine wisdom that it associates the most ordinary reality to exceptional things, and thus elevates the former while rendering the latter more accessible: *Nunc vero ita inter Deum et homines mediator apparuit, ut in unitate personae copulans utramque naturam et solita sublimaret insolitis et insolita solitis temperaret.*[50]

* * *

The notion of *unio inconfusa* seems to be a taproot of neo-Platonic psychology and neo-Platonic thought generally. We encounter it again each time that two beings, at least one of which is incorporeal, enter into contact. The relations between spirits and their union with God, the action of God upon the world and that of the soul on the body, fall under this type and are conceived analogously. It is a way of affirming the perfection of spiritual beings, to whom it pertains to conserve their very integrity, above all when they are united to a higher being, and on the other hand not to undergo harm when they are joined in the natural order to a material being. Unity here never implies confusion, any more than the friendship which can exist between two beings entails the annihilation of their personality. Unity in no way contradicts the love they feel for themselves.[51] By this consistency and this differentiation, spiritual natures are radically opposed to corporeal beings which are confused when they unite and tend by nature towards homogeneity and the most complete anonymity.

This doctrine would be widely used by Christians especially from the fifth century on. In the passage examined above, Nemesius already exhibits the same skill as Augustine in defending the dogma of the Incarnation with it.[52] Of course, we find it again in the well known definition of the Council of Chalcedon.[53] We believe that Pseudo-Dionysios Areopagite, who uses it

50 St. Augustine, *Epistula 137*, 9, p. 108, 13 Goldbacher.

51 Proclus, *In Timaeum*, 32 C, vol. 2, p. 53, 15 Diehl.

52 Nemesius, *De Natura Hominis*, *Patrologia Graeca*, vol. 40, col. 601 A.

53 *Apud* Mansi, *Sacrorum Conciliorum Nova et Amplissima Collectio*, vol. 7, col. 115 B: ἕνα καὶ τὸν αὐτὸν Χριστὸν υἱὸν, κύριον μονογενῆ, ἐκ δύο φύσεσιν ἀσυγχύτως, ἀτρέπτως, ἀδιαιρέτως, ἀχωρίστως γνωριζόμενον, οὐδαμοῦ τῆς φύσεων διαφορᾶς ἀνῃρημένης διὰ τὴν ἕνωσιν, σωζομένης δὲ μᾶλλον τῆς ἰδιότητος ἑκατέρας φύσεως . . .

constantly and with precision, conceives the union of the two natures in Christ as a function of this doctrine.[54] Eucher, bishop of Lyon, following Augustine's *Epistula 137*, develops the doctrine in a sermon which we know only by *De Statu Animae*.[55] Claudianus Mamertus and after him Cassiodorus take it up in their own way.[56] Lastly, the creed *Quicumque Vult* includes it, again, it seems, following St. Augustine.[57]

Furthermore, these reflections can shed light on the real reasons for pagan opposition to the dogma of the Incarnation. In his thesis, *L'universe dionysien*, Fr. René Roques deplores the fact that Dionysios did not

54 E.g., *Ecclesiastical Hierarchy*, 444 C. The principal passages have been recorded by René Roques, L'univers dionysien, Paris: Aubier, 1954. See the index for the term ἀσύγχυτος.

55 Eucher *apud* Claudianus Mamertus, *De Statu Anima,* p. 135, 20 ff: "Quaerere quidam solent, quo modo in Christo misceri potuerit homo et Deus. Quaerunt rationem huius mysterii, quod semel factum est, cum ipsi reddere rationem nequaquam possint eius rei, quae fit semper, quo modo societur anima corpori, ut fiat homo. Ergo quo modo corporea res incorporeaque coniungitur et corpori anima miscetur ut homo efficiatur, ita homo coniunctus est Deo et factus est Christus: et tamen ut fieret Christus, duo illa incorporea, id est anima et Deus facilius coniungi permiscerique potuerint, quam miscetur una incorporea aliaque corporea, id est anima et corpus ut persona hominis existat."

56 Claudianus Mamertus, *De Statu Animae*, p. 37, 4: "Quia sicut anima et corpus ex diversa substantia unus est homo, ita Deus et homo ex diversa substantia unus est Christus." *De Statu Animae*, p. 34, 9: "Nunc porro superest, ut quoniam Christus homo verus et Deus verus ex duplici substantia una persona et Deus homo et homo Deus est, idem gloriae dominus et non sit crucifixus pro inviolabili divinitate et crucifixus sit in homine pro unitate personae." These two texts were repeated verbatim by Cassiodorus (Pseudo Primasius), *In Epistulam ad Romanos*, *Patrologia Latina*, vol. 68, col. 466 B and *In Epistulam Primam ad Corinthios*. *Patrologia Latina*, vol. 68, col. 511 A-B.

57 "Symbolum Athanasianum," p. 6, 32–35 Burn *(The Athanasian Creed and Its Early Commentaries. Texts and Studies*, IV, 1, Cambridge, England: Cambridge University Press, 1896): "Qui licet Deus sit et homo, non duo tamen, sed unus est Christus, unus autem non conversione divinitatis in carnem sed assumptione humanitatis in Deum, unus omnino non confusione substantiae, sed unitate personae. Nam sicut anima rationalis et caro unus est homo, ita Deus et homo unus est Christus," For an attempt to justify this comparison, see, E. Schlitz, "La comparaison du Symbole *Quicumque vult*," in *Éphémérides de Theologique du Louvain*, vol. 24, 1948, pp. 440 ff.

further develop the question of the mode of union of Christ's two natures:

> We may regret that he [Dionysios] should have completely neglected the Incarnation's human element and that he did not make himself clearer about the problem of the union of divinity and humanity in Christ. Perhaps the difficulty of making minds with a Hellenic formation and orientation admit the cohabitation of the two natures, that they found scandalous, discouraged him from such an endeavor and by reaction led to putting into very vivid relief the ineffable, mysterious, and incomprehensible character of the Incarnation of the Word. For the rest, the care in expounding this mystery by means of neo-Platonic notions and schemes can only confirm this attitude in Dionysios.[58]

These remarks are all the more striking in that, as we have seen, the neo-Platonists are the first to insist on the new and ineffable character of the ἀσύγχυτος ἕνωσις. Since the problem had been amply treated by them, and since agreement had been reached on the subject after long consideration, perhaps we might formulate the inverse hypothesis, with the caution appropriate in such a difficult subject: it is because a mind imbued with neo-Platonism like Dionysios considers the solution to be so obvious that he does not feel the need to insist on it and can be content with a few allusions.

What collided head-on with pagan mentality in Christ's case is exactly the suppression of those intermediaries that play such an important role in the neo-Platonic system, and whose presence has precisely the goal of making the divine perfection stand out. It does not befit God to be joined directly to man: *At enim urgens causa et artissima cogit daemones medios inter deos et homines agere, ut ab hominibus adferant desiderata, et a diis referant inpetrata. Quaenam tandem ista causa est et quanta necessitas? Quia nullus, inquiunt, Deus miscetur homini*.[59]

58 René Roques, *L'univers dionysien*, p. 318.

59 St. Augustine, *De Civitate* Dei, VIII, 20, (*Corpus Christianorum*, vol. 47, p. 237); *De Civitate Dei*, IX, 12, 5 ff, p. 259; *Sermo Guelferb*. III, 3, *Miscellanea Agostos-*

The tendency, especially from the imperial period on, was to elevate God more and more above the creature, to always push him further into the domain of transcendence.[60] How, then, could it be conceived that this God, perfect in all ways and, as Numenius had said,[61] withdrawn into himself, ἑυατῷ συγγινόμενος, had "dwelt among us" (John, I, 14) and had accepted being directly united with a nature occupying a lower rank in the hierarchy of beings? Therein was the scandal, the novelty that jolted accepted ideas and put everything in doubt. At the bottom of this debate between Christians and neo-Platonists we find, in the first place, not the impossibility of conceiving a way in which the union of two natures might be effected in Christ, and still less the Manichaean idea that matter is evil in itself and capable of polluting a being joined to it,[62] but rather the idea of an utterly perfect God who cannot, without demeaning himself, enter into direct contact with man and become one with him. The Incarnation had become unbelievable exactly because there was a more exalted idea of God than ever; therein lies the paradox in which ended these struggles between the pagan elite and Christians anxious to engage in discussion on a legitimately theological plane and which rendered the struggle so poignant.[63]

tineana, vol. 1, p. 454, 14: "Sed deus, inquiunt, homini misceri non potuit, et cum illo fieri Christus unus."

60 On this subject see André-Jean Festugière, *L'hermétisme,* Lund: W. K. Gleerup, 1948, pp. 19–21.

61 *Apud* Eusebius, *Praeparatio Evangelica*, XI, 17, 3 vol. 2, p. 40, 20 Mras.

62 St. Augustine, *De Civitate Dei*, XIV, 5, 11 (*Corpus Christianorum*, vol. 48, p. 420): "Non quidem Platonici sicut Manichaei desipiunt, ut tamquam mali naturam terrena corpora detestentur."

63 Setting aside other applications that have been made of the conception of a close bond between body and soul, let us note simply how useful it was for St. Augustine in explaining the intensity of the suffering of Christ at the moment of the Passion; cf, *Epistula 140*, 33, p. 183, 23 ff Goldbacher (*Corpus Scriptorum Ecclesiasticorum Latinorum*, vol. 44): "Nihil est autem animae sua carne propinquius. Ideo mundi huius quilibet magnus perfectusque contemptor cum alibi patitur, nihil patitur. Potest enim adhibere vigilem rationem, cum amittit bona, quae extrinsecus sunt et ab animo sapientis, qui ex cupiditate non haeret, sine dubio longe sunt, et non curare, quod patitur, quia nec patitur. Cum vero amittit praecipua corporis bona, id est corporis vitam ac salutem, iam tribulatio

* * *

Yet, the doctrine of *unio inconfusa* is what certain passages of *De Statu Animae* develop or suppose, interesting passages to which scholarship does not seem to have paid attention but which, however, are not without interest. Returning to an idea he had already articulated, Mamertus recalls that in the world of bodies we seek in vain the divine image of which *Genesis* speaks. Only souls have been created in the likeness of God and more precisely of the Trinity. But now it is by their union to each other, according to the Apostle's phrase, *unus credentium, unusque volentium erat animus et cor unum*,[64] and by their union to God according to another text of Scripture, *Pater, sint isti in nobis unum, sicut et nos sumus unum*,"[65] that souls are deemed to achieve that likeness. Indeed, both of these unions are spiritual unions, which in no way affect the nature of the beings put into relations, and which thereby reflect "the ineffable union" of the three divine persons. All these souls which form a single soul in God do not become more or less great quantitatively when they are united among themselves or when they are separated, any more than the three persons of the Trinity grow or diminish according to whether we consider them individually or in their union with each other.[66] The reason, says Claudianus, again in a very typical way, is that souls are spiritual "powers" and not bodies: *potentiae sunt illae, non corpora*.[67]

proxima est animi bonis, quibus ipse intus tamquam corporis dominus est. Quid facit qualibet ratione, ut non doleat, cum corpus vulneratur aut uritur, cui tanto implicatur consortio, pati possit, dolere non possit?" Cf. *De Cura pro Mortuis Gerenda*, III, 5: "Si enim paterna vestis et anulus ac si quid huius modi tanto carius est posteris, quanto erga parentis maior affectus, nullo modo ipsa spernenda sunt corpora, quae utique multo familarius atque coniunctius quam quaelibet indumenta gestamus."

64 *Acts of the Apostles*, 4, 32; Cf. *De Statu Animae*, p. 60, 7.

65 *John* 17, 22; Cf. *De Statu Animae*, p. 59, 17.

66 Claudianus Mamertus, *De Statu Animae*, p. 60, 8: "Non tamen reor multas animas ita sibi fuisse coniunctas, ut maior quaedam ex multis animabus anima fieret, quia trinitas, per quam et cum qua omnes bonae animae fiunt unum, nec in ulla ex eadem trinitate persona minor est quam in tribus, nec in tribus maior est quam in singulis."

67 Claudianus Mamertus, *De Statu Animae*, p. 60, 16: We know no example of a Latin author using *potentia* to define the soul. Marius Victorinus utilizes the

Bodies are quite different; nothing analogous is found in them: *Nec vero credi licet quorumque coniunctionem corporum unitatem Trinitatis imitari aut eidem* inconfusibiliter *posse* misceri.[68] Indeed, a body cannot take on another body without increasing its volume. However small it may be, it has three dimensions, which can only be added to those of the body to which it is joined.[69] Similarly, how could we admit that a body might be joined to God in the sense in which St. Paul affirms that whoever adheres to God, forms a single spirit with him?[70] For that, the body would have to become a soul, or else, if we deny that there could be any incorporeal being other than God, God himself should become a body.[71]

The scripture texts which form the skeleton of this development have in common the idea of unity; they are evidently interpreted with the help of the doctrine of ἀσύγχυτος ἕνωσις, in a way that allows us to foresee the expression *inconfusibiliter misceri*, which exactly corresponds to the Greek ἀσυγχύτως κεραννύναι, a recognized technical term designating this spiritual union. Mamertus is even the first Latin author to employ the

Greek word ἐνέργεια without translating it; cf. *Adversus Arium*, IV, 13, *Patrologia Latina*, vol. 8, col. 1122 C: "Ergo semper in motu est [anima], quod est semper agere, et esse ipsam ἐνέργειαν, ut sit ei substantia, ille motus." Cf. above Chapter three, note 60. On the soul as ἐνέργεια, cf. Plotinus, *Enneads* II, 5, 3 (pp. 160–165 *Plotinus II,* Loeb Classical Library, A. H. Armstrong trans.,Cambridge, Mass.: Harvard University Press, 1980); Plotinus, *Enneads* V, 1, 6 (pp. 29–33 *Plotinus V*, Loeb Classical Library, A. H. Armstrong trans., Cambridge, Mass.: Harvard University Press, 1984); Plotinus, *Enneads* V, 2, 1 (pp. 58–61 *Plotinus V*, Loeb Classical Library). See also *De Statu Animae*, p. 82, 5, where God is designated by the expression *principalis potestas*, which seems to correspond to the Greek πρώτη ἐνέργεια; cf. Plotinus, *Enneads*, V, 3, 5 (pp. 84–89 *Plotinus V*, Loeb Library edition). Marius Victorinus employs the formula *potentia actuosa* in the same sense, *Adversus Arium*, 1, 37, *Patrologia Latina*, vol. 8, col. 1069 A.

68 Claudianus Mamertus, *De Statu Animae*, p. 59, 23.

69 Claudianus Mamertus, *De Statu Animae*, p. 59, 25: "Patet enim liquido quodlibet unum corpus paris corporis adiunctione duplicari . . . esse illic pro modo magnitudinis longitudinem, latitudinem, altitudinem." By contrast, the Stoics maintained, that although the soul is material, it does not increase the volume of the body when it is intimately mixed with it.

70 I *Corinthians*, 6, 17, cf. Claudianus Mamertus, *De Statu Animae*, p. 59, 4.

71 Claudianus Mamertus, *De Statu Animae*, p. 59, 11

word *inconfusibiliter* in this sense.[72] What is more, the new application of this doctrine to the union of spiritual beings with each other is no more peculiar to Christian authors than the theory of the union of soul and body. The neo-Platonists themselves knew these ἀσύγχυτοι φιλίαι, and it is again the formula ἀσύγχυτος ἕνωσις which Hierocles employs to describe the intimate union of the three kinds of spiritual beings: gods, demons, and men.[73]

Finally, we note that for Mamertus, the *analogum princeps* is no longer the union of the two natures in Christ, but rather the indescribable union of the three persons of the Trinity, a doctrine he fervently congratulates Plato for having discovered before it was revealed, but which is really more neo-Platonic than Platonic, and which he takes from Porphyry's *De Regressu*, as Pierre-Paul Courcelle has effectively shown.[74]

These remarks are ample indication that Mamertus was not content to simply enunciate revealed truth. We perceive in him the ability of a philosopher and theologian to scrutinize the divine word by means of reason, *adminiculante ratione*,[75] to extract its presuppositions and develop its consequences. To be sure, his enthusiasm led him to see in paganism what brought it close to Christianity rather than what separated it. Nevertheless, passages like these would suffice to place him, as he would put it, among those who prefer the soul of reason to the body of words.[76]

72 The word soon became common. Cf. Cassiodurus, *Expositio in Psalmum 9, 1*, *Patrologia Latina*, vol. 70, col. 80 B: *inconfusibiliter humanatum*, applied to the Incarnation. Fulgentius of Ruspa, *Ad Tras.*, III, 6, *Patrologia Latina*, vol. 65, col. 273: *inconfusibiliter unit utrumque naturam*; Fulgentius of Ruspa, *Ad Tras.*, III, 8, col. 274: *veritate divinae humanaeque substantiae inconfusibiliter permanente*. We find *inconfuse* in Vigilius of Thaspe, *Adversus Eutychetem*, 4, 19 and 5, 25; Pseudo Felix II, *Epistula I*, 11; Marius Mercator, *Contradictio in Blasphemias Nestorii*, *Patrologia Latina*, vol. 48, col. 914 B; Facundus, *Pro definitione Trium Capitulorum*, 9, 7.

73 The text comes to us by way of Photius, *Bibliotheca*, CCXIV, *Patrologia Graeca*, vol. 103, col. 701 A. On this quotation, see Edward Zeller, "Ammonias Sakkas und Plotinus," in *Archiv für Geschichte der Philosophie*, vol. 7, 1894, pp. 295–312.

74 Pierre-Paul Courcelle, *Les lettres grecques en Occident*, p. 226 ff.

75 Claudianus Mamertus, *De Statu Animae*, p. 81, 9; cf. p. 125, 1.

76 Claudianus Mamertus, *De Statu Animae*, p. 21, 12

We are better situated now to examine some special applications of the doctrine of *unio inconfusa* in *De Statu Animae*.

II

The first of these applications concerns the idea, rather curious at first sight, that the soul is the "place" of the body. As a little noticed chapter of *De Statu Animae*[77] basically says, properly speaking, the soul does not reside in the body, as Faustus of Riez would have it.[78] Rather, it is the body which is in the soul: *Vide ne non corpus contineat animam, sed contineatur ab anima.*[79] There is no way in which the soul could be in the body as something which inheres in a subject, for instance, as the sciences are in the soul or color in a body. In that supposition, the soul's fate would be linked to that of the body, and the dissolution of the body would involve its own disappearance.[80] Are not the intellectual disciplines and color inextricably linked to their respective subjects, to the point of not being able to exist without them?[81] Now experience shows us that far from sharing the destiny of the body, the soul is fortified and renewed when the body becomes feeble. Instead of withering away in its turn, the soul carries on better without the body.[82]

Scripture taught the same thing, and Mamertus gives an ingeniously personal interpretation of *Wisdom* 9:15: "For the corruptible body is a load upon the soul." There is a bearer and his burden. Which of these two beings weighs upon the other? Evidently the second. To affirm the contrary would be absurd. The burden is in what bears it and not vice versa.[83] If as the

77 Claudianus Mamertus, *De Statu Animae* III, 3, p. 157, 8 ff.

78 Faustus of Riez, *Epistula 3*, p. 175, 7 and *passim* (*Corpus Scriptorum Ecclesiasticorum, Latinorum*, vol. 21).

79 Claudianus Mamertus, *De Statu Animae,* p. 158, 5.

80 Claudianus Mamertus, *De Statu Animae,* p. 157, 16: " . . in rebus corporalibus subiectum est corpus et color corporis in subiecto, in incorporeis animus et disciplina, quae ita sibi nexa sunt, ut nec sine colore corpus nec sine disciplina sit rationalis animus . . ."

81 Claudianus Mamertus, *De Statu Animae,* p. 157, 21.

82 Claudianus Mamertus, *De Statu Animae,* p. 158, 7: "Illa [anima] sine hoc [corpore] vivit melius." Cf. p. 158, 1.

83 Claudianus Mamertus, *De Statu Animae,* p. 158, 18: "Onus videlicet in portitore, non portitor in onere."

sacred text says, it is the body which is a weight for the soul, we are obliged to acknowledge that it is in the soul and not the soul which is in the body. In this again the soul is again revealed to be like its creator. Properly speaking, God is not in the world, it is the world which is in God. Just as the soul contains the body, God contains the world, although in a completely spiritual manner.[84]

To be sure, the originality of these views must not be exaggerated. Mamertus is not the first to affirm that the soul contains the body in this paradoxical fashion, and the idea of comparing man and the world on this point would occur quite naturally to the mind of an ancient. This is no more than a variation of the theme of microcosm, so widely found in antiquity. Few ideas were as familiar and imposed themselves earlier in classical thought. We find it already in Anaximander, Heraclitus, and Pythagoras, that is to say at the dawn or almost the dawn of scientific thought.[85]

However, we should pay attention to the precise turn taken by the analogy between the relations of soul and body on the one hand, and God and the world on the other hand. René de la Broise, who had already pointed it out,[86] saw only a play on words in the verb *continere* (συνέχειν), which meant "contain" like a receptacle in one case, and in the other meant "maintain united." Perhaps this is not completely false, but it does not adequately capture the richness of thought expressed by the antithesis. Mamertus says that the body is *in* the soul and not merely that it is "contained" by it.[87] There is every reason to believe that when Claudianus speaks that way, he is not simply indulging in a facile and banal play on words which has been handed down to him, but that he maintains, certainly with more subtlety than depth, a thesis which had a well defined meaning for his contemporaries.

84 Claudianus Mamertus, *De Statu Animae,* p. 158, 19: "Magnam animae auctoris sui inesse similitudinem maximo illud indicio est, quod pro similitudine sicut inlocaliter mundus in Deo est, sic inlocaliter corpus in anima."

85 On this matter, see Rudolf Allers, "Microcosmus from Anaximandros to Paracelsus," in *Traditio*, vol. 2, 1944, p. 338 ff.

86 René Marie De la Broise, *Mamerti Claudiani vita eiusque doctrina de anima hominis*, Paris: Retaux-Bray 1890, p. 90.

87 Claudianus Mamertus, *De Statu Animae*, p. 158, 18 and *passim*.

In so far as we can tell, Mamertus does not owe this position to any of his Christian predecessors. We look in vain in Augustine for the idea that the soul is not in the body, and still more for a comparison between the soul and God in this regard.[88] The doctor of Hippo perhaps makes allusion to it once in *De Quantitate Animae* (XXX, 61) but without stopping and above all without declaring himself on the subject: "Any idea that the soul does not reside in the living, animated body seems quite absurd," he declares to Evodius. "However, there have been very learned men who adopted it. We still find them today, I believe. But you perceive correctly, this is one of the most delicate questions, and to envisage it, it is most necessary to purify the eye of our intelligence."

Victorinus notes the same idea, refuses to adhere to it, and indicates that it conflicts with the contemporary manner of speaking: *Quoniam multi in anima corpus esse dicunt, sed nunc secundum dicendi usum anima sit in corpore.*[89]

88 However, St. Augustine recognized that, although the soul is in the body, it is not there as in a place, because it does not have corporeal dimensions. Cf. *De Quantitate Animae*, XXX, 60 (Tourscher, p. 166): "Ex quo cui non videatur, nullo loco animam contineri." *De Genesi ad Litteram*, VIII, 21: "Cum anima non sit natura corporea nec locali spatio corpus inpleat, sicut aqua utrem sive spongiam, sed miris modis ipsi incorporeo nutu commixta sit vivificando corpori, quo et imperat corpori quadam intentione, non mole." We also find the parallel between soul and God in Augustine, although in another form: God is the life of the soul as the soul is the life of the body. Cf. *De Libero Arbitrio*, II, 16, 41; *Confessions*, X, 6, 10; *De Immortalitate Animae*, 9, 16; *De Genesi ad Litteram*, VII, 3, p. 203, 1 Zycha, etc. It will be noted that in Augustine the preferred comparison is between God and the soul and not between God and the world. In general considerations περὶ κόσμου have little room in his work. On man as microcosmus, cf. Democritus, fragment 34 B, Diels (*Vorsokratiker*, vol. 2, p. 153, 8); Plato, *Philebus*, 29 a ff.; Aristotle, *Physics*, VIII, 2, 252 b 26; Macrobius, *In Somnium*, II, 12, 10–11: "The soul governs the body in the same way that God governs the universe, This is the reason why philosophers have called the universe a large man and man a microcosmos." Chalcidius, *In Timaeum*, ch. 202, p. 243, 13 Wrobel, etc. For the different forms that the idea of microcosmos assumes in antiquity, cf. Rudolf Allers, "Microcosmos from Anicamandros to Paracelsus," pp. 338 ff.

89 Marius Victorinus, *Adversus Arium*, I, 32, *Patrologia Latina*, vol. 8, col. 1064 D.

It is not impossible that Mamertus knew it directly through the *doctissimi* or the *multi* to whom these testimonies remit. But we should first dwell for a moment on this doctrine which played such a great role in antiquity from the pre-Socratics to neo-Platonism, passing through Aristotle and Stoicism.[90] Indeed, studying it thoroughly would familiarize one with a whole sector of ancient thought, and although an exhaustive investigation is not at all required here, it seems indispensable to set out at least some of its riches, if only to better grasp everything implied by the texts we want to comment. It is difficult to find a more typical example of the complex interplay and exchanges of ideas from which neo-Platonism issued.

Even if the idea that the soul is the envelope and support of the body is definitely not Stoic in origin, by integrating this doctrine into its overall system so as to make it one of the central axes of its thought, Stoicism

90 Anaximines, fragment B 2 Diels, vol. 1, p. 95, 17): "Just as our soul, which is air, keeps us united, similarly breath and air contain the whole universe." Plato, *Timaeus*, 34 b, p. 65, R.G. Bury trans., London: Heinemann, 1961: "And in the midst thereof he set Soul, which He stretched throughout the whole of it, and therewith He enveloped also the exterior of its body." Cf. *Timaeus*, 36 e. For Plato, the universal soul surrounds the body, but not the individual soul, which itself is enclosed in the body, as in a prison or tomb; cf. *Phaedo*, 62 b; *Gorgias*, 493 a and 525 a; *Cratylus*, 400 c etc. Plotinus admits having gone beyond his master in extending the doctrine about the soul of the world to particular souls. *Enneads* IV, 3, 22 (p. 103, *Plotinus IV*, Loeb Classical Library):: "That is why Plato rightly does not put the soul in the body when he is speaking of the universe, but the body in the soul, and says also that there is a part of the soul in which body is and part in which there is no body, clearly the powers of the soul of which the body has no need. And the same principle clearly applies to other souls." See likewise the parallel between the action of the soul upon the body and that of the gods who organize and "contain" (συνέχοντες) the universe, Xenophon, *Memorabilia*, IV, 3, 13; *Cyropedia*, VIII, 7, 22. Aristotle *De Anima*, I, 5, 411 b 5 ff (pp. 553–554, Richard McKeon, ed. *The Basic Works of Aristotle*, New York: Random House, 1941) on the subject of the human soul not the soul of the world: "Some hold that the soul is divisible, and that one part thinks, another desires. If, then, its nature admits of its being divided, what can it be that holds the parts together? Surely not the body; on the contrary it seems rather to be the soul that holds the body together (συνέχειν); at any rate when the soul departs the body disintegrates and decays." Cf. *De Caelo*, IV, 5, 312 b 12.

certainly gave it extraordinary diffusion. One attribute of πνεῦμα, that fiery breath which, though material, is divine and immanent to the universe, will be to coordinate the different parts of the κόσμος and to guarantee its cohesion at the same time as that of every individual being by spreading through all things and mixing itself closely with them. Two texts among many others[91] can be selected as representative: one, from Chrysippus's immediate disciple Diogenes of Seleucia, affirms that "Zeus *contains* (περιέχειν) the world as the soul *contains* man."[92] In the other, Posidonius proclaims in turn that, "It is not bodies that contain (συνέχειν) souls, but souls which *contain* bodies."[93] Adapted to a Stoic context and directed against the Epicureans, the idea serves the philosopher of Apameus to show that the soul is not dissipated like an exhalation at the moment of death, but that it possesses something in itself which assures its subsistence for a very long time.

From the second century A. D., that is from the moment when the texts begin to be abundant, we can say that this idea is part of the epoch's philosophical κοινή, formed of the most diverse elements and utilized for no less diverse ends. We find it in the Aristotelian Alexander of Aphrodisias, who notes its Stoic links,[94] in the Platonists Albinus,[95]

91 Abundant documentation on this subject is found in Gérard Verbeke's thesis, *L'évolution de la doctrine du pneuma du stoïcisme à saint Augustin*, Paris-Louvain: Desclée de Brouwer, 1945.

92 Diogenes of Seleucia, *apud* Diels, *Doxographi Graeci*, 549, B. Cf. Arius Didymus, *apud* Eusebius, *Praeparatio Evangelica*, XV, 15, 1, vol. II, p. 379, 12 Mras: "The Stoics call the whole κόσμος with its parts God . . . he contains (περιέχειν) all things." Zeus is often identified with the soul of the world. An etymological relationship can be seen between ζεύς and ζῆν: "That is why the κόσμος is also called Zeus, since it is from him that life comes to us." On this basic identification of God and the world soul, cf. Seneca, *Naturales Quaestiones*, I, *praefatio*, 13; St. Augustine, *De Civitate Dei,* VII, 6, 1 (*Corpus Christianorum*, vol. 47, p. 191) and IV, 31, 24 (vol. 47, p. 125); *De Genesi ad Litteram*, VII, 4, p. 203, 24 Zycha.

93 Posidonius, *apud* Achilles Tatius, *Isagoge in Arati Phaenomena*, ch. 13, Cf. Gérard Verbeke, *L'évolution*, p. 128; Max Pohlenz, *Die Stoa*, Göttingen: Vandenhoeck und Ruprecht, 1948, p. 229.

94 Alexander of Aphrodisias, *De Mixtione*, III, p. 216, 14 Bruns (*Supplementum Aristotelicum* II, 2): Ἡνῶσθαι μὲν ὑποτίθεται [Chrysippus] τὴν σύμπα-

Plutarch,[96] and Maximus of Tyre,[97] and even in the skeptic Sextus Empiricus.[98] Is it necessary to recall what certain Fathers of the Church owe to it, notably the Alexandrians, Clement of Alexandria and Origen?[99] Referring to the same idea, the author of the *Letter to Diognetus* can say very happily of Christians that they are the soul of the world.[100]

What we see above all and what directly interests us is that around this time the doctrine is first linked to the notions of the spirituality and immortality of the soul. Later authors will hardly innovate on this point or on that of the ἀσύγχυτος ἕνωσις. It will suffice for them to rummage in an already well stocked arsenal. Numemius and Ammonius, who exercised considerable influence on neo-Platonism, deduced the spirituality of the soul from the fact that it *contained* the body, a role that only an immaterial

σαν οὐσίαν, πνεύματός τίνος διὰ πάσης αὐτῆς διήκοντος, ὑφ' οὗ σύνέχεταί τε καὶ συμμένει, καὶ σύμπαθές ἐστιν αὐτῷ τὸ πᾶν . . . Cf. Alexander of Aphrodisias, *De Anima*, p. 114, 24 Bruns.

95 Albinus, *Epitome*, XIV, 4

96 Plutarch, *Moralia*, 881 B; 886 E; 1054 F, etc.

97 Maximus of Tyre, *Dissertatio* XV, 5: Ἐν γοῦν τῇ συστάσει τὸ μὲν σῶμα συνέχεται, ἡ δὲ ψυχὴ συνέχει.

98 Sextus Empiricus, *Adversus Mathematicos*, IX, 72: Οὐδὲ γὰρ πρότερον τὸ σῶμα διακρατητικὸν ἦν αὐτῶν [sc. ψυχῶν], ἀλλ' αὐταὶ τῷ σώματι συμμονῆς ἦσαν αἰτίαι, πολὺ δὲ πρότερον καὶ ἑαυταῖς.

99 Clement of Alexandria, *Stromata*, V, 8, 48, 2, vol. II, p. 358, 17 Stählin; *Stromata*, VII, 5, 28, 1, vol. 3, p. 20, 18. Origen, *Contra Celsum*, VI, 71, p. 141, 5 Koetschau (*Die griechischen christlichen Schriftsteller*, vol. 3); *De Oratione*, 23, 1 p. 349, 19; *De Principiis*, II, 1, 3, p. 108, 11 (*Die griechischen christlichen Schriftsteller*, vol. 22), and earlier Philo, *De Confusione Linguarum*, 136, vol. 2, p. 254, 22 Cohn-Wendland; *De Migratione Abrahami*, 181, vol. 2, p. 303, 22, etc.

100 *Letter to Diognetus*, VI, 7. See the commentary by Henri-Irenée Marrou, *A Diognète*, Paris: Éditions du Cerf, 1951, pp. 137 ff. Lactantius seems to refer to the same Stoic idea, when he affirms that the city of Rome "sustains everything" and that its ruin will entail that of the universe. *Divinae Institutiones*, VII, 25, 6–8. A tradition rooted in *Apocalypse*, 17, 1 ff, considered that the fall of the "eternal city" must be the sign foretelling the end of the world. That partly explains the dismay when Rome fell to the Visigoths in 410. We know that St. Augustine stood against this interpretation in *The City of God*. Cf. E. T. Mommsen, "St. Augustine and the Christian Idea of Progress, The Background of *The City of God*," in the *Journal of the History of Ideas*, vol. 12, 1951, pp. 346–374.

principle is capable of assuming. "Matter is a violent, impetuous river the limits of whose depth, breadth, and length, escape our vision and remain unfathomable."[101] How could such pure dispersion and agitation subsist, if there were nothing to dominate and retain it? This unifying principle could not be another body, however subtle we suppose it to be; such a body would have to be itself dominated by another body, and so on to infinity.[102] Only what is incorporeal in the strict sense of the word can compensate for the mobility of material beings and save them from the dispersal and corruption to which they are destined.[103]

Here again we find new specifications beyond Plato. The polemic against Stoicism again obliged the defenders of the spirituality of the soul to deepen their thought. The word ἀσώματος, which is never employed to qualify the soul in the *Dialogues*, is at the center of discussion here. The neo-Platonists and their immediate predecessors even dared to take over the expression συνέχειν, already assimilated by Stoicism, which also did not belong to primitive Platonism in this sense. But this is only a material loan. They hastened to add that the action by which the soul "contains" the

101 Numenius *apud* Eusebius, *Preparatio Evangelica*, XV, 17, 2, vol. 2, p. 381, 16 Mras. The image of the stream that is swept away is already in Plato, *Timaeus*, 43 a, and, of course, in Heraclitus, fragment 49 a B, vol. 1, p. 161, 11 Diels, and 91 B, p. 171, 9. Cf. Chalcidius, *In Timaeum*, ch. 214, p. 244, 16 Wrobel.

102 Numenius *apud* Eusebius, *Praeparatio Evangelica*, *ibid*. Nemesius, *De Natura Hominis*, *Patrologia Graeca*, vol. 40, col. 540 A, where the same idea is again attributed to Numenius.

103 Numenius *apud* Eusebius *Praeparatio Evangelica*, ibid., Cf. Albinus, *Epitome*, XI, 2, p. 65 Louis: "Furthermore, efficient causes can only be incorporeal. Bodies, indeed, are passible and fluid, they are never similar to themselves, they lack stability and permanence. Thus, just as a purely passive element exists, it likewise is necessary that a definitely active element exist; now, this agent can only be incorporeal." Proclus, *In Timaeum*, 90 A, vol. 1, p. 293, 22 Diehl: what contains (συνετικόν) is necessarily incorporeal (ἀσώματον). According to a fragment recalled by Mamertus, *De Statu Animae*, p. 129, 13, this doctrine was already in the two Sextiuses: "Incorporalis, inquiunt, omnis est anima et inlocalis atque indeprehensa vis quaedam, quae sine spatio capax corpus haurit et *continet*." The fact that Mamertus attributes this quote to both philosophers at once indicates that he had not read their works himself. Cf. Pierre-Paul Courcelle, *Les lettres grecques en Occident*, pp. 232–233.

body does not at all resemble that of bodies. It is accomplished in a spiritual, not local manner, οὐ τοπικῶς, ἀλλὰ νοητῶς.[104]

The same principle was used to establish the immortality of the soul, the other dogma of neo-Platonic psychology. The soul *contains* the body, but it *contains* itself as well and thereby its duration in being is assured. The ultimate conclusions are now drawn from this argument, which was already sketched by Posidonius: the soul does not survive the body just for a time, it is imperishable by nature.

The discussions related to the eternity of the world are linked to the same order of ideas. Indeed, the two questions are connected. The importance of the later topic in ancient thought is well known. Like bodies taken individually, the material world in totality is intrinsically perishable. It is nonetheless eternal due to the conserving action of God or of the universal soul. In this sense, it can be said to be "simultaneously perishable and incorruptible, but not in the same regard, which would be absurd. It is incorruptible according to time, since it had no beginning (and what has no beginning, has no end); but it is perishable, if that means it cannot *contain* itself."[105] Thus there are two kinds of immortality, one belonging to beings which have no intrinsic principle of corruption, the other peculiar to beings maintained in existence by a force external to them. The first is the immortality of the soul; the second, that of the κόσμος.[106] Like Christian authors later on, Plutarch refers this conserving action to divine providence.[107]

Plotinus was to develop the doctrine admirably, no longer against Stoicism, but against the theory of the demiurge's repentance, in a passage which allows us to measure the distance which separates him from the Gnostics, against what is sometimes affirmed.[108] This repentance of the soul

104 Nemesius, *De Natura Hominis*, col. 540 A; Proclus, *Institutio Theologica*, 176, p. 154, 30 Dodds (Oxford, 1933).

105 Proclus, *In Timaeum*, 90 A, vol. I, p. 293, 19 Diehl.

106 E.g., Macrobius, *In Somnium*, II, 13, 7.

107 Plutarch, *Moralia*, 886 E.

108 Cf. Hans Jonas, *Gnosis und späntike Geist*, Göttingen: Vandenbroeck & Ruprecht, 1934. Appropriating in his turn the Spenglerian concept of pseudomorphosis, the author tends to view the gnostic attitude as the spiritual style of the first millennium after Christ. Under ancient forms which are maintained and mask it, the gnostic sprit would dominate this whole period. Regar-

(μετάνοια τῆς ψυχῆς) is something ridiculous for him, since the world soul governs without fatigue (ἄπονος) and without wear and tear (ἀβλαβής).[109] If the world soul really regrets having produced the world, why does it wait to destroy it?[110] Its "marvelous powers" are such that things lodged in it can only escape it by being annihilated. The supreme cause which "contains" (συνέχειν) all things is stronger than any other bond: "For it would be absurd for the soul, if it is able to hold (συνέχειν) the universe together for any length of time, however short, not to do so forever, as if it held it together (συνέχειν) by force and the natural state of affairs was other than this existing one which is in the nature of the universe and the noble disposition of things, or as if there was someone who was going to dissolve the universal structure by violence and depose the nature of soul as if from some sort of kingship or magistracy."[111]

Has it been sufficiently emphasized how much the development of the Christian notion of conservation, or as it is sometimes put, continuous creation, owed to the doctrine we have just briefly traced, if only in its formulation? Even setting aside the theory of the world soul, which would haunt the minds of the Fathers for a long time,[112] we see that ecclesiastical writers recur to the idea of συνοχή to explain God's preserving action toward creatures. The two main scriptural texts on which they base the doctrine were inviting. Do we not read in the Book of *Wisdom* that "The spirit of

ding the demiurge's repentance, cf. G. Quispel, "Die Reue des Schöpfers," in *Theologische Zeitschrift*, 1942, 2, p. 151 ff.

109 Plotinus, *Enneads* II, 1, 4 (pp. 16–21, *Plotinus II*, Loeb Classical Library, A. H. Armstrong trans., Cambridge, Mass.: Harvard University Press, 1990). On the ease and absence of effort with which the soul governs according to Plato, see the charming remarks of Pierre-Maxime Schuhl, *La fabulation platonicienne*, Paris: Presses Universitaires de France, 1947, p. 118: "Nature, of whose silent contemplation action is but a shadow, resembles the soul which governs the life of a great tree, it is without fatigue and in silence." [How can one not be struck by the astonishingly romantic character of this observation, so sensitive to the taciturn demeanor of the vegetative world – not at all *nature morte*, but *still life*]." St. Augustine, *De Quantitate Animae*, XXXIII, 71 (Tourscher, p. 192): "sine labore [anima] ordinat membrorum concordiam."

110 Plotinus, *Enneads* II, 9, 4 (pp. 234–239 *Plotinus II*, Loeb Classical Library).

111 Plotinus, *Enneads* II, 1, 4 (p. 19 *Plotinus II*, Loeb Classical Library).

112 Cf. Rudolf Allers, "Microcosmos from Anaximandros to Paracelsus," p. 356.

the Lord . . . containeth [συνέχειν] all things . . .",[113] and on the other hand in the *Acts of the Apostles* that "in him we live and move and have our being"?[114] Once more pagan philosophy was clearly ahead of revelation: "How can we say that in God we have life, movement, and being," asks Origen, "except by his comprehending and holding together the whole world by his power?"[115]

In the early Fathers, as in Stoicism, this action is still conceived in a completely static manner. Once the world is created and adorned, the role of the conserving action is limited to preventing its dissolution.[116] Above all, the action maintains equilibrium without explicitly involving the notion of progress. Origen and subsequently Augustine will add the idea of divine government to that of conservation.[117] God is not satisfied with obtaining

113 *Wisdom*, I, 7. The verse itself has been influenced by the philosophical vocabulary of the period.

114 *Acts of the Apostles*, XVII, 28. Cf. *Romans*, II, 36; *Colossians*, I, 16.

115 Origen, *De Principiis*, II, 1, 3 (*Origen*, De *Principiis*, *The Ante-Nicene Fathers*, vol. IV, ed. Alexander Roberts and James Donaldson, Grand Rapids, Michigan: William B. Eerdmans, N.D., revised by A. Cleveland Coxe from T&T Clark, Edinburgh, p. 269). In the same passage we detect the parallel between the soul and God already noted: "Sed sicut corpus nostrum unum ex multis membris aptatum est et ab una anima continetur, ita et universum mundum velut animal quoddam immensum atque immane opinandum puto, quod quasi ab una anima virtute Dei ac ratione teneatur." Like Plutarch, Origen refers this action to divine providence, *Contra Celsum*, VI, 71, p. 141, 10 Koetschau (*Die griechischen christlichen Schriftsteller*, vol. 3). Without thus admitting that the body is in the soul Augustine frequently develops the idea that the world is in God; cf. *De Genesi ad Litteram*, IV, 18, p. 115, 20 Zycha; VIII, 26, p. 265, 19; *Sermo 342*, 3 etc. See the texts gathered by Stanislaus J. Grabowski, *The All Present God, A Study in St. Augustine*, St. Louis and London: Herder, 1954, pp. 112–117. Furthermore, Augustine excuses himself for having employed this metaphorical language, *De Genesi ad Litteram*, IV, 18, p. 117, 16; *De Diversis Quaestionibus 83*, quaestio 20.

116 Athenagoras, *Legatio,* 10, *Patrologia Graeca*, vol. 6, col. 908; Theophilus of Antiochia, *Ad Autolycum*, I, 4, *Patrologia Graeca*, vol. 6, col. 1029; Clement of Alexandria, *Stromata*, VII, 3, 17, 2, vol. 3, p. 13, 1 Stählin.

117 Origen, *De Principiis*, I, 2, 9, p. 40, 2 Koetschau (*Grieschen christlichen Schriftsteller der ersten Jahrhunderte*, vol. 22): "Intellegenda est ergo virtus Dei, qua viget, qua omnia visibilia et invisiblia vel instituit vel continet, vel gubernat,

and keeping the order of the universe. He disposes and directs its destinies. He mysteriously leads the world through the vicissitudes of history towards a goal which he already knows and which will be infallibly attained. His action is exercised without fatigue, without clashes, and most freely. For God has no need of the creature, and nothing could trouble the rest of the seventh day.[118] This establishes the scheme of the divine operations *ad extra* which would later become classical.[119]

As we see, the doctrine that makes God the "place" of the world was very familiar both to Christians and pagans. Indeed, we still say today that the world is in God, but in a rather different sense. We normally understand by this that the exemplary cause of creatures is in God or that created perfections are encountered in the creator eminently and purified of their limitations. That was not primarily the idea that the ancients tried to express through this formula. In Aristotelian and scholastic terms, we would say that they meant more efficient causality than exemplary causality. When St. Augustine tells us that God is in himself and that the soul or the creature is in God, he wants first to persuade us that God is the cause of all beings, who assigns everything its measure and limit, and that everything only subsists in as much as it is actually submitted to the influence of this first

qua ad omnia sufficiens est . . . quibus velut unita omnibus adest." On the question of the time of history or of the divine economy in Origen, where these considerations will lead us if they are pursued, see Henri de Lubac, *Histoire et esprit*, Paris: Aubier, 1950, especially pp. 246 ff. St. Augustine, *Sermo CXXVI* Mai *apud Misc. Agost.*, vol. I, p. 360: "Sed fuerunt alii dissimiles, qui per istam creatarum potuerunt pervenire ad intellegendum creatorem, et dicere de his quae fecit Deus: ecce quae fecit, gubernat et continet." Cf. *De Genesi ad Litteram*, IV, 12, p. 108, 25 Zycha.

118 St. Augustine, *De Civitate Dei*, VII, 30, 37 (*Corpus Christianorum*, vol. 47, p. 212): " . . . implens caelum et terram praesente potentia, non indigente natura"; *Enarratio in Psalmum 113*, 1, 14 (*Corpus Christianorum*, vol. 40, p. 1641): "Ergo in quibus est ipse, tamquam indigentia continet, non ab eis tamquam indigens continetur;" *Epistula 187*, 15, p. 92, 14 Goldbacher (*Corpus Scriptorum Ecclesiasticorum Latinorum*, vol. 57): "sic est Deus per cuncta diffusus, ut non sit qualitas mundi sed substantia creatrix mundi sine labore regens et sine onere continens mundum . . ."

119 E.g., St. Thomas, *Summa Theologiae*, Prima Pars, Quaestiones 103–104.

cause.[120] By contrast, God is in himself because he is his own reason of being and needs no other to exist.

In this same sense Mamertus can say that the world is in God as the body is in the soul. In this regard his doctrine is very much within Christian tradition. Still, since it is hardly likely that he took it from his Christian predecessors[121] in this form, we would be inclined to think that he owes it directly to neo-Platonism, in which it appears very frequently. Plotinus several times affirms and often develops at length the idea that the body is in the soul and not vice versa, just as the world is in the principle which contains it.[122] The same thought is present in Porphyry,[123] Proclus,[124] and Nemesius in a passage already studied in relation to the union of soul and body, which is inspired by Porphyry.[125]

It flourishes well beyond our fifth century. We find it again, as we might expect, in the Aristotelian commentators[126] and later in the polymath Psellos[127] and William of Saint-Thierry.[128] In the Carolingian period, the author of *De Diversa Animae Ratione* attacked it violently[129] and Hincmar of Reims considered it as heretical or only slightly less,[130] which seems to

120 Similarly, in the order of final causality, God is the place toward which creatures tend and where they find rest; cf. St. Augustine, *De Genesi ad Litteram*, IV, 18, p. 117 Zycha.
121 See above in this chapter.
122 Besides the texts already cited, see *Enneads* IV, 3, 20 (pp. 94–101, *Plotinus IV*, Loeb Classical Library); V, 5, 9, (pp. 180–185 *Plotinus V*, Loeb Classical Library, A.H. Armstrong trans., Cambridge, Mass.: Harvard University Press, 1984) and *passim*.
123 Porphyry, *Sententiae ad Intelligibilia Ducentes*, XXXI.
124 Proclus, *In Timaeum*, 90 A-B, vol. I, p. 267, 25 ff Diehl.
125 Memesius, *De Natura Hominis*, *Patrologia Graeca*, vol. 40, col. 536.
126 John Philoponus, *De Anima*, I, proemium, p. 12 Hayduck; Themistius, *De Anima*, p. 37, 10 Heinze.
127 Psellos, *De Anima*, *Patrologia Graeca*, vol. 122, col. 1043 B.
128 William of Saint Thierry, *De Natura Corporis et Animae*, II, *Patrologia Latina*, vol. 180, col. 712.
129 Pseudo Hincmar, *De Diversa Animae Ratione*, *Patrologia Latina*, vol. 125, col. 929.
130 Hincmar de Reims, *De Praedestinatione Dissertatio Posterior*, ch. XXXI, *Patrologia Latina*, vol. 125, col. 296 D.

indicate that it was current in their environment. Finally, St. Thomas himself will not hesitate to welcome it into the *Summa Theologiae*.[131]

* * *

A detailed exposition like the one just given is even more justified if we briefly consider discussions in recent years provoked by the neo-Platonic concept of man as microcosm. Ernst Cassirer and after him certain modern critics have denied that the conception is compatible with the overall system of neo-Platonism and deplored as useless efforts carried out by neo-Platonists to integrate into the system a whole series of doctrines foreign to its most basic inspiration, while recognizing the dramatic, even touching character of this attempt, predestined to failure. The result would be an amalgam of considerable historical interest but without much consistency, having nothing to do with organic, coherent thought, that is to say, with anything normally called "philosophical system" in the best sense of the term. Typical in this regard are the reproaches formulated by Rudolf Allers in the very rich article to which we have already referred:

> It should be noted . . . that the strictly Platonic interpretation of human nature creates certain difficulties when combined with the notion of the microcosm. If the body is a substance in itself, and the soul imprisoned therein – *hoc corpus, hoc est tenebrosum carcer*, as Augustinus wrote, *Contra Academicos*, I, 3, 9 – then man can hardly be a microsom, because the essential unity of the κόσμος is missing; there is a break in his nature. This difficulty, apparently, has not been noticed, or if noticed not felt as serious, by those writers who unhesitatingly speak of man as a *minor mundus* and, at the same time, as consisting of two independent substances, united one to the other in a more or less accidental manner.[132]

131 St. Thomas, *Summa Theologiae*, I, 52, 1; cf. *In Aristotelis Librum De Anima*, I, lectio 14, no. 206.

132 Rudolf Allers, "Microcosmos from Anaximandros to Paracelsus," in *Traditio*, vol. 2, 1944, p. 354, note 86.

And further on:

> The idea of microcosm presents some particular difficulties when envisioned in the background of neo-Platonism. History, of course, shows that neo-Platonism became associated with various types of microcosm. But historical factuality and systematic possibility are very different problems.[133]

We suddenly perceive how deeply neo-Platonic thought is challenged by such an accusation of eclecticism. To proclaim "its fundamentally syncretist nature"[134] in this way, is already to decide on its value and considerably restrict the philosophical significance of a system which still possesses greatness. What remains of a doctrine stripped of norms, whose principal merit would be to have accepted the most divergent ideas of its period with as much generosity as indifference toward its own principles?

Also, given the stature of some representatives of the neo-Platonic school, among whom the mere mention of the name Plotinus suffices, it is perhaps prudent to express certain reservations. Is it evident that neo-Platonism presents a hidden contradiction? Certainly, the microcosm-macrocosm scheme had been vigorously impressed upon ancient thought, and it was normal that a philosopher would try to color his thought with it. But to make this scheme function as the only reason of the approximation between man and universe is, it seems, to employ it quite mechanically. Does not rather the very mindset of the neo-Platonists push them to conceive things this way? Because they had a genuine notion of the nature of incorporeal being, they could dream of a parallel between the individual soul and the body on the one hand, and the universal soul and the world on the other. Though inferior, the human soul fully realizes the notion of soul, and therefore, its relations with the body can only conform to the mode

133 Rudolf Allers, "Microcosmos," p. 357.

134 Rudolf Allers, Microscosmos, p. 357. Allers remits to Ernst Cassirer, *The Individual and the Cosmos in Renaissance Philosophy* (Oxford: Blackwell, 1963), p.18: "Plotinus and neo-Platonism tried to unite the fundamental ideas of Platonic and Aristotelian thought; but in fact, they only succeeded in producing an eclectic mixture."

characteristic of spiritual beings. Allers himself is obliged to recognize that in Stoicism the gap between soul and body was attenuated thanks to the notion of συμπάθεια,[135] which tends to legitimate that of microcosm in its eyes. But we can similarly observe that in neo-Platonism this break is far from being as marked as the formulas bequeathed by Plato would make us suppose. Whatever criticisms can be directed against this doctrine, it is beyond doubt that its presence would not harm the overall unity of neo-Platonism.

In what particularly concerns the place of the soul, there is no doubt. For a neo-Platonist, the idea of physical place no longer has sense since we are dealing with an incorporeal being, that is to say, a being whose characteristic is precisely to lack dimensions and which, consequently, cannot situate itself at a determined point in space.[136] In this regard, matters are the same for God, the world soul, and the human soul.

But, inversely, in what sense can the body be said to be in the soul? Is this a simple metaphor? Is it not unwittingly falling back into the same materialistic terminology which expresses itself in this way? Perhaps the difficulty stems simply from Greek usage, quite different from ours. Reviewing the several ways in which a thing is said to be in another, Aristotle notes that which consists in affirming that "the affairs of Greece center in the king (ἐν βασιλεῖ) and in general events center in their primary motive agent."[137] Without doubt the place in question, if we can still speak of place, is free of all spatial determination. I can say that a thing is in me because it is in my power to do it, that I act on it or that in one way or another it depends on me. It is in this sense that the soul, which governs the body, maintains it, and is responsible for the ordering of its parts, "contains" that body and is its "place."

So we again meet the idea already emphasized of a close bond, conceived in a new way, between body and soul. We also see how this doctrine,

135 Allers, "Microcosmos," p. 354, note 86.

136 However, it must be recognized that because the soul vivifies the body and acts upon it, it acquires a certain local determination κατὰ συμβεβηκός; cf. Nemesius, *De Natura Hominis*, *Patrologia Graeca*, vol. 40, col. 540 C; Priscian, *Solutiones*, p. 51, 18 Bywater: "Manet ergo [anima] inconfuse unita, ac per hoc impertibilis quidem natura, partita vero connaturalitate quae est ad corpus." Mamertus wrongly neglects this distinction.

137 Aristotle, *Physics*, IV, 3, 210 a 21 (*Basic Works of Aristotle*, McKeon, p. 273).

far from betraying the spirit of neo-Platonism, has a profound link to one of its most original features.

III

The idea of the separation of soul and body ties in quite naturally with that of the place of the soul. The end of chapter XX of *De Statu Animae*, which immediately precedes the chapter we would like to examine now (book I, chapter XXI, p. 71, 12 ff), announces an explanation of the faculties of the soul: memory, judgment, will. But the author has decided to first give us some clarifications about the problem of death, a topic which has just been touched upon. Carried off by his subject, he will only return to the question posed at the outset fifteen pages later (p. 85, 22 ff).[138] This long digression has never been studied. We believe it too forms a unit whose inspiration is completely neo-Platonic.

The new chapter's title – that memory is common to men and animals and that man is a microcosm – is obviously applicable only to its first lines and hardly gives a precise idea of its content.[139] What is its real subject?

The doctrine presented can be summed up briefly as follows: at the moment of death, it is not the soul which leaves the body, but the body which abandons the soul.[140] Since the soul is not enclosed in the body, as we have just seen and does not occupy a place in any sense for Mamertus,[141]

138 There are similar digressions elsewhere in *De Statu Animae*, e.g., p. 105, 6, where the author introduces a quote from Philolaos, which will only be given 15 pages later: "Nunc ad Philoaum redeo, a quo dudum magno intervallo digressus sum," p. 120, 12. Sidonius had already pointed out this stylistic trait in Claudianus; *Letters*, vol. II, Book IV, 3, 4 (p. 72, Loeb Library): "At vero in libris tuis iam illud quale est, quod et teneritudinem quamquam continuata maturitas admittit interseritque tempestivam censura dulcedinem, ut lectoris intentionem per eventilata disciplinarum philosophiae membra lassatam repente voluptuosis excessibus quasi quibusdam pelagi sui portubus foveat?"

139 Nothing guarantees that the author made the division into chapters or the titles.

140 The idea is expressed for the first time on p. 70, 17: "Hinc est quod emoriens corpus animatum non amittit animam sed dimittit."

141 *De Statu Animae*, p. 70, 18: "non egreditur quod non includitur, nec amittitur quod non tenetur."

it is false to say that it departs from the body. It is rather the body which escapes from its influence.

In the pages that follow, the author tries to show that this principle is applicable not only to man but to all animated beings; first of all to plants. The latter have no soul, a monopoly of beings endowed with knowledge and local movement.[142] They are nonetheless vivified by an incorporeal principle. When they are about to die, it is not this vital principle which withdraws from the body, it is the body which escapes its action.[143] Like all material beings, plants are formed out of the four elements, each tending by nature toward its proper place; hence the necessity of a higher principle

142 *De Statu Animae*, p. 72, 4: "quaereo a te herbas et arbusta utrumne neges vivere, an forsan dicas his ipsis viventibus aliquibus ut vivant animas inesse. Sed animata si essent, motu proprio non carerent, quia sunt quae moventur motu non proprio. Sentirent etiam vulnus inflictum. Sed haec talibus non inesse vel de ossuum sectione et capillorum atque unguium praecisione cognoscimus, quae sine ullo sensu doloris abscidimus. Est ergo ibi vita, ubi non est anima." The same distinction between soul and life is found in St. Augustine in response to the Manichaeans, who held that plants were endowed with sensation and that they felt pain when they were mistreated; cf. *De Genesi ad Litteram, Liber Imperfectus*, V, 24, p. 474, 7 Zycha (*Corpus Scriptorum Ecclesiasticorum Latinorum*, vol. 28, 1): "Non ergo qui his causis non sentit, caret ista luce; sed cum talis potentia non est in anima, quae iam nec anima dici solet sed tantum vita, qualis perhibetur esse vitis et arboris et quarumque stirpium, si tamen eas vel talem habere persuaderi ullomodo potest, quas nonnulli nimis errantes haeretici non solum sentire per corpus, id est videre et audire et calorem ignemque discernere sed etiam intellegere rationem et cogitationes nostras nosse arbitrantur." Cf. *Confessiones*, III, 10, 18; *De Genesi ad Litteram*, VII, 16; *De Moribus Ecclesiae Catholicae*, II, 17, *Patrologia Latina*, vol. 32, col. 1368. Old Stoicism likewise denied that plants had a soul and only attributed the latter to animals and men; Cf. Émile Bréhier, *The History of Philosophy. The Hellenistic and Roman Age*, trans. Wade Baskin (Chicago: The University of Chicago, 1965), p. 54. For Aristotle, by contrast, everything that lives has a soul; *De Anima*, II, 1, 412 B 1 and *passim*. For what concerns the Platonic school, see the discussions on the subject in Plato, *Timaeus*, 76, 3; Porphyry, Πρὸς Γαῦρον, 38, 1 ff. Kalbfleisch (trad. Festugière, *La révélation d'Hermès Trismégiste*, vol. 3, p. 272); Nemesius, *De Natura Hominis*, *Patrologia Graeca*, vol. 40, col. 580 B, etc.

143 *De Statu Animae*, p. 72, 2: "herbarum quoque et fruticum vitam incorpoream esse poteat eandemque non amitti a corpore, sed dimitti . . ."

capable of achieving their harmony. Each being only subsists in the measure in which these elements lend themselves to the action of a unifying principle. When they escape its grasp, whether they become too abundant or scarce, harmony is broken; the being perishes and dies. But once again, it is always the elements which leave the vital principle, and not the opposite.[144]

What has just been affirmed about plants can be said even more of animals and men, both endowed with a soul, however different it may be in the two cases.[145] Allowing for the differences, the same observations hold in any sick part of the body. Mamertus asks whence it comes that the soul does not move a healthy and a sick member in the same way. It is not the soul which has withdrawn from that part of the body. Where would it go?[146] It is the member itself which no longer has the disposition required to carry out the soul's orders.[147] The soul has lost none of its vigor, but the hand is no longer capable of being useful.

This rapid overview was necessary to familiarize the reader with the content of these pages and to bring out the central idea which risks passing unobserved in a flood of details. We can now return to the notion of the body abandoning the soul and examine it more closely. As before, this is not a purely gratuitous affirmation and still less an invention of our author.

The explanation which first comes to mind is that we are dealing with an anti-Stoic polemic, at least in its origin. Indeed, Stoicism believed that it had found a new proof of the soul's corporeality in the phenomenon of the separation of soul and body. The argument was developed especially by Chrysippus: since no contact is possible between an incorporeal substance and a corporeal substance, to say that one separates itself from the other has no sense. Now, that is just what happens at the moment of death. It is enough to proffer, as Chrysippus does, Plato's own definition: Θάνατος . . . χωρισμὸς ψυχῆς ἀπὸ

144 *De Statu Animae*, p. 73, 10. On the lack or excess of the elements as the cause of illness, cf. Plato, *Timaeus*, 82 a; Albinus, *Epitome*, XXII, p. 109 Louis.

145 *De Statu Animae*, p. 74, 17 ff.

146 *De Statu Animae*, p. 75, 9.

147 *De Statu Animae*, p. 75, 18.

σώματος.[148] However, the reasoning loses all its cogency once this contact between the two substances is admitted and explained, as we have seen. The union which results is completely spiritual and their separation is in no way local. Besides, it would have been of no use to turn the proposition around and say that the body separates itself from the soul. The same principle could hold in both cases. There is no place where the neo-Platonists responded to the Stoic syllogism in this way. All the evidence indicates that the solution to the problem was not to be sought in this direction.

It is much more important to note that our doctrine reappeared elsewhere in a famous and already disputed text of Macrobius. Let us recall the essential elements of the problem.

In the passage in question, basing himself on the *Phaedo*, Macrobius distinguishes two kinds of death in man, one obtained by nature, the other by virtue. The first takes place when the soul leaves the body according to the laws of nature, the second when the soul, while remaining united to the body, loosens itself from desires and other carnal passions. The first happens to everyone; the other requires the practice of virtue whose possession is reserved to philosophers. One can and one should search for the latter; it is forbidden to provoke or even hasten the former.[149]

Macrobius tells us that this doctrine has been deepened by Plotinus, and here we find, clearly formulated, the initial antithesis on the subject of the separation of body and soul. At the moment of death, the soul should be free of any passion, which is not always the case when there is a suicide. Far from freeing the soul, the suicide only attaches it more closely to the body.[150]

148 Plato, *Phaedo*, 67, d; cf. 64 c; Chrysippus, fragment 790 (Diels, *Fragmente der Vorsokratiker*, vol. 2, p. 219, 24); cf. Alexander of Aphrodisias, *De Anima*, p. 117, 21 Bruns; Nemesius, *De Natura Hominis*, *Patrologia Graeca*, vol. 40, col. 549 A-B.

149 Macrobius, *In Somnium Scipionis*, I, 13, 5 ff. Franz Cumont already observed that this distinction between physical and spiritual death is not found in this form either in Plotinus or Plato; for Plato, to free the soul by the practice of virtue is not properly speaking to die, but to prepare for death, μελέτη θανάτου; "Comment Plotin détorna Porphyre du suicide," in *Revue des études grecques*, vol. 32, 1919, p. 114.

150 Macrobius, *In Somnium Scipionis*, I, 13, 7.

Only spiritual death, that is to say the philosopher's, and the natural death, which occurs precisely when it is the body which abandons the soul and not the soul which abandons the body, are licit.[151]

That said, it is useful to compare certain representative passages of the *Commentary* and the *De Statu Animae*. Note that we are not presenting strictly parallel texts at all, but simple doctrinal similarities. Nothing indicates that Mamertus used or even knew Macrobius's work.

Macrobius, *In Somnium Scipionis*, I, 13, 11	Claudianus Mamertus, *De Statu Animae*, p. 70, 17
Addit etiam illam solam esse naturalem mortem, ubi *corpus animam, non anima corpus relinquit*. Constat enim numerorum certam constitutamque rationem, animas sociare corporibis. Hi numeri dum supersunt, perserverat corpus animari; cum vero deficiunt, mox arcana illa vis solvitur, qua societas constabat, et hoc est quod fatum et fatalia vitae tempora vocamus.	Hinc est quod emoriens omne *corpus animatum non amittit animam, sed dimittit* . . . (73, 13) Cernis istic dissonantibus ab unitatis concinentia corporis partibus *vitam potius* **a corpore deseri**, *quam corpus a vita dimitti*.
(12) *Anima ergo ipsa non deficit*, quippe quae immortalis atque perpetua est, sed impletis numeris, corpus fatiscit; *nec enim lassatur animando, sed officium suum* **deserit corpus**, cum iam non possit animari. Hinc illud est doctissimi vatis 'explebo numerum reddarque tenebris.' (13) Haec est igitur naturalis vere mors, cum finem corporis solus nu-	(75, 16) ... *non anima imperandi vim perdidit, sed vires serviendi manus amisit*. Illo enim ut puta sanguinis inpetu coniventium elementorum harmonia turbata corpori adimitur serviendi possibilitas, et animo dominandi accidit difficultas . . . *Non tamen anima movendi vim* perdidit, sed membrum convenienter se necessariae motioni non praebuit . . . (73,9) Ex his autem elementis quattuor, quae moderate musiceque in arboris vita sibi concinunt, si quid

151 Macrobius, *In Somnium Scipionis*, I, 13, 11.

merorum suorum defectus adportat, non cum extorquetur vita corpori adhuc idoneo ad continuationem ferendi; nec levis est differentia vitam vel natura vel sponte solvendi. (14) anima enim cum **a corpore deseritur**, potest in se nihil retinere corporeum, si se pure, cum in hac vita esset, instituit. . .	contra mensuram vel superfuit forte vel defuit, aegrescit arbor ipsa primum, dehinc emoritur veluti victa languore.

Of course there are considerable differences between these two series of texts. The idea of suicide, which is at the center of the discussion in Macrobius, has disappeared completely in *De Statu Animae*. That is hardly surprising. Besides the fact that suicide has no role in the general scheme of the work, Mamertus did not have to point out its dangers to the Bishop of Riez. With those reservations, the two authors coincide on several precise points which ought to be emphasized.

Both conceive the union of soul and body as the result of a passing harmony, thanks to which the body submits for a time to the soul's vivifying action. When this harmonic bond, which controls the production and extent of earthly life,[152] is broken, the body wears out, it becomes unusable and, overcome by illness, dissolves. That, Macrobius says, is what is understood by "the destiny and fatal time of life."[153] By contrast, the soul conserves all its vigor, because it is immortal and always in movement. Just as animating the body does not occasion fatigue for the soul,[154]

152 See the references given by Franz Cumont, "Comment Plotin détourna Porphyre du suicide," p. 118, note 2; similarly, St. Augustine, *De Quantitate Animae*, XXXIII, 70 (p.188 Tourscher): "Haec igitur primo, quod cuivis animadvertere facile est, corpus hoc terrenum atque mortale praesentia sua vivificat; colligit in unum, atque in uno tenet, diffluere atque contabescere non sinit . . . congruentiam eius modumque conservat, non tantum in pulchritudine, sed etiam in crescendo atque gignenendo."

153 Macrobius, *In Somnium*, I, 13, 11: "Fatum et fatalia vitae tempora."

154 St. Augustine, *De Quantitate Animae*, XXXIII, 71 (Tourscher, p. 192): "sine labore ordinat membrorum concordiam."

similarly, the soul does not undergo essential modification because of the fact of ceasing to animate; this activity is secondary. The soul will only be freer thereafter to be at leisure for its proper activity, which is to contemplate the Ideas. This is the doctrine of εἱμαρμένος θάνατος, whose Pythagorean inspiration in Macrobius has been demonstrated by Franz Cumont.[155]

It is striking that among the texts which best illustrate it, we find precisely this quote from Philolaos, which *De Statu Animae* has preserved for us and which can be usefully juxtaposed with one of the phrases of the *Commentary* that has just been read:

Philolaos *apud* Claudianus Mamertus, *De Statu Animae*, p. 120, 15	Macrobius, *In Somnium Scipionis*, I, 13, 11
Anima inditur corpori per numerum et immortalem eandemque incorporalem convenientiam.	Constat enim numerorum certam constitutamque rationem animas sociare corporibus.

So, book I of *De Statu Animae* already substantially contains a doctrine which book II attributes to the pagans, and more specifically to the Pythagoreans.[156]

Besides, we can ask in what measure it would not be more justified to speak of neo-Pythagoreanism. In any case the conception which these passages offer differs appreciably from what Philolaos's disciple, the Pythagorean Simmias, defends in the *Phaedo*.[157] According to this theory, the soul is not only the artisan of the harmonious mixture (κρᾶσις καὶ ἁρμονία) of contrary elements which constitute the body; it is this harmony itself. To employ a musical metaphor, the soul is the harmony of the

155 Franz Cumont, "Comment Plotin détourna Porphyre du suicide," p. 118

156 F. Boemer, "Der lateinische Neuplatonismus," pp. 143–154 tries to show that this quote from Philolaos could not go back to early Pythagorism. Heinrich Gomperz defends its autenticity, ᾿Ασώματος, in *Hermès*, vol. 67, 1932, p. 156, whose conclusions are accepted by Diels, *Fragmente der Vorsokratiker*. Vol. 1, Berlin,: Weidmann,1951, 16th ed., p.149.

157 Plato, *Phaedo*, 86 b ff. See Plato's criticism, *Phaedo*, 92 a ff.

lyre which is the body.[158] The soul does not survive the dissolution of the body, any more than harmony, however incorporeal and divine, subsists once the cords of an instrument have been loosened.[159]

By contrast, harmony is not identified with the soul here; it is only an effect of the soul, as Olivieri quite rightly notes.[160] To make the soul the harmony of the body would amount to saying that the soul is responsible for the ordering and sustenance of the different elements that compose the body. Through a kind of inclination[161] and active presence[162] in the midst of the material world, the soul gathers and vivifies scattered elements. The soul thereby forms a true body[163] from this indeterminate mass, empty of any thought. The harmoniously constituted body in its manner participates in the world of ideas.

158 Plato, *Phaedo*, 86 a 1. There are innumerable references to this doctrine of the harmony-soul, which assumes both a medical and a musical character. E. Rohde traces it back to Zeno of Elea; cf. *Psyché*, trans. A. Remond, Paris, 1952, p. 392, and note 2. For the terms ὁμολογία, ἁρμονία, συμπάθεια and their Latin equivalents, *harmonia*, *convenientia*, *coaptatio*, etc., cf. F. Boemer, "Der lateinische Neuplatonismus," p. 147, note 1.

159 Yet it is not clear how this doctrine is compatible with the Pythagorean belief in the soul's immortality; cf. Eduard Zeller, *Die Philosophie der Griechen*, vol. I, 1, p. 147.

160 A. Olivieri, "Osservazione sulla dottrina di Filolao," in *Rivista Indo-greco-italica*, vol. 5, 1921, p. 40; F. Boemer, "Der lateinische Neuplatonismus," pp. 144, note 1.

161 Claudianus Mamertus, *De Statu Animae*, p. 76, 3: *animae intentio vivax*. Cf. St. Augustine, *Epistula 166*, 4, p. 551, 7 Goldbacher (*Corpus Scriptorum Ecclesiasticorum Latinorum,* vol. 44): "Per totum quippe corpus, quod animat [anima] non locali diffusione sed quadam vitali intentione porrigitur." *De Genesi ad Litteram,* VII, 19, p. 216, 14 Zycha (*Corpus Scriptorum Ecclesiasticorum Latinorum*, vol. 28, 1); *De Genesi ad Litteram*, VIII, 21, p. 261, 10.

162 On this "presence" of the soul (παρεῖναι, παρουσία) Cf. Plotinus, *Enneads* I, 1, 7, (pp. 108–111 *Plotinus I*, Loeb Classical Library); I, 8, 15 (pp. 314–317 *Plotinus I*, Loeb Classical Library); IV, 3, 22 (pp. 102–103 *Plotinus IV*, Loeb Classical Library); Porphyry, Περὶ ψυχῆς πρὸς Βόηθον, *apud* Eusebius, *Praeparatio Evangelica*, XV, 11, 2, vol. 2, p. 374, 12 Mras; Nemesius, *De Natura Hominis*, *Patrologia Graeca*, vol. 40, col. 597 A; St. Augustine, *De Quantitate Animae*, XXXIII, 70 (Tourscher, pp. 188–190).

163 Cf. St. Augustine, *De Immortalitate Animae*, XV, 24: "Tradit speciem anima corpori, ut sit corpus in quantum est."

Above all, it is significant that death is presented in Mamertus as the desertion of the body, an idea which offers a new and very peculiar specification in relation to the traditional definition. We have seen how Plato defined death simply as a separation of soul and body, and this notion is what we always find prior to neo-Platonism.[164] The *Phaedo* simply taught that the soul is detached from the body by philosophy and science; but here for Plato and the Platonic school we are only dealing with spiritual death.[165] It was, to be sure, reported that before giving himself up to death, Cato reread this dialogue and that the perusal of these pages had caused the suicide of one Cleombrotus of Ambratia.[166] However, these two cases in no way modify the traditional doctrine. Nowhere is death presented as abandonment of the soul by the body. When he attributed this doctrine to Plotinus, Macrobius was fully aware of its novelty.

Similarly, Ambrose and Augustine, who often revisited the topic, limit themselves to the usual definition of death: it is either separation of soul and body without further specification, or the abandonment of the body by the soul.[167] Barring oversight on our part, neither alludes to the doctrine we find here. Even in *De Immortalitate Animae*, where the question is studied at length in a context which frequently recalls ours, the soul or life is always said to abandon the body.[168] Consequently, it hardly seems plausible that Mamertus took these views from Augustine.

From whom did he get them? We know that the passage from

164 See note 148 in this chapter; Albinus, *Epitome*, XXV, 2, p. 119 Louis.

165 Plato, *Phaedo*, 66 e; Xenophon, *Cyropaedia*, VIII, 7, 22; Albinus, *Epitome*, IX, etc.

166 Cicero, *Disputationes Tusculanae*, I, 34, 84; *Pro Scauro*, 5; Lactantius, *Divinae Institutiones*, III, 18, p. 238 12 Brandt (*Corpus Scriptorum Ecclesiasticorum Latinorum*, vol. 19); St. Augustine, *De Civitate Dei*, I, 22, 12, (*Corpus Christianorum*, vol. 47, p. 23); pseudo-Jerome, *Epistula 6*, *Patrologia Latina*, vol. 30, col. 87.

167 Ambrose, *De Bono Mortis*, 2, 3, p. 704 Shenkl (*Corpus Scriptorum Ecclesiasticorum Latinorum*, vol. 32, 1); *De Bono Mortis*, 3, 8, p. 708, 12 and *passim*; St. Augustine, *Enarrationes in Psalmos XLVIII*, *Sermo* II, 2, 8 (*Corpus Christianorum*, vol. 38, p. 565); *Enarrationes in Psalmos LXX*, *Sermo II*, 3, 59, vol. 39, p. 962; *De Civitate Dei*, XIII, 2, 7 (*Corpus Christianorum*, vol. 48, p. 385); *De Civitate Dei*, XIII, 16, 3, p. 396; *De Trinitate*, IV, 3; *Patrologia Latina*, vol. 42, col. 890, etc.

168 St. Augustine, *De Immortalitate Animae*, IX, 16 and *passim*.

Macrobius presented above gave rise to a controversy between Franz Cumont and Fr. Henry. The former held that Macrobius was inspired in Porphyry's *De Regressu*;[169] the latter, that he followed Plotinus textually.[170] Despite Fr. Henry's pertinent remarks, it now seems to be established that Porphyry was certainly the immediate source.[171] Besides, we know that Mamertus was familiar with *De Regressu* and that he used it.[172] Notably, he found there the extract from the *Phaedo* that he reproduces in the second book of *De Statu Animae*, precisely the passage used to support Macrobius's dissertation on suicide.

Finally, a somewhat enigmatic remark in the same passage of *De Statu Animae* suggests that we not let our intelligence be clouded "to the point of believing that souls, once freed from the body, remain prisoners of the air, or of some other element."[173] It is possible that we have a veiled allusion to the popular belief that the soul of the Βιαιοθάνατοι conserved a portion of matter or was condemned to wander for some time around the corpse, an idea that Macrobius also knew and which, like the others, must have come from Porphyry.[174]

All together these indications render the hypothesis about borrowing

169 Franz Cumont, "Comment Plotin détourna Porphyre du suicide," in *Revue des études grecques*, vol. 32, 1919, pp. 113–120.

170 Paul Henry, *Plotin et l'Occident,* Louvain: Spicelegium Sacrum Louvainense, 1934, pp. 163–182.

171 See remarks by Pierre-Paul Courcelle, *Le lettres grecques en Occident*, pp. 27–28. The idea of a double death, as it has just been explained, is still found in Porphyry, *Sententiae ad Intelligibilia Ducentes*, 8–9, and in the *Commentary on the Phaedo* published by Norvin under the name of Olympiodorus, pp. 21, line 22 ff. Regarding the work's authenticity, see the reflections of Rudolf Beutler, "Olympiodorus," in P.W., R.E., vol. 18, 1, col. 211 ff. The two references to Porphyry and to Olympiodorus are noted by Franz Cumont, "Comment Plotin détourna Porphyre du suicide," p. 119. Cf. also Psellos, *De Omnifaria Doctrina*, 64 Westerink,.

172 Cf. Pierre-Paul Courcelle, *Les lettres grecques en Occident*, pp. 226 ff.

173 *De Statu Animae*, p. 76, 10.

174 Franz Cumont, "Comment Plotin détourna Porphyre du suicide," p. 116. On the distinction between natural (or inevitable) death and premature death (accidental or violent), cf. Franz Cumont, *Lux perpetua*, Paris: Paul Geuthner, 1948, ch. VII, "L'astrologie et les morts prématures," especially pp. 312 ff.

from Porphyry quite plausible. The continuation of *De Statu Animae* will confirm this supposition.

* * *

In fact, the next chapter (I, 22, p. 78, 15 ff), which at first sight appears to be a commentary on two texts from scripture,[175] is simply a series of considerations on spiritual death and essentially just glosses the *Phaedo* text, which in Macrobius was close to the Plotinian doctrine of suicide. To facilitate its exposition, we again place the relevant passages from chapter XXII and the translation of the *Phaedo* which we find in the second book with the commentary which highlights it. The quotation marks indicate the passages translated from Plato.[176]

Claudianus Mamertus, *De Statu Animae*, p. 77, 17	Claudianus Mamertus, *De Statu Animae*, p. 125: 14
Cum sumus in corpore, peregrinamur a Domino.	"Donec *corpus habeamus* . . . numquam nos id quod iam olim concupiscimus satis plane consecuturos . . ."
(79, 10) [Corpus] adgravat animam *occupando* eam atque inliciendo vel necessariis vel voluptuosis defigendo eandem in pulchra corpora et *a contemplatione summae pulchritudinis abducendo*. Istud ergo quod vel **esui aut potui necessario** in salutem corporis opus inpenditur,	Corpus enim nobis primum *innumerabiles* et infinitas **occupationes** infert, quibus conterimur ob **necessarium victum** et alimenta cotidiana. Deinde si qui *morbi* ingruerunt, inpedimento sunt, quominus inquirere et invenire veritatem possimus. Nam *cupiditatibus*

175 *II Corinithians*, 5, 6: "Dum sumus in corpore peregrinamur a Domino"; *Wisdom*, 9, 15: "Corpus quod corrumpitur adgravat animam."

176 For the moment we set aside the question of knowing whether the translation is by Mamertus himself. In regard to the text, p. 79, 14, it is reasonable to omit the parentheses introduced by Engelbrecht following Hartelius, which the meaning of the phrase does not demand at all; cf. Einar Harleman, *De Claudiano Mamerto gallicae latinitas scriptore quaestiones*, Uppsala: A. Landequistkahekhandeln, 1938, ch. 1, *Critica ad locum*.

vel superflue *voluptatum* nugis animus **occupatur** vel *plagis ac doloribus* per corpus adfligitur, adgravari eandem et *pro multitudine ac difficultate actionis* **onerari** perspicuum est.	*et cupidinibus* et timoribus innumerabilibus, variarum rerum *adpetitionumque visionibus* et infinita quadam dementia corpus **oneratur**, ut prae illo ne sapere quidem ulla in re possimus.
(77, 9) Sed *occurrunt animae phantasiae corporum*, quibus per sensus corporis adfecta non locis, sed falaciis circumscribitur, et quia illorum tantum meminit, quorum species per corpus accepit, nihil esse credit quidquid tale non fuerit . . .	"Et si quando tempus aliquod ad philosophandum vacuum vel habuerimus vel fecerimus, tunc quoque *in ipsis cogitationibus nostris corpus intercurrit* turbam erorum inferens menti, ut obcaecante illo veritatem pervidere non possimus."
(80, 9) Sed in tantum istic peregrinatur, in quantum *per voluptatem ac dolores corporis* per loca vel tempora, per phantasias et phantasmata **a summi boni contemplatione revocatur** . . .	(127, 10) . . . quidnam sit illud quod, ut aiunt [philosophi], corporeus animus ab omni inventione occursante sibi semper extrarii corporis praepediatur obstaculo aut cur extrarium corpus in reatum vocet, quod semet **a contemplatione veri devocet** . . .
(77, 15) Peregrinam se vero in corpore scire non poterit, **si corpus esse se credit** . . .	(122, 22) Si forsan praecipiti lapsu stultitiae ulla anima corpus esse iudicanda est, illas equidem corporeas iudicaverim, **quae corpus esse se credunt**.

Both passages use similar approaches and images that are often very close to one another to develop the general theme of the body as obstacle to contemplation, a Platonic idea, if ever there was one, but in which a Christian like Mamertus could see a stunning anticipation of St. Paul's texts describing the soul's wandering in exile far from its true homeland. "While we are in the body, we are exiled from the Lord," affirmed *II Corinthians* 5: 6, quoted in the same passage of *De Statu Animae*. But what is more pre-Pauline than the opening of the excerpt from the *Phaedo* (65 b) where we read, "So long as we have the body, and the soul is contaminated by such an evil, we shall never attain completely what we desire."

What follows in both passages simply enumerates the several obstacles. Some involve life here below, and we cannot avoid them: humans must obtain nourishment to survive, we have daily occupations, illness. Other obstacles come from our allowing material beings to sweep us up against our true nature and from our succumbing to their attraction. Such are desires and greed, images and illusions of the senses.

Everything makes it seem that the passage from Book I is only a commentary and enlargement of the ideas contained in Book II. Is not the distinction between necessary obstacles (*necessaria*) and those due to our weakness (*voluptuosa*), which is merely implicit in the *Phaedo*, a commentator's distinction? Further, where Plato's text talks generically about nourishment (ἀναγκαία τροφή), Mamertus specifies necessary food and drink. To the multiplicity of occupations, he adds their difficulty: *pro multitudine ac difficultate actionis*. To the vague idea of illnesses (*morbi*), he adds that of internal pain (*dolores*) and external injuries (*plagae*).

We can even ask whether certain expressions in Book I do not achieve their complete sense through reference to the Greek original, which they strangely approximate. This is the case for the *voluptatum nugae*, which might well remit us to the text of the *Phaedo*: ἐρώτων . . . καὶ φλυαρίας ἐμπίπλησιν ἡμας πολλῆς, rather imperfectly translated as *infinita quadam dementia corpus oneratur*. Similarly, by its Greek sense ἐμπίπλησιν, *occupatur* is closer than *oneratur*.

In both passages, error, the soul's evil, appears as a result of an attack by sensorial images which burst into the soul (*occurrunt*, *intercurrit*) and somehow besiege and blind it, so that in the end only the crowd of shadows and images taken from bodies seem real to the soul – and it comes to believe itself to be of the same nature as they are: *corpus esse se credit*. Here again new elements are to be observed, notably the allusion to beautiful bodies,[177]

177 *De Statu Animae*, p. 79, 10: "[Corpus] adgravat animam . . . defigendo eandem in pulchra corpora et a contemplatione summae pulchritudinis abducendo." E. Harleman, *De Claudiano Mamerto Gallicae Latinitatis Scriptore Quaestiones*, p. 79, compares the text of Cicero, *Academica*, II, 46: "Parum defigunt animos

which does not figure in the passage from the *Phaedo* and which instead makes us imagine Plotinus's treatise *On the Beautiful*. Indeed, a resonance of this famous treatise, perhaps indirect but unquestionable, is found in a passage of *De Statu Animae* which ostensibly connects with our present passage. "Here," says Claudianus, "is what has been given to the heart's eye to contemplate. To where do we flee, to where we allow ourselves to be dragged, why, while remaining in ourselves, are we outside ourselves? Why do we insist on seeking our homeland just anywhere, for to tell the truth, we abandon it not by traveling but by doing evil? Why do we take the shadows for light, because to see them is surely to not see? No doubt we seek the truth but it must not be sought in some corner of the earth, nor is there any hope of finding it among bodies."[178]

et intendunt in ea quae perspicua sunt," and *De Finibus*, V, 87: ". . . ut quam minime animus a cogitationibus abduceretur, patrimonium neglexit, agros deseruit incultos [sc. Democritus]." Cicero, *De Natura Deorum. Academica*, H. Rackham trans., Cambridge, Mass.: Harvard University Press, 1979, *Academica* II, chapter XV, 46. P. 534; Cicero, *De Finibus*, trans. H. Rackham, Loeb Classical Library, Cambridge, Mass.: Harvard University Press, 1983, book V, XXIX, 87, p. 490). However the comparison loses much of its value because what characterizes Claudianus's text, namely the mention of beautiful bodies and supreme beauty, is missing in Cicero. Let us note in passing that the parallel established by Harleman between *De Statu Animae*, p. 107, 14, and Cicero, *De Natura Deorum*, I, 62: *sed vide quam tecum agam liberaliter*, does not suppose a direct influence of Cicero. Claudianus could have found the same expression in St. Augustine, *De Quantitate Anima*, IV, 5 (Tourscher, p. 12), *liberaliter mecum agis*, supposing that he had to have taken it from somebody.

178 *De Statu Animae*, p. 94, 1: "Ecce quod oculo cordis videre concessum est. Quo diffugimos, quo distrahimur, cur in nobismet ipsis extra nos sumus? Cur patriam nostram localiter quaerimus, de qua utique non ambulando, sed peccando discessimus? Cur tenebras splendere credimus, quas videre ipsum est utique non videre? Veritatem certe quaerimus: non illam per spatia locorum oportere quaeri, non per corporeum aliquid aestimis inveniri." Cf. Plotinus, *Enneads* I, 6, 8–9 (pp. 255, 257, 279 *Plotinus I*, Loeb Classical Library): "But how shall we find the way? What method can we devise? How can one see the 'inconceivable beauty' which stays within the holy sanctuary and does not come out where the profane may see it? Let him who can, follow and come within, and leave outside the sight of his eyes and not turn back to the bodily splendors which he saw before. When he sees the beauty in bodies he must not run after them; we must know that they are images, traces, shadows, and hurry away to that

Consequently, just as in the previous reflections about death, we are dealing with a neo-Platonic development of the *Phaedo*, quite probably Porphyry's *De Regressu*. Together with what we already know about Mamertus, this double coincidence leads us to such a conclusion.

It is hardly necessary to add that the tactic of taking over whole pages of a pagan author, usually without naming him, was no longer new. After recent research, we are more aware of the extent to which Victorinus, Ambrose, Augustine, and others practiced it. Mamertus could appeal to the example of illustrious precursors. But neither is it necessary to exaggerate his dependence on those Christian teachers. Other than certain expressions which he has perhaps taken,[179] or borrowed from a common source, we do

which they image. For if a man runs to the image and wants to seize it as if it was the reality (like a beautiful reflection playing on the water, which some story somewhere, I think, said riddlingly a man wanted to catch and sank down into the stream and disappeared) then this man who clings to beautiful bodies and will not let them go, will, like the man in the story, but in soul, not in body, sink down into the dark depths where intellect has no delights, and stay blind in Hades, consorting with shadows there and here. This would be truer advice, 'Let us fly to our dear country.' What then is our way of escape, and how are we to find it? . . . Our country from which we came is there, our Father is there. How shall we travel to it, where is our way of escape? We cannot get there on foot; for our feet only carry us everywhere in this world, from one country to another. . . . And what does this inner sight see?" The passage cited from Mamertus clearly goes back over the ideas developed in the chapter that we are examining; cf. *De Statu Animae*, p. 76, 12: "Intellectum tuum . . . intellege, cui soli cum angelo haec videre concessum est," and *De Statu Animae*, p. 94, 1: "Ecce quod oculo cordis videre concessum est."

179 We note here the following coincidences of detail:

De Statu Animae, p. 94, 1	St. Augustine, *De Civitate Dei*, X, 29, 12 (*Corpus Christianorum*, vol. 47, p. 304)
Ecce quod oculo cordis videre **concessum est.**	Ad eum per virtutem intellegentiae pervenire pacuis dicis **esse concessum.**
p. 94, 3 Cur patriam nostram localiter quaerimus, **de qua** utique non ambulando, sed **peccando** *discessimus.*	St. Augustine, *De Civitate Dei*, XI, 28, 39 (*Corpus Christianorum*, vol. 48, p. 348)

not find that these chapters have been directly inspired by Augustine. It does not seem necessary to us to hold that their genuine source is any of the some hundred fifty more or less elaborate commentaries that the bishop of Hippo devoted to the two texts of Scripture which Mamertus here explains in his fashion.

Even more than for other periods, history certainly presents itself here as a science of gaps. Because we lack important work like Manlius Theodorus, *De Anima*,[180] or St. Ambrose, *De Philosophia*, which must have contained neo-Platonic and perhaps Porphyrian elements,[181] or that whole

	In nobis autem ipsis eius imaginem contuentes tamquam minor ille evangelicus filius ad nosmetipsos reversi surgamos et ad illum redeamus, **a quo peccando** *recesseramus*.
p. 94, 6 Non illam per **spatia locorum** oportet quaeri.	St. Augustine, *Confessions*, I, 18, 28 Non enim pedibus aut **spatiis locorum** itur abs te aut reditur ad te.
p. 122, 17 **Patrem Deum paternamque mentem**, artem sivi consilium . . . docuit.	St. Augustine, *De Civitate Dei*, X, 23, 10 (*Corpus Christianorum*, vol. 47, p. 296) Dicit enim **Deum patrem** et Deum Filium, quem graece appellat paternum intellectum vel pa**ternam mentem**
p. 128, 16 Si **beati**, inquit [Porphyrius] **esse volumus, corpus est omne fugiendum.**	St. Augustine, *De Civitate Dei*, X, 29, 89, vol. 47, p. 306 Ut **beati** simus, **omne corpus fugiendum** esse opinamini.

Regarding the last two parallels and the conclusions that can be drawn from them, see Pierre-Paul Courcelle, *Les lettres grecques en Occident*, pp. 226 ff.

180 Lastly, on Manlius Theodorus see Pierre-Paul Courcelle, *Les lettres grecques en Occident*, pp. 122–128, and "Recherches sur les *Confessions* de saint Augustin," pp. 153–155.

181 Cf. Pierre-Paul Courcelle, "Recherches," p. 137.

part of Victorinus's work which has disappeared, not to mention many pagan works, it is not always possible to fit together the scattered pieces which our documents provide. Despite these reservations, we can confidently deny that Mamertus drew from pagan sources; all the more because we have his own professions before us.[182] The absence of more exact or more elaborate indications should not surprise us. Our author did not purport to say everything. He often pointed out that because of lack of time, he had to limit himself to what was essential and that he had not used all the material at his disposition.[183] What we have been able to uncover about *De Statu Animae* seems to corroborate these affirmations thoroughly.

IV

Thanks to this basic data, it is not difficult to perceive how our author's thought is constructed. These pages simply offer a Christian transposition of the soul's drama as the neo-Platonists had come to conceive it, and whose basic stages we can reconstruct in the following way:

The soul is spiritual and God-like by nature. From its originally elevated state, the soul has fallen through its own fault and called upon itself the ills it now suffers: *Illa namque si in statu pristini sublimitate mansisset, a quo sponte dilapsa est, numquam contra spiritum caro, nec contra carnem spiritus*

182 Cf. *De Statu Animae*, p. 191, 6 quoted above chapter three, note 70. *De Statu Animae*, p. 19, 13: "Abhinc itidem ad erudiendum in ea quae sunt obscuriora lectorem quippiam ex geometricis et arithmeticis atque etiam ex dialecticis et nonnullis, prout interfuit usui, philosophomenon regulis modeste ac moderate et quam potuit parciter praelibavit habita identidem cum adversa parte congressione, sicque adiectis nostris aliquot sine alienorum interpolamento finem liber accepit."

183 *De Statu Anima*, p. 18, 13: "Scripsi igitur pauca haec veluti quaedam rationum semina." Cf. p. 97, 13: "Ecce de statu vel visione rationalis animae infinitarum pro quaestionis magnitudine rationum tactis breviter potius causis quam satis usque discussis arbitor me de inlocalitate atque incorporalitate animae sufficiens dedisse responsum"; p. 99, 4: " . . . quamlibet multa brevitatis studio omissa fecerim, non tamen omnibus pro causae excellentia supersedi"; p. 129, 5: "Multosque ex eadem Graecia, si vel causa posceret vel ratio sineret, proferre possemus"; p. 189, 10: "Pauca haec et exilia, prout arctum temporis sivit, responsa redhibui."

concupisset.[184] For the soul this fall consisted in turning away from God and toward lower beings; yielding to the deceitful beauty of material things, it became enmeshed in bodies.[185] Evidently, this fall is to be understood in the moral sense, but the terms which describe it recall the fall of the souls through the spheres and their gradual corporalization, according to an old belief inherited from eastern paganism,[186] metaphorically interpreted as psychic transformation by the neo-Platonists themselves.[187]

The immediate result of this abasement is the alienation of the soul in the body. By turning away from God, the soul became foreign to itself. From the domain of certainty, it fell into that of opinion and doubt. Whereas it normally is transparent to itself and knows itself better than anything else, now it takes itself for a body. Sensible images have become a screen between the soul and the intelligible reality to which it belongs, so that it ends by believing that only the corporeal is real and that everything else is nothing.[188] Whatever its efforts to attain God by thought, the soul always finds itself led by the vortex of these phantasms or images toward the realm of bodies.[189]

How will this soul thus turned outside itself tend toward a homeland whose existence it does not even suspect?[190] Like the children Plotinus

184 *De Statu Animae*, p. 85, 12.

185 *De Statu Animae*, p. 85, 9: "Inlecebris pellecta corporeis defluxit in corpus."

186 Cf. Franz Cumont, *Oriental Religions in Roman Paganism* (New York, Dover, 1911, 1956, trans. Grant Showerman), p. 269–270, note 54.

187 E.g., Plotinus, *Enneads* I, 6, 7 (pp. 248–253 *Plotinus I*, Loeb Classical Library); Macrobius, *In Somnum Scipionis*, I, 11, 11–12

188 *De Statu Animae*, p. 77, 11: "quia illorum tantum meminit, quorum species per corpus accepti, nihil esse credit quidquid tale non fuerit."

189 *De Statu Animae*, p. 85, 18: "Hinc est ille prae oculis eius imaginum corporearum tumultus se semper obiectans, ut si quando vel ad se vel ad Deum suum rationcinando nititur, semper ad corporea phantasiis corporis avocetur."

190 *De Statu Animae*, p. 77, 13: "nec suspirare potest illi patriae, de qua in hanc perigrinationem merito praecipitata est, cum peregrinari, se nesciat." Cf. Macrobius, *In Somnium Scipionis*, I, 10, 10. The theme of lack of awareness frequently reappears in St. Augustine's *Confessions*, with a slightly different sense: by a secret disposition, God snatches the soul from its misery and leads it to himself without the soul knowing it; *Confessions*, I, 12, 19; VII, 6, 10; VII, 7, 11, and *passim*."

describes as brought up far from their father, the soul is ignorant of its true dwelling place and does not know itself: *in recognitione sui fallitur*.[191] Its punishment is precisely here.[192] This did not need to be imposed externally; it is part and parcel of the fault. By attaching itself to the mirage of bodies, the soul has been cut off from the possibility of rising to its true good. Plato already held that this blindness was what best characterized the fate of the wicked and made their state desperate. A just person is consciously just, μετὰ φρονήσεως. His happiness is found in virtue, and by virtue, in the divine likeness which men attain in this life according to their abilities.[193] As for the unjust person, he is unaware of his injustice and no longer is even conscious of the error of judgement that he commits.[194] In thinkers at the end of antiquity, this doctrine takes on more pronounced mystical tints and deliberately situates itself in the eschatological mentality dear to the period.

Of course, the soul never becomes a body, but only like a body (σωματοεδής). It must remain what it is by nature, but unfortunately, it is no longer in a position to perceive that and seeks itself as if it were absent.[195] No psychological contact corresponds to the soul's ontological contact with itself.[196]

Perhaps these views partly explain Mamertus's rather surprising harshness toward Faustus of Riez. Since the soul spontaneously recognizes itself for what it is – it has some sort of intuition of its own spiritual essence –

191 *De Statu Animae*, p. 84, 12. Cf. Plotinus, *Enneads* V, 1, 1 (pp. 13–15, *Plotinus VI*, Loeb Classical Library, A. H. Armstrong trans. Cambridge, Mass.: Harvard University Press, 1988); *Enneads* VI, 9, 7 (p. 326–331 *Plotinus VII*, Loeb Classical Library, A. H. Armstrong trans., Cambridge Mass.: Harvard University Press, 1988).

192 *De Statu Anima*, p. 85, 7: "haec illi non naturalia, sed poenalia sunt." Cf. p. 82, 14

193 Plato, *Theaetetus*, 176 b 1 ff; *Gorgias*, 478 e 1 and *passim*; *Laws*, I, 631 c 7, etc.

194 Plato, *Theaetetus*, 176 e 3 ff.

195 *De Statu Animae*, p. 84, 14: "eotenus inplicatur errore, ut tamquam absens sibi se quaerat, cum ipsa sit quaerens se."

196 *De Statu Animae*, p. 80, 3 ff; Cf. Plotinus, *Enneads* I, 1, 11 (p. 117 *Plotinus I*, Loeb Classical Library): "But then does not the 'we' include that which comes before the middle? Yes, but there must be a conscious apprehension of it. We do not always use all that we have . . ."

any error on this point can only come from the clouding of the intelligence by the passions and sin.[197] Strictly speaking, it should not even be necessary to demonstrate the soul's spirituality; what is evident is not proved. Inversely, no proof of its spirituality is effective without preliminary purification. The rational part of the soul is suited by nature to perceive the incorporeal, but on condition that that part is disengaged from adventitious, deforming elements which color its exercise.[198]

Here we touch on one of the points where neo-Platonic spiritualism clearly separates from the Aristotelian current as well, evidently, as from most modern thought. For most contemporary philosophers, the ideas of God and of the spirituality of the soul appear to be among the highest and most difficult reaches of the mind. By contrast, the Platonic tradition often gives the impression that these truths are connatural and appropriate for the mind. That is why error on these subjects can only be imputed to moral failure or vicious inclination on the part of the knower.

Hence the acerbic and uncompromising tone that the discussion usually takes when these problems are treated. We seldom witness a serene exchange of ideas in this area. Nothing is odder than the lack of thoughtfulness evinced by Mamertus toward a bishop whose reputation seems to have been considerable, and who was considered one of the most eminent personalities in Gaul during this period. His rigor is that of someone who, never having had to overcome error on his part, is not inclined to excuse it in others. His ideas here are not especially different from Augustine's, but the bishop of Hippo manages to demonstrate more indulgence for his opponents. The memory of his own wandering remains alive. The tone of *De Statu Animae* may be contrasted with the following passage directed to a Manichaean, which manifests the exquisite goodness and understanding of someone who has been the victim of the same confusion for many years:

197 *De Statu Animae*, p. 156 1 ff.

198 *De Statu Animae*, p. 96, 18: "Nequaquam me vel incorporeus nisi purgatus videt." See Porphyry, *De Abstinentia* I, 30, p. 107, 21–108, 27 Nauck, for considerations on this exile of the soul mixed with ἀλλότρια of which it must be stripped, if it wishes to remember itself and take possession again of real goods. *De Abstinentia* chapters XXVIII and XXIX also frequently recall the views set forth here.

> Let those rage against you who know not with what labor the truth is to be found and with what difficulty error is to be avoided. Let those rage against you who know not how rare and hard it is to overcome the fancies of the flesh by the serenity of a pious disposition. Let those rage against you who know not the difficulty of curing the eye of the inner man that he may gaze upon his Sun, - not that sun which you worship, and which shines with the brilliance of a heavenly body in the eyes of carnal men and of beasts, – but that of which it is written through the prophet, "The Sun of righteousness has arisen upon me;" [Malachi 5:2] and of which it is said in the gospel:. "That was the true Light, which lighteth every man that cometh into the world." [John 1:9] Let those rage against you who know not with what sighs and groans the least particle of the knowledge of God is obtained. And, last of all, let those rage against you who have never been led astray in the same way that they see that you are.[199]

However, it must be understood exactly where neo-Platonism situates this drama of the soul. It is not that corporalization as such is bad. We have already seen that since the union of soul with body does not touch the soul in its essence, it does not involve any harm for the soul in itself. Only the disordered, excessive love of the body constitutes a fall. As the sun of bodies, the soul remains intact and free as long as its action is limited to illuminate them and turn bodies towards itself. "If the declension is no more than the illuminating of an object beneath, it constitutes no sin," says Plotinus. "The shadow is to be attributed not to the luminary but to the object illuminated." The soul's descent is natural and simply means that " the thing which receives light from it lives with it."[200] St. Augustine is not simply

199 St. Augustine, *Contra Epistulam Manichaei Quam Vocant Fundamenti*, *Against the Epistle of Manichaeus Called Fundamental*, 2 (pp. 129–130, *Nicene and Post-Nicene Fathers*, vol. IV, St. Augustin, *The Writings against the Manichaeans and against the Donatists*, ed. Philip Schaff, Grand Rapids Michigan: Eerdmans, reprinted, 1983).

200 Plotinus, *Enneads* I, 1, 12 (p. 119–121 *Plotinus I*, Loeb Classical Library).

reacting against Manichaeism when he presents the union of soul and body as a good. Speaking thus, he does not have to depart from the neo-Platonic line.[201] It would be a crass error to attribute to neo-Platonism the typically Manichaean doctrine which regards the earthly body as an evil in itself. Augustine himself puts us on guard against such contempt,[202] and the same conclusion clearly flows from a passage of the *Enneads* relating to the soul of the heavenly bodies, which contains an implicit reference to the passage from the *Phaedo* cited above: "For, as there are two reasons why the soul's fellowship with body is displeasing, that body becomes a hindrance to thought and that it fills the soul with pleasures, desires and grief, neither of these things could happen to a soul which has not sunk into the interior of its body, and is not anyone's property, and does not belong to the body, but the body belongs to it, and is of such a kind as to want nothing and be defective in nothing; so that the soul will not be filled with desires or fears; for it will never have any frightening expectations about a body of this kind, nor does any business make it turn to what is below and take it away from the better, blessed vision . . ."[203]

201 St. Augustine, *De Fide et Symbolo*, IV, 10, p. 14, 9 Zycha (*Corpus Scriptorum Ecclesiasticorum Latinorum*, vol. 41): "Non enim cum regit corpus atque vivificat, sed cum eius bona mortalia concupiscit, de corpore anima maculatur." On this point one should review the beautiful passage in *De Libero Arbitrio*, III, 9, 27, about the slave employed in the lowliest task and whose simple presence adorns the humblest corner of the house: "Indeed, what is there in a house greater than man, and what is there lower and more abject than the sewer of the house: However, the slave caught in a fault which makes him subject to cleaning this sewer, adorns it by his very shame; and these two things, the slave's shame and the sewer's cleaning, together form a kind of special unity, adapting themselves to the house's good order and inserting themselves in it so well that they come together in an arrangement full of beauty . . . Thus is there anything lower than a body made of mud? Yet, even the sinful soul so adorns this corruptible flesh that it gives it an admirably constituted form, as well as movement and life. That is why, if it is not suitable that such a soul dwells in heaven because of its sin, it is suitable for it to live on earth for its punishment . . ."

202 St. Augustine, *De Civitate Dei*, XIV, 5, 11 (*Corpus Christianorum*, vol. 48, p. 420): "Non quidem Platonici sicut Manichaei desipiunt, ut tamquam mali naturam terrena corpora detestentur."

203 Plotinus, *Enneads* IV, 8, 2 (p. 405, *Plotinus IV*, Loeb Classical Library).

No matter that this union with the body is full of dangers, which the soul generally does not escape. As soon as its love for the body goes beyond what is required, the soul ceases to belong to itself. Renouncing its vocation, which is to stay in contact with the Ideas and to make the body participate in them, the soul turns itself towards the body, rather than returning itself towards the soul. Then, and only then, does the body become a tomb and an evil.[204] This is the primary sense of the tropism or conversions of the soul, which play such a large role in neo-Platonic psychology and stem from the effort to offer a philosophical explanation for the lived experience to which Plotinus himself, ordinarily so abstract, referred.[205]

Precisely because the soul remains what it is by nature, even if it no longer is aware of that nature, it retains the possibility of returning to its first state. This return is achieved by purification, whose goal is to detach us from the body. Whoever desires this purification must not only reject carnal goods, but even avoid thinking about them, because all thought is contact and supposes or creates a resemblance between the one who knows and the object known.[206] The separation from everything corporeal thus takes the form of a return to the self and, by that very fact, a return to God. Thanks to this separation the soul re-encounters its previous state, again coincides with itself, and can henceforth realize itself fully through divine contemplation.

These few pages of Mamertus, whose illustrious ancestry from Plato to Plotinus and Porphyry we have tried to show, seem to us to be among the most felicitous in his work. They offer one of the striking examples which late antiquity has bequeathed us of the capacity to harvest the purest echoes of paganism and mold them to the demands of Christianity. Through these pages we better grasp the originality of the tendency to which Mamertus belonged, so open to philosophy, and the distance which separates him from those like Cassian and Faustus of Riez, who believed

204 Plotinus, *Enneads* IV, 8, 3 (pp. 404–497 *Plotinus IV*, Loeb Classical Library).
205 Plotinus, *Enneads* IV, 8, 1 (pp. 396–402 *Plotinus IV*, Loeb Classical Library).
206 *De Statu Animae*, p. 94, 8: "Satis ex corpore non solum tangendo, sed etiam cogitando se separabit qui huic [i.e. veritati] adhaerebit." The neo-Platonists saw an etymological connection between *contagio* and *cogitatio*. Macrobius makes a similar play on the two words, *In Somnium Scipionis*, I, 11, 11, p. 529, 26 ff, Eyssenhardt.

they never served their shared faith better than when they carefully sheltered it from any contact with alien thought.

* * *

We can already draw some general conclusions from these analyses. First, in what concerns the passage from the *Phaedo* in the second Book, it seems more and more difficult to agree with Boemer that we are dealing with a translation made in the first century AD.[207] Since we know that Mamertus found this passage in a neo-Platonic work, most probably Porphyry's *De Regressu*, and that his commentary on it is steeped in neo-Platonic ideas, it is hardly probable that the translation in question is earlier than Porphyry. So far our conclusions coincide and confirm those of Einar Harleman and Pierre-Paul Courcelle. Is it certain that the translation was made by Mamertus himself? Unfortunately, the arguments marshaled by Harleman do not allow us to settle the problem definitively.[208] Until we have further information, nothing prevents us from thinking that the author of *De Statu Animae* had a Latin version of *De Regressu* before him, that of Marius Victorinus for example, where he would have found both the passage from the *Phaedo* and Porphyry's commentary which accompanied it.

In the second place, these considerations shed light on our author's methods of composition. Evidently, in the whole first Book of *De Statu Animae*, Mamertus did not hold to a strict plan. We know that ancient requirements on this point were quite different from ours. However, it is no less true that this long passage is controlled by an internal structure which a superficial reading will hardly detect. The idea of the soul's place from which we start, leads naturally to that of its separation from the body, which in turn poses the problem of the soul's fall, of the nature of its union with the body, and finally the purification indispensable for its return. Even if

207 F. Boemer, "Der lateinische Neuplatonismus," pp. 1–30.

208 Einar Harleman, *De Claudiano Mamerto Gallicae Latinitatis Scriptore Quaestiones*, Uppsala: Lundequistkabokhandeln, 1938, pp. 57–80. In the absence of parallel texts from St. Augustine, Pierre-Paul Courcelle came to believe like Harleman, that Mamertus read *De Regressu* in Greek; *Les lettres grecques en Occident*, p. 232. See, however, the comparisons above in note 179 in this chapter.

we momentarily set aside the strictly dialectical level of proofs of the soul's spirituality, we never completely lose it from view. It is not the least of the merits of our author's originality to utilize data which were normally set in a different context, all the while opportunely calling to mind this notion of the soul's spirituality which they suppose and upon which they rest.

Lastly, if we admit that these pages are inspired by a pagan work we can better explain the reticence and even hostility of certain Christians towards a doctrine whose origins they knew, and which was often mixed, as in *De Regressu*, with violent attacks against Christianity. Beyond the spirituality of the soul, there is the whole corpus of pagan thought, with its pronounced anti-Christian bias, which was viewed and condemned as a whole, in the certainty that to do so was an eminently Christian work.

Chapter Five
De Statu Animae's "Rhetoric"

> Non autem hoc est occultare veritatem, quod est proferre mendacium. Quamvis enim omnis qui mentitur velit celare quod verum est, non tamen omnis, qui vult quod verum est celare, mentitur. Plerumque enim vera non mentiendo occulimus, sed tacendo.
>
> St. Augustine, *Contra Mendacium,* X, 23

It is hardly possible to study *De Statu Animae*, as we have done, without going into its most notable features in depth. This painstaking work will be amply recompensed if we can reassemble the elements that analysis forces us to isolate and offer a perceptive interpretation of the overall work.

From what has been said it is apparent that our author frequently merely reproduces and comments in a more or less personal fashion doctrine borrowed from pagan philosophers, whose testimony has been presented in another part of his treatise. At first sight the procedure might seem quite singular. Is Claudianus not too casual when he presents as his own ideas substantially inspired and often literally taken from writers upon whom praise is subsequently heaped because they have expressed similar notions? We immediately imagine the slightly ridiculous professor who is delighted to see that a famous scholar to whom the theory that the professor explains is due, has the same opinion as the professor. However, let us not be quick to call this naive. It would be significant if Mamertus wanted to do precisely this, and if, as everything indicates, he recurred to this method quite deliberately.

The Fathers saw clearly, and it was already one of the great lessons of Socratic rhetoric, that it was not always opportune to say everything to anyone at all. Not only error, but truth can be harmful. "For there are some passages," St. Augustine said, "which are not understood in their proper force, or are understood with great difficulty, at whatever length, however clearly, or with whatever eloquence the speaker may expound them; and these should never be brought before the people at all, or only on rare occasions when there is some urgent reason."[1] Does not what is said here of the holy mysteries hold, *mutatis mutandis*, for any science whatsoever? Not all men have the aptitudes or the formation required to grasp the highest truths. To want to make them philosophers or theologians at any cost would be to strikingly lack good sense and expose oneself to grave dangers: "He who dares to thrust himself into the study haphazardly and without order does not become studious, but curious, not learned, but credulous, not prudent, but incredulous."[2] Again, what well advised, conscientious orator will dare to state his whole thought before an audience where workers are mixed with intellectuals and sometimes non-believers with believers? What writer conscious of his responsibility will fail to envelop himself in precautions when he publishes a book that might fall into absolutely any hands?[3] We

1 St. Augustine, *De Doctrina Christiana*, Book IV, chapter 9, 23, *A Select Library of the Nicene and Post-Nicene Fathers of the Christian Church*, ed. Philip Schaff, volume II, *St Augustine's City of God and Christian Doctrine*, Grand Rapids: William B. Eerdmans reprinted 1983, p. 581.

2 St. Augustine, *De Ordine*, II, 5, 17; cf. *De Ordine*, I, 11, 31.

3 Cf. Plato, *Phaedrus*, 275 d 4 – e 6 (*Euthyphro, Apology, Crito, Phaedo, Phaedrus*, translated by H. N. Fowler, Loeb Library edition, Cambridge, Mass.: Harvard University Press, 1914, 1968, pp. 565-567): "Socrates – Writing, Phaedrus has this strange quality, and is very like painting; for the creatures of painting stand like living beings, but if one asks them a question, they preserve a solemn silence. And so it is with written words; you might think they spoke as if they had intelligence, but if you question them, wishing to know about their sayings, they always say only one and the same thing. And every word, when once it is written, is bandied about, alike among those who understand and those who have no interest in it, and it knows not to whom to speak or not to speak; when ill-treated or unjustly reviled it always needs its father to help it; for it has no power to protect or help itself." See the continuation of this passage up to 277 a 4. See also St. Augustine's reflection in *Epistula CXX*, 1: "Proinde voluit, ut quaedam nostra opuscula, quae arbitratus sum tibi esse necessaria, non procul a nobis positus sed potius apud nos legeres, ut ea, quae forte minus intellexisses, non difficulter praesens interrogares ..." Hence the indisputable superiority of oral or acroatic teaching, which permits a judgement about the hearer's dispositions and degree of understanding. Regarding

have here, it seems, a rule of elementary prudence which the best minds heed spontaneously.

Note that the issue is not simply expressing what needs to be said in simple, non-technical language.[4] That is a given. Rather, it is to *hide* in some measure truths likely to be misunderstood by the mass of the faithful, while allowing them to be seen by those to whom they can be useful. This way of acting cannot clash with or offend the laws of sound morality. It is not a lie to silence, for good reason, certain matters of which the still inadequately formed common folk can appropriately remain ignorant.[5]

the dangers of writing, cf. Plato, *Phaedrus*, 274 c 5 ff; 275 a 6 (Loeb Library edition, pp. 563-565) : " ... you offer your pupils the appearance of wisdom not true wisdom, for they will read many things without instruction and will therefore seem to know many things, when they are for the most part ignorant and hard to get along with, since they are not wise, but only appear wise." A Platonic dialogue aims at imitating oral teaching and, as far as possible, stave off the pitfalls of written discourse. For a description of this philosophical or "Socratic" rhetoric, which is different from what is usually understood as rhetoric, see Plato, *Phaedrus*, 269 d 3 ff. and chapter two above.

4 Cf. St. Augustine, *De Genesi contra Manichaeos*, I, 1, 1, *Patrologia Latina*, vol. 34, col. 173; Cassiodorus, *Institutiones*, I, 22: "That great mind [Augustine] is able to become so simple that he becomes accessible even to children."

5 St. Augustine, *Contra Mendacum*, X, ch. 23 (*To Consentius*: *Aganst Lying*, *The Nicene and Post-Nicene Fathers* vol. III, ed. Philip Schaff, Grand Rapids, Michigan: William Eerdmans, reprinted 1980, p. 491): "It is not, however, the same thing to hide the truth as it is to utter a lie. For although everyone who lies wishes to hide what is true, yet not everyone who wishes to hide what is true, tells a lie. For in general we hide truths not by telling a lie, but by holding our peace. For the Lord lied not when he said: 'I have many things to say unto you, but ye cannot hear them now.' [*John* 16: 12] He held his peace from true things, not spake false things; for the hearing of which truths he judged them to be less fit. But if he had not indicated this same to them, that is, that they were not able to bear the things which he was unwilling to speak, he would indeed hide nevertheless somewhat of truth, but that this may be rightly done we should peradventure not know, or not have so great an example to confirm us." The same doctrine is in *De Mendacio*, X, 17: "Licet igitur vel dissertori ac disputatori atque praedicatori rerum aeternarum vel narratori aut pronuntiatori rerum temporalium ad aedificandam religionem atque pietatem pertinentium occultare in tempore quidquid occultandum videtur, mentiri autem numquam licet, ergo nec occultare mentiendo." In this regard, the remarks in

Writers in the late period had not forgotten the role which white lies played in Plato's dialogues.[6] Certain of them even occasionally reproached

Confessions VI, 5, 8, about Scripture's esotericism can be consulted. Boethius, *De Trinitate*, prologue, (p. 4, H. F. Stewart, E. K. Rand, S. J. Tester, trans. *Tractates, De Consolatione Philosophiae*, Cambridge, Mass.: Harvard University Press, 1978): "quocumque igitur a vobis deieci oculos, ut contumeliam videatur divinis tractibus inrogare qui talibus hominum monstris non agnoscenda haec potius quam proculcanda proiecerit. Idcirco stilum brevitate contraho et ex intimis sumpta philosophiae disciplinis novorum verborum significationibus velo, ut haec mihi tantum vobisque, si quando ad ea convertitis, conloquantur; ceteros vero ita submovimus, ut qui capere intellecto nequiverint ad ea etiam legenda videantur indigni." Cf. Plato, *Phaedrus*, 276 a 5 (p. 576 Loeb Library edition): "Phaedrus. What is this word and how is it begotten, as you say? – Socrates. The word which is written with intelligence in the mind of the learner, which is able to defend itself and knows to whom it should speak, and before whom to be silent." Plato went further and judged that it was even permitted to lie in certain cases; cf. *Republic* III, 389 b 3 (pp. 64-65, M. A. Grube trans., revised by C. D. C. Reeve, Indianapolis: Hackett Publishing Company, 1992): "Moreover, we have to be concerned about truth as well, for if what we said just now is correct, and falsehood, though of no use to the gods, is useful to people as a form of drug, clearly we must allow only doctors to use it, not private citizens. – Clearly. – Then if it is appropriate for anyone to use falsehoods for the good of the city, because of the actions of either enemies or citizens, it is the rulers. But everyone else must keep away from them, because for a private citizen to lie to a ruler is just as bad a mistake as for a sick person or athlete not to tell the truth to his doctor or trainer about his physical condition or for a sailor not to tell the captain the facts about his own condition or that of the ship and the rest of the crew - indeed it is a worse mistake than either of these." It is to this text that Origen, *Contra Celsum*, IV, 19, and Maximus of Tyre, *Dissertationes*, XIX, 3, refer when they attempt in turn to justify lying, at least in certain circumstances. Origen's "Christian gnosticism," so careful to shelter truth from any injury, is largely inspired by the same concerns. See, for example, the texts quoted by Adolf Harnack, *Texte und Untersuchungen,* XLIII, 3, pp. 73-74.

6 Cf. St. Augustine, *De Civitate* Dei, VIII, 4, 38 (*Corpus Christianorum*, vol. 47, p. 220): "Cum enim magistri sui Socratis, quem facit in suis voluminibus disputantem, *notissimum morem dissimulandae scientiae vel opinionis suae servare adfectat*, quia et illi ipse most placuit, factum est ut etiam ipsius Platonis de rebus magnis sententiae non facile perspici possint." Cf. Origen, *Contra Celsum*, IV, 39 (*Origen against Celsus, The Ante-Nicene Fathers*, vol. IV, ed. Alexan-

Plato for having abused the procedure, for cloaking his thought in such obscurity that it became almost impossible to penetrate it. If each must try

der Roberts and James Donaldson, Grand Rapids Michigan: William Eerdmans, N.D., reprint revised by A. Cleveland Coxe of Edinburgh: T&T Clark, p. 515: "But if, on investigating in a philosophic spirit what is conveyed in the dress of a myth, they should be able to discover the meaning of Plato, [they will admire] the manner in which he was able to conceal, on account of the multitude, in the form of this myth, the great ideas which presented themselves to him, and to speak in a befitting manner to those who know how to ascertain from the myths the true meaning of him who wove them together." Augustine, it may be recalled, explained the errors attributed to the new Academy in this way, *Epistula I*, 1 (*The Letters of St. Augustin. Nicene and Post-Nicene Fathers*, vol. I, ed. Philip Schaff, Grand Rapids, Michigan: William Eerdmans, reprinted, 1983, p. 219): "I would not presume, even in playful discussion, to attack the philosophers of the Academy; for when could the authority of such eminent men fail to move me, did I not believe their view to be widely different from those commonly ascribed to them? Instead of confuting them, which is beyond my power, I have rather imitated them to the best of my ability. For it seems to me to have been suitable enough to the times in which they flourished, that whatever seemed pure from the fountainhead of Platonic philosophy should be rather conducted into dark and thorny thickets for the refreshment of a very few men, then left to flow in open meadow-land, where it would be impossible to keep it clear and pure from the inroads of the vulgar herd. I use the word here advisedly; for what is more brutish than the opinion that the soul is material? For defense against the men who held this, it appears to me that such an art and method of concealing the truth was wisely contrived by the new Academy. But in this age of ours, when we see none who are philosophers, – for I do not consider those who merely wear the cloak of a philosopher to be worthy of that venerable name, – it seems to me that men (those, at least, whom the teaching of the Academicians has, through the subtlety of the terms in which it was expressed, deterred from attempting to understand its actual meaning) should be brought back to the hope of discovering the truth, lest that which was then for the time useful in eradicating obstinate error, should begin now to hinder the casting in of the seeds of true knowledge." *Contra Academicos* develops the same ideas extensively; cf. II, 4, 10; II, 10, 24: "I do not believe that the Academics were men who failed to know how to give things the names that were necessary; but they seem to me to have chosen these names at the same time to hide their doctrine from mediocre minds and to reveal it to keen minds." *Contra Academics*, III, 7, 14; III, 17, 38; III, 20, 43. Cf. *Confessions*, V, 10, p. 79 Sheed trans-to discover it on his own, "the peasant or the worker who hammers bronze, the carpenter or the pilot, every man who lives by the work of his hands would have to abandon his trade and die of hunger before acquiring the notion of Justice."[7] But can the Fathers who spoke thus dispense completely with such artifices? The bishop who directs himself to all Christians alike and who has a common responsibility toward them, must take into account the demands and capacities of each. He must act so that the educated can find in his statements a teaching suited to their needs, without shaking the belief of the simple faithful. Less than anyone else, would it be licit for him to open a cistern without also covering it. "He, who in sacred teaching has penetrated the depths of the doctrine," Gregory the Great will say, "must conceal by silence the sublime meanings from those who do not comprehend them, in the fear of killing by spiritual scandal a simple Christian or even an infidel who might have been able to become a believer."[8]

We encounter some difficulty in correctly interpreting the thought of an author forced to recur to this method, or even simply to emit a judgment on the persons who surround us. How many "admirable" people are unknown to us, "because to accommodate himself to the words of vicious men, the just man says certain things that he seems to approve or desire. There are also many things he does reluctantly, whether to avoid the hate of others, or to avoid eccentricity."[9] That is why, before taking the statements of a writer literally, we would do well to ask ourselves if he did not have "some reason or some pretext to lie."[10]

lation: "The notion began to grow in me that the philosophers whom they call Academics were wiser than the rest, because they held that everything should be treated as matter of doubt and affirmed that no truth can be understood by men. For so it seemed clear to me that they thought – and so they are commonly held to teach – though I did not yet understand their real meaning."

7 John Chrysostom, *Homiliae in Matthaeum*, I, 5, *Patrologia Graeca*, vol. 57, column 19.

8 Gregory the Great, *Moralium Libri*, XVII, 26, *Patrologia Latina*, vol. 76, col. 28 B; *Regulae Pastoralis Liber*, ch. 39: *Quod infirmis mentibus omnino non debent alta praedicari*, *Patrologia Latina*, vol. 77, col. 124.

9 St. Augustine, *De Ordine*, II, 10, 29. See Aristotle's observation about the magnanimous man, who always tells the truth, except when he uses irony to address the crowd, *Nicomachean Ethics*, IV, 3, 1124 b 30.

10 St. Augustine, *De Ordine*, II, 10, 28.

Recalling such notions will allow us to grasp the astuteness demonstrated by the author of *De Statu Animae*. It is likely that a similar problem presented itself to Mamertus. At his time and in a work destined to enjoy some diffusion, could he defend against a Catholic bishop a position which was largely inspired by pagan philosophers without provoking scandal and casting the mind of many of his readers into confusion? Was it not more suitable to show the specifically Christian side of their religion to the mostly uneducated mass of the faithful and therefore shelter them from mistakes to which too direct a presentation of his thought might have given rise? The task was rather complicated, but there was a way of getting out of the quandary with a bit of ingenuity.

The author first assumed the stance of speaking in his own name, of expounding, as if it were his own, a doctrine which was not always that, namely of only putting anything forward with great support of scriptural texts. At the point where he prepares to quote pagan authors in support of his thesis, he remembers to excuse himself and pretends to act in this fashion only because his adversary has brandished the term philosophy "like a bogey"[11] which is no doubt literally true, although the remark hardly gives an accurate impression of the tone of Faustus's letter. It would have occurred to nobody but Claudianus to accuse the bishop of Riez of sympathy for philosophers. Certainly, Mamertus gives Plato praise that might appear excessive or misplaced,[12] but it is almost equally compensated by equal expressions of praise for Christian authors, particularly St. Ambrose and St. Augustine.[13] Moreover, Plato was not a bad choice. Of all the pagans, he was he one who en-

11 *De Statu Animae*, p. 104, 19: "Neque mihi profecto cordi foret mutuum ex his [philosophis] carpere quippiam, nisi iste corporis amicus sola philosophici nominis mentione terriculamenta quaedam nobis scientiae profundioris ostentavisset." Faustus had, indeed, made passing reference to philosophy, *Epistula 3*, p. 171, 11 Engelbrecht (*Corpus Scriptorum Ecclesiasticorum Latinorum*, vol. 21).

12 *De Statu Animae*, p. 122, 11: "Quo fit ut mirari admodum digne nequeam huius Platonis animum, qui tantis equidem saeculis ante puerperium virginis, ante incarnationem Dei, ante hominis resurrectionem, ante praedicatam summae Trinitatis in gentibus unitatem ineffabilem una tres in divinitate personas laudabili ausu, mirabili ingenio, inimitabili eloquio quaesivit invenit proditit ..." Cf *De Statu Animae*, p. 124, 1; p. 127, 3, p. 128, 9; p. 204, 10.

13 *De Statu Animae*, p. 131, 4 ff; p. 133, 10, etc.

joyed the highest repute among the Fathers. Was he not, in St. Augustine's phrase, the philosopher who would have become Christian, if he had lived in the Christian era?[14] Even Arnobius, who seems to be indifferent to all philosophers, whoever they are, speaks of Plato only in terms of praise.[15]

It was still necessary to explain how the pagans had arrived at the truth. If there is only one truth, which is possessed by Christians, it might seem strange to find it among the philosophers as well. We know how much this question concerned church writers and the different answers they successively formulated. Some maintained that the pagans stumbled on the truth by chance, and as it were, despite themselves,[16] or even that this truth had been dictated to them by reason or common sense.[17] More often we find the notion that all profane science is contained in Scripture and non-Christian

14 St. Augustine, *De Vera Religione*, IV, 6-7. Cf. *Contra Academicos*, III, 17, 37. It is true that later Augustine will reproach himself for having praised Plato and the Platonists excessively, *Retractationes*, I, 1, 4.

15 Arnobius, *Adversus Nationes*, I, 8, p. 10, 3 Marchesi: "Plato ille sublimis apex philosophorum et columen." (Cf. *De Statu Animae*, p. 204, 10: "Platon apex culmenque philosophiae.") *Adversus Nationes*, II, 36, p. 107, 23: "Plato ille divinus." Blame is mixed with praise in Lactantius, *Institutionum Epitome*, 33, p. 708, 14 Brandt (*Corpus Scriptorum Ecclesiasticorum Latinorum*, vol. 19): "solus [Plato] omnium sic philosophatus est, ut ad veritatem propius accederet, tamen quia Deum ignoravit, in multis ita lapsus est, ut nemo deterius erraverit."

16 Tertullian, *De Anima*, 2, 1: "Plane non negabimus aliquando philosophos iuxta nostra sensisse; testimonium est etiam veritatis eventus ipsius. Nonnunquam et in procella confusis vestigiis caeli et freti aliqui portus offenditur prospero errore, nonnunquam et in tenebris aditus quidam et exitus deprehenduntur caeca felicitate ..." Clement of Alexandria, *Stromateis*, 1, 19, 94, 1 (*Sources chrétiennes*, vol. 30, p. 119): "Therefore, if we are told, it is 'by accident' that the Greeks professed certain theories in agreement with true philosophy, this accident is part of the divine plan – chance will not, I believe, be divinized to fit into the puzzle. If it is 'by coincidence,' the coincidence is providential." Origen, *Contra Celsum*, IV, 39. Lactantius, *Epitome Divinarum Institutionum*, III, 18. See the observations of J. H. Waszink, *Tertulliani De Anima*, pp. 99-100.

17 Tertullian, *De Anima* 2, 1: "Sed et natura pleraque suggeruntur quasi de publico sensu, quo animam Deus dotare dignatus est." Clement of Alexandria, *Stromates*, I, 19, 94, 2: "Someone will say: 'But didn't the Greeks have natural rea-

thinkers were able to discover it there.[18] Another solution was to affirm like Mamertus that the pagans themselves were inspired by God.[19] Thus, whatever Cassian and his disciples thought, St. Paul did not condemn philosophy as such. He only reproached pagans for having scorned that truth after having known it.[20] So, we can explain how their doctrine often agreed with

son?' Nature is the work of the one God, as far as I know ... Will they say, 'They only had common sense'? Then let us examine who is its father, and whence comes the justice which presides over its bestowal." Justin, *Second Apology*, 8. On this idea and its relations with the Stoic doctrine of κοιναὶ ἔννοαι, cf Waszink, *Tertulliani de Anima*, p. 100.

18 The latter belief, which goes back to second century BC Hellenizing Judaism, was much more widely held than the others. The Jews of that period, considered barbarians by the Greeks, responded to the scorn in which they were held in this way. Cf. Clement of Alexandria, *Stromates*, I, 22, 150, 1: "Aristobulus, in the *Studies* dedicated to Philometor, book I, writes literally: 'Plato himself underwent the influence of our reception of the Laws, and it is obvious that he examined every article with care.'" Numenius is famous for making Plato a Greek-speaking Moses, Μωυσῆς ἀττικίζων, Clement of Alexandria, *Stromateis*, I, 22, 150, 4; Cf. *Pedagogue*, II, 10, 90, 8, where Plato is called ὁ ἐκ Μωυσέως φιλόσαφος. *See* likewise Tatian, *Oratio ad Graecos*, 40; Justin, *First Apology,* 59; Tertullian, *Apologia,* 47, 2; Origen, *Contra Celsum*, IV, 39; Origen adds that Plato slightly modified Jewish doctrines so as not to offend the Greeks. Celsus had accused the Jews of plagiarizing from the Greek philosophers. Eusebius, *Praeparatio Evangelica*, VIII, 10; XIII, 12; Ambrose, *De Noe et Arca*, VIII, 24; In *Psalmum CXVIII, expositio* XVIII, 4. For the same reason Ambrose sought to establish the great antiquity of Jewish wisdom in *De Philosophia*; cf. Pierre-Paul Courcelle, "Recherches sur les *Confessions* de saint Augustin," p. 174; St. Augustine, *De Civitate Dei*, VIII, 11; Cassiodorus, *Institutiones*, praefatio, *Patrologia Latina*, vol. 70, col. 1108 C, and I, 4, col. 1115 C, etc. We also find the idea in ancient literature that pagan philosophy goes back to the apocryphal books or to the fallen angels, cf. Waszink, *Tertulliani de Anima*, pp. 104-106.

19 *De Statu Animae*, p. 125, 2 ff. Cf. Clement of Alexandria, *Protrepticus*, VI, 72, 5.

20 *De Statu Animae*, p. 101, 12: "Unde etiam doctor gentium non tam ignaros veri philosophos iudicat, quam cogniti contemptores accusat inquiens: 'invisibilia Dei a creatura mundi per ea quae facta sunt intellecta conspiciuntur, sempiternerna quoque virtus eius et divinitas, ut sint inexcusabiles, quoniam cum cognovissent Deum, non sicut Deum magnificaverunt.' Ergo cognoverunt, et ingressa est divinitatis abditae mens humana secretum ...".

Christian thought, and instead of seeing the two currents as opposed, it becomes necessary to see how they are made compatible.

Even when this principle is accepted, the problem is not entirely resolved. One could always ask why God had inspired the pagans, supposing that he had done so. Was not this inspiration a second activity alongside Revelation so that the latter lost a bit of its grandeur by becoming merely one conduit of the sole truth among others? The response is simple, and frankly, rather provocative. While St. Augustine was content to say, in the passage studied above, that philosophy allows us to fight against the pagans with the same weapons, Mamertus will not hesitate to affirm that philosophy has been given to us to refute "our people," that is to say Christians themselves.[21] The very facility with which, thanks to Revelation, we now possess the truth is a temptation and a snare for us.[22] This truth demands an effort on the part of man. It is a value which must be won and which at each instant we run the risk of losing by our indolence or our bad will.[23] Pagan philosophy was willed by God as a remedy to the insensitivity and routine that threaten us. Its function is to stimulate us and call us to order. Far from contradicting Revelation, in its own way pagan philosophy protects Revelation against the bad use we might make of us. There are more elements than necessary to reassure the mass of the faithful about the primacy of Christianity and orthodoxy of the doctrine that was proposed to them. After that, how can we doubt the worth of the author's affirmations and the sentiment which inspires them?

Seen in this perspective, the work already acquires a complete significance. It excuses anyone satisfied with it from looking further. One cannot even say that this "purely Christian" interpretation is mistaken, because the author de-

21 *De Statu Animae*, p. 125, 10: "Aut cur non haec eadem per philosophos nobis in usum veri caelitus procurata credamus, quae ad redarguendam nostrorum quoque inperitiam utilia fore cognoscimus?" Cf. p. 104, 14: "Huius modi igitur rationibus utentium philosophorum quoad potui voluminibus perdagatis ignobilium plebe reiecta potiores quosque delegi, qui veritati in praesentiarum testificarentur, quorum quidem ex abundanti est proferre sententias, non quo propriis deficiamur, sed quo magis mirum sit adversum nos dimicare nostros et extraneos pugnare pro nobis."

22 *De Statu Animae*, p. 122, 6

23 *De Statu Animae*, p. 101, 6; p. 22, 12 ff.

sired it for at least some of his readers. In the same way, modern critics who hold that Mamertus's only merit is to have cashed in on the doctrine of his Christian predecessors are not completely mistaken. Those critics give his treatise a doubtless superficial, though legitimate, interpretation, in accordance with at least one of the author's intentions. They have read *De Statu Animae* like the average readers of whom Mamertus did not lose sight in writing.

It is still the case that Claudianus himself saw that the problem was less simple than he pretended. He was not taken in by his own maneuver, and he did not want to hoodwink all his readers. He informs us from the start that anyone who wishes to take the trouble can find in its pages all the elements required to understand the work.[24] Anyone who was even slightly informed about neo-Platonist teaching could not fail to make the inevitable connections with *De Statu Animae*. If he was ignorant of pagan doctrine, it would be enough to compare the passages where pagan doctrine is clearly set forth and those where the author speaks on his own authority. The link between them stands out immediately. The same phrases, repeated literally from one book to the other, could have no other goal than to underline the relationship which exists between Claudianus's thought and that of the philosophers he quotes. But those phrases were also an invitation to reverse the terms of the comparison and to see that these were truths whose discovery went back to the pagans. The same thing follows from the praise of Plato in book II and the selection from the *Phaedo*, whose length as well as the importance attributed to it by our author immediately catches our attention. If this praise seemed inoffensive for the reasons we have indicated, it still has the value of a sign and could furnish one of the keys to the work. It can be demonstrated indeed that it was taken from a work by Porphyry, whose name is skillfully disguised at the end of the same passage.

Does not this interpretation square with what contemporary testimony tells us about Claudianus? Claudianus makes a show of protesting that he only had recourse to philosophers because he has been provoked to it by his adversary. However, thanks to Sidonius we still know his proclivity for

24 *De Statu Animae*, p. 18, 12: " Scripsi igitur pauca haec veluti quaedam rationum semina, quae studiosus quisque si non otiose capessat, ut ego arbitror, multa exinde derivare poterit, quae etsi angustis emanantia venulis in magnos tamen amnes longiore procursu exuberabunt."

philosophy and the enthusiasm with which he devoted himself to it. His friends seem not to have been mistaken in recognizing him as the first of their philosophers.[25] Besides, how can we be surprised that the doctrine he defends is primarily philosophical? To realize that Mamertus hardly had another choice, we have only to consider how little the Bible could furnish on the subject, and what those like Faustus got from the Bible when they based themselves exclusively on it as a matter of principle. Anyone trying to develop the thesis of the spirituality of the soul saw himself obliged to draw on non-biblical sources.

But, it will be said, why such subtlety? All things considered, would it not have been better to simply state matters as they were, without engaging in this somewhat childish game and without introducing all sorts of precautions which today seem quite superfluous? We are long accustomed to all sides of the question and used to regarding the spirituality of the soul as being an integral part of Christian teaching, so that we find it odd that it might have awakened such suspicion at a certain moment. We must not forget that the ancients did not view spirituality of the soul in the same terms as we do. Beyond retaining a pagan flavor by its origin, in the most popular philosophers it was identified with the idea of the divinity of the soul and seemed as inadmissible as the latter. As long as Christians who worked to distinguish the notions of incorporeality and divinity had not succeeded in making their views prevalent, the doctrine as a whole would continue to seem dangerous and was capable of leading refined minds into error.

Such is the reason Mamertus ultimately had to recur to this subterfuge. Instead of being able to reach his goal directly, he strove to smuggle in his ideas, to utilize an oblique path, which was no less efficacious for being longer. The proof that he was successful is that for several centuries, he will be placed in the first rank of the defenders of the spirituality of the soul and will obtain the praise even of those who do not share his views.[26]

25 Sidonius, *Epistula V*, 2, 1, and *IV*, 11, 1, quoted above in chapter one, note 69.

26 E.g., Gennadius, *De Viris Inlustribus*, 83, p. 90, 11 Richardson (*Texte und Untersuchungen*, XXIV, 1, Leipzig, 1896).

Chapter Six
Conclusion

In the course of this study we have generally refrained from passing judgment on Mamertus and his work, since our only goal was to interpret it as exactly as possible in order to understand it as the author wished it to be understood and as he might hope that it would be by an attentive reader. Because of that, it is important to not try to second guess him by going beyond the text to explain it by considerations which would have escaped Mamertus. If we may be permitted, we will abandon this point of view now, and, by getting behind the work in a sense, risk a few words of so-called "explanation." We restrict ourselves to two lines of reflection.

The first concerns the culture of the period as reflected in *De Statu Animae*, which accounts for some of the book's peculiar characteristics. For an author to be able to suitably expound a fairly difficult question, it was surely necessary that culture should not have faded away into nothingness. Thanks to Mamertus, we may again take stock of the importance of the role played by neo-Platonism in philosophical thought. It is neo-Platonism which definitively established the thesis of the spirituality of the soul to a degree that the fate of the idea often seemed tied to the acceptance or rejection of this philosophy as a whole or at least of some of its essential features. We already know the revelation that the reading of "Platonic books" constituted for St. Augustine. It was necessary again that someone should take over the neo-Platonic doctrines in the second half of the fifth century in Gaul to defend the notion of the incorporeality of the soul against increasingly frequent attacks.

However, what makes Mamertus's sympathy for philosophy almost unique is that perhaps for the first time in the West we are faced with a "Christian philosopher" in the full sense of the word. He is a thinker who is neither a pagan convert like Marius Victorinus, who remains more or less faithful to his old ideas,[1] nor an author who, after undergoing the profound impact of pagan culture during one period of his life, retains some mistrust toward it. Claudianus seems to have only encountered pagan philosophy in an already Christianized version, or at least after his precursors believed they had interpreted it in a Christian fashion. He thus possesses "inner freedom" from the start and in the most complete way, something that was hardly possible in a previous period. His attitude already announces that of the theologians of the following period who no longer feel the hostility of their patristic era predecessors toward profane culture,[2] now fragmented and rendered inoffensive.

Nevertheless, if his work proves the existence of a philosophical movement in Gaul, it also bears witness to other less elevated facets of this culture. We observe dogmatism that is a bit crude, a tendency towards emphasis and a kind of youthful enthusiasm that brings to mind the authors of the high Middle Ages[3] and the first theologians of the Carolingian

1 Consider the even more typical case of Synesios of Cyrene: "Helene *and* Christian," as Christian Lacombrade recently showed (Paris: Belles Lettres, 1951). Synesios agreed to become a bishop on two condition: that he be permitted to keep his wife and . . . his ideas! Like the metal and clay of Nebuchadnezzar's statue, Christianity and neo-Platonism never were fused in the mind of this curious personage.

2 It has often been observed that it was the Irish monks, protected by their isolation from the seduction of Mediterranean paganism, who would become the intermediaries who introduced the pagan muses into the Carolingian world. See, for example, Étienne Gilson, *Les idées et les lettres*, Paris: Vrin, 1932, "L'humanisme médiéval", pp. 171–196; Ernest Fortin, "Translatio studii," in *Folia, Studies in the Christian Perpetuation of the Classics*, vol. X, 2, 1958, pp. 43–51.

3 The tendency is in full flower, for example, in the *Hesperica Famina* or in the work of Virgil the Grammarian, where the vocative of *ego* or the frequentative of some Latin verb are endlessly discussed. A century and a half later we come to overblown style, a taste for mystery, knowledge for the initiated, secret alphabet, deliberate and savored obscurity, naiveté and fantasy. What exactly is this fantastic, unreal, and a slightly grotesque world? Solemn caricature? Erudite sham or professorial joke? The pedantic dream of one who only knew grammar, that is, all that remained of the classical literary epoch in full retreat? In any case, one idea stands out: the obsession with a high culture that the drought of scholarship rendered impossible.

period.[4] In many ways, Mamertus is like a man who discovers thinking, one who for the first time feels the inebriating joy of refuting an opponent. Alone in a century given over to ignorance or to literary games, he understands the seriousness of thinking, which is not to deny that he grazes pedantry at certain instants. Nothing seems more pleasant to him than trampling under the feet of his science and erudition a poor adversary who can only beg for mercy. Without doubt, had more cultivated minds been present in his environment, a more moderate tone and a livelier sense of nuance would have imposed themselves on Mamertus's work and on its author.

A second series of observations is suggested not by Mamertus's or his contemporaries' culture, but by the very nature of the subject with which he deals. Evidently, the majority of the Fathers did not pose the problem of the human soul on a purely philosophical plane. As we have seen throughout the present study and as the prominence given scriptural considerations in *De Statu Animae* indicate, the problem of the soul is also, and sometimes rather, a theological problem. This is perhaps the characteristic which most clearly distinguishes it from our treatises of philosophical psychology. The task which thus fell to our ecclesiastical authors was to harmonize the doctrine of the philosophers with revealed data. In this perspective, our subject is only one aspect of a vast problem which dominated or almost dominated doctrinal history in the first centuries, the relation between faith and reason.

Christians had to resolve this problem on a very concrete level. This becomes evident if we concentrate on what philosophy was for the ancients, namely, not just a speculative science, one form of mental operation among others, even if the most noble one, but also a way of life, comprising the whole of human activities and often expressing itself by a "conversion" with clearly defined outward behavior. In this sense, the philosopher was a person who had chosen reason as the highest norm and who understood he was conforming his whole life to it. Now it follows necessarily that between two postures which both present themselves as ultimate and which attempt to offer a definitive answer to the fundamental questions, a choice must be

4 By way of example, the dissertation of Fridugisus on being and nothingness, can be read in Monumenta Germaniae Historica, *Epistula IV*, 2, pp. 552–555.

made. One cannot be Christian and philosopher at the same time, without giving the words a new sense or without attempting a reconciliation between the two.

At that time, two extreme solutions were possible: either one sacrificed philosophy to faith showing that the former was false and did not keep its promises, which is what numerous Christians did, notably the authors belonging to the Marseilles group. Or else one tried to show there was no real opposition between divine science and human science; the deep and "hidden" teaching of one being somehow identical to the openly professed doctrine of the other. Such is roughly the solution towards which Mamertus leaned, seeing an almost perfect agreement between Revelation and reason; most of the time the former is simply the surer guide and all the more necessary because philosophy is always only the prerogative of a small number of privileged minds, whereas divine science has the role of making Revelation better understood, of shaking off Christian torpor, and responds to the need of refuting foolishness among Christians.

This way of looking at things is not completely wrong, because philosophical teaching comes to coincide with that of the Bible. Nevertheless, what the author lacks, what sometimes makes his demonstration less than completely satisfactory, is a more precise notion of the respective domains of faith and natural thought. Without having been able to trace clear limits between these two orders of truth, he comes to present things like the dogma of the Trinity as purely rational mysteries whose profundity escapes human reason, and inversely, attributes a sort of philosophical teaching to the Bible that it does not claim to give at all. This is to fall back into an impasse similar to the one with which Faustus of Riez struggled, and to expose oneself successively to the reproaches of philosophers and Christians. Certainly, when Mamertus affirms that the pagans were inspired by God, he posits a principle intended to safeguard the transcendence of Christianity and to give his position solid theological support. But we must understand that this notion of inspiration is intrinsically ambiguous and that it calls for certain clarifications. The question is postponed, not resolved.

Having acknowledged these deficiencies, let us not be too severe toward Mamertus. His problem was difficult, and we cannot say that it always found a fully satisfactory solution in antiquity. It would be somewhat inelegant to reproach Claudianus for not succeeding where minds of greater capacity had failed before him. Even more, if we place ourselves at the vantage point of the Christian faced with secular culture, we discover that the question recurs ceaselessly, and that each period, if not each individual, must resolve it on its own. Has not this secular culture always found, even in our era, defenders and adversaries, equally staunch on both sides? Viewed from this perspective, the problem is eternal, and it is of some importance to see how it is reflected in the work of an author who certainly does not deserve to be situated among the giants of Christian literature, but who in spite of everything, is an excellent representative of one of the most attractive tendencies of his time.

Appendix
The Concept of *Paideia* in Aristotle

If we closely examine the passages where Aristotle treats teaching philosophy to the young, we come to ask whether the usual method of the ancients did not sometimes contradict their principles. The practice, strongly asserted in the Platonic dialogues, whose resonance is detectable everywhere during this period, required that once the cycle of preliminary studies in the grammarian and rhetorician's school had ended, the pupil who aspired to philosophy was immediately initiated in this discipline under the tutelage of an accredited master. Now on at least two occasions, Aristotle, who had been brought up in this tradition himself, seems to deny the appropriateness and even the possibility of teaching philosophy to a youth of this age. One might deem this a trifling problem which stems from a misunderstanding, so simplistic does its articulation seem. However, when we pause, we soon perceive a frequently ignored dimension of ancient education which the problem reveals and forces us to ponder. Let us first reproduce the two relevant passages without comment.

In book I, chapter three of the *Nicomachean Ethics*, Aristotle briefly explains the way of studying moral theory and wonders immediately to whom it is suitable to teach this science. We learn that a young man is not suited for lessons of moral philosophy for two reasons. First, he lacks experience of life and men. This experience is only acquired with time, and it is indispensable, because human actions are precisely what constitute the subject of moral discourse and give it its proper principles.[1] Second, a young man has not yet sufficiently mastered his passions. From the purely speculative point of view, indeed, moral philosophy only has moderate interest. The only benefit we have the right to expect from it, is that it helps us to become

1 *Nicomachean Ethics*, I, 3, 1905 a 2.

better, facilitating the acquisition of moral virtues. But for this to happen, it is necessary for the pupil to be disposed to regulate his conduct according to the requirements of reason. Now a young man, and by young man we must also understand he who is young in character, lets himself too easily be led by his passions to the detriment of reason.[2]

Book VI, chapter 18, deals with intellectual virtue and returns to the same question from a slightly different viewpoint. Aristotle insists again that a young man, lacking experience, cannot attain practical wisdom.[3] He now adds that the beginner also does not have the preparation required to study natural science and first philosophy or, as it will be called later, metaphysics. It is difficult to accede to metaphysics, which requires a training that a youth hardly has undergone. At most the pupil will be able to repeat words he has heard, without grasping their sense. As for natural science, it covers the entire realm of nature in its formidable extension – Aristotle himself spent a whole part of his life doing an inventory of nature and classifying species and sub-species and tracing their "history" – impossible for a young person to have covered. What a youth lacks is the adequate experience, this time not of life, but of nature, on which this science rests.[4] In truth, there is only one subject within his reach, namely mathematics. Less difficult than metaphysics, and furthermore, less linked to knowledge of singulars, mathematics can be mastered without too much difficulty and be an object of truly scientific study even by an adolescent.[5]

2 *Nicomachean Ethics* VI, 8, 1095 a 4 ff. Cf. Shakespeare, *Troilus and Cressida*, 11, 2, 163–171:

Paris and Troilus, you have both said well;
And on the cause and question now in hand
Have gloz'd, but superficially; not much
Unlike young men, whom Aristotle thought
Unfit to hear moral philosophy.
The reasons you allege do more conduce
To the hot passions of distempered blood
Than to make up a free determination
Twixt right and wrong . . .

3 *Nicomachean Ethics*, VI, 8, 1142 a 14 ff.

4 *Nicomachean Ethics*, 1142 a 18 ff.

5 Cf. *Nicomachean Ethics*, 1142 a 12, 17, where the youth is characterized as σοφός in what concerns mathematics.

If we accept this argument, the initiative of a philosophy professor who tries to communicate his science to youthful minds is condemned to failure beforehand. Rather than waste his time and that of his students, it would be better, as Hamlet would have it, to buy a cart and drive mules. We can only smile at the naiveté of a master who begins by gravely explaining to a group of young people the impossibility of his teaching them such a subject and who then proceeds, before the very same pupils, to all kinds of scholarly discussions which he has established they will not understand at all. Not only ancient education, but a good part of medieval education,[6] and even our own, in the measure in which it is inspired by Aristotle, are victims of a rather crude illusion, when we consider these things. It would be astonishing that such an illusion, if it is an illusion, has not at least been denounced. We nowhere see philosophy professors renouncing their profession because of the reason given. The problem, one may guess, is more complex than the remarks above allow. What we would like to show is that this did not escape Aristotle's notice, and that it is possible to find the elements of a solution in his works.

These elements are clustered around a concept which has not yet enjoyed serious study by modern critics and historians; we refer to the Aristotelian notion of παιδεία. Of course the term *paideia* has become very familiar since the now classical work of Werner Jaeger, *Paideia, The Ideals of Greek Culture*.[7] However, Jaeger's study stops at Plato, and in any case, takes the idea of *paideia* in its broadest acceptation, without always clearly distinguishing the different uses of the term. Let us agree henceforth that the expression has possessed different meanings during its history, since its humble beginning in Aeschylus,[8] as a synonym of τροφή, the traditional

6 Cf. Étienne Gilson, "Note sur un texte de saint Thomas," in *Revue Thomiste*, vol. 54, 1954, pp. 148–152, where the same problem is raised in connection with St. Thomas, without an attempt to resolve it. In a lecture published at about the same time under the title, "Thomas Aquinas and Our Colleagues," Princeton, 1953, Gilson suggests that, for a Christian, faith can come to the aid of reason, to help it understand the very abstract notions of metaphysics; cf. p. 17 ff. But he is the first to acknowledge that this solution, which he does not consider definitive, would not hold for a pagan like Aristotle, *ibid.*, p. 18.

7 We use the title of Gilbert Highet's English translation, three volumes, Oxford, Oxford University Press, 1939 ff.

8 *Seven against Thebes*, 18.

word to indicate care bestowed on a child, up to the Hellenistic period, when it was extended to cover the whole of human intellectual and moral development.[9] Aristotle himself will apply it equally to animal taming[10] and to all the stages of physical, moral, and intellectual formation of human beings from early childhood to the age of about twenty-one.[11] Elsewhere in his work, the term seems to cover something more restricted, which we will make every effort to delimit precisely. Although he never devoted a sustained analysis to this question, by assembling the texts where παιδεία is employed in this restricted and specialized sense, we can capture the essence of his thought.

* * *

To discover the first feature of this thought, we begin by attending to the famous discussion about the first principle of knowledge in Book IV of the *Metaphysics*.[12] Aristotle says that this principle, upon which all subsequent knowledge depends in some manner, is indemonstrable, not because it is not true, but because it is immediately evident. To try to establish it deductively from previously known premises would be absurd. It is impossible to demonstrate everything. Sooner or later it is necessary, if we are not to fall into an infinite regress and thereby renounce any demonstration and any science, to arrive at a proposition which is a principle and not a conclusion in any way, in other words, at a proposition whose truth does not depend on that of another proposition previous to it. Among these principles known of themselves, there is none more obvious than the one which enunciates the opposition between being and non-being or, as it is called ordinarily, the principle of non-contradiction. However, there are those who demand that even this principle should be strictly demonstrated. To demand this is to reveal oneself incapable of becoming aware of what is

9 Cicero tried to render this idea in Latin by *humanitas*. On *paideia* in this sense, see, for example, Henri-Irenée Marrou, *Saint Augustin et la fin de la culture antique*, Paris: E. de Brocard, 1938, pp. 552–555.

10 See *Historia Animalium*, IX, 46, 630 b 19 for the anecdote from Hecateus about the elephant who had been taught (*paideuein*) to bend his knee before the king.

11 For example in the treatise *Peri Paideias* of the *Politics*, VII, 13 to the end.

12 *Metaphysics*, IV, 4, 1006 a 4 ff.

evident, which can only be explained, Aristotle adds, by their lack of education, ἀπαιδευσία.

We can already infer from this that a pupil who wants to acquire παιδεία ought first to learn to recognize a principle in distinction from a conclusion or, what comes to be the same, to distinguish between that which is known and not known. The pupil will only be "disciplinable," that is to say capable of receiving a teaching, in the measure in which he has acquired this aptitude. Take the philosophy of nature. Before being able to demonstrate anything in this science, it is necessary to accept the existence of nature as Aristotle defines it in Book II of the *Physics*.[13] That nature, in the precise sense in which Aristotle understands it, exists is immediately evident.[14] To attempt to demonstrate this existence is once again to seek to establish what is manifest by what is not, and by that very fact, to attack this science at the root by destroying its principle. Anyone who reasons in this way is in the same relation to the science of nature as someone born blind in relation to colors: he can always speak of them, but the words he uses will have no sense for him.[15]

It is not difficult to see that such an aptitude already requires some training of the pupil. Of course, there are principles which are based on very common notions, whose simple enunciation is enough for them to be understood by everyone. However little one knows what is a part and a whole or what the word equal means, one will easily agree that the part is not greater than the whole, or that two things equal to a third are equal among themselves. To deny these truths would be to completely forbid oneself to think. The same is not the case when we reach the principles proper to each science. It no longer suffices here to learn what the words mean. Although indemonstrable, these principles require explication. By making their truth apparent through examples or in some other manner, the teacher already performs a considerable service to the pupil. Thus, properly speaking, that every changeable being is composed of matter and form, or that nature acts for an end, is not demonstrated, but the pains Aristotle takes to go over these propositions from every side indicates clearly enough

13 *Physics*, II, 1, 192 b 22.
14 *Physics*, II, 1, 193 a 2.
15 *Physics*, II, 1, 193 a 7.

that they are not within the grasp of just anyone.[16] It is all the more important to get hold of these principles well because even a slight error about them has the greatest consequences. It is understandable that in this situation *paideia* ought first of all to be directed to elucidate them, and that only when this preliminary work is accomplished can the pupil go on to something else.

However important this initial determination may be, it only constitutes the first element of philosophical *paideia* elaborated by Aristotle. We uncover another if we go back to our Book I of the *Nicomachean Ethics* (I, 3, 1094 b 12 ff). This time the discussion deals with moral sciences' *characteristic method*. Positing in principle that the method according to which the truth is manifested in any science stems from the subject of this science, Aristotle recalls that we must not expect the same precision from each science. Again, it will be the mark of the πεπαιδευμένος, to know the method of these sciences, and thereby the degree of rigor or of exactness which each is capable of attaining.[17] Thus, given the extraordinary contingency of its subject, human acts, moral philosophy only offers low certainty. Anyone who undertakes to write this sort of treatise will have to be content with indicating the truth very roughly.[18] Unlike natural beings, who present great uniformity everywhere – the properties of fire are the same in Greece and in Persia – the noble, the just, and the legal vary from one country to another.[19] Without denying natural law, as some have been tempted to do, the philosopher is forced to keep to general principles which govern human conduct, while recalling that these principles lose their edge when they are applied to particular cases. It is true in general that we are obliged to return something entrusted to us. That is the very definition of justice or almost so. But it is not difficult to imagine a situation where it would be dangerous and even opposed to justice to give back to its owner an object which belonged to him by right. Such examples could be multiplied indefinitely.

16 *Physics*, 1, 7, 189 b ff; II, 8, 198 b 10 ff.

17 *Nicomachean Ethics*, I, 3, 1094 b 24: πεπαιδευμένου γάρ ἐστιν ἐπὶ τοσοῦτον τἀκριβὲς ἐπιζητεῖν καθ᾽ ἕκαστον γένος ἐφ᾽ ὅσον ἡ τοῦ πράγματος φύσις ἐπιδέχεται.

18 *Nicomachean Ethics*, I, 3, 1094 b 20.

19 *Nicomachean* Ethics, V, 7, 1134 b 25; I, 3, 1094 b 14; cf. Plato, *Laws*, X, 889 e.

General principles of moral science never dispense the person who acts from taking into account the infinitely variable circumstances of each human act.[20] A physician cannot prescribe the same remedy for all his patients, even if they are affected by the same sickness. It often happens that one of these patients cannot endure the remedy in question because of something peculiar to him.[21] Similarly, a trainer cannot mold each athlete with whom he deals in exactly the same manner, unless they all have the same physical dispositions.[22] His art consists precisely in bringing the best result out of each individual's own potential. These remarks show the danger of teaching moral philosophy to a student who has no idea of the method of this science nor, consequently, of the nature or the scope of its conclusions.

Thus each science has its peculiar method, which must be settled before we come to the problems that the science seeks to resolve. If we must pursue this research and extend it to other disciplines, we find for example, that mathematics, thanks to the rigor of its method, permits us to attain the highest degree of certainty and constitutes the prototype of scientific approach. We find that, by contrast with mathematics, that abstracts from sensible matter and change, natural philosophy does demonstrate, starting with the four chief causes, but most of the time must be content with *a posteriori* reasoning.[23] We find that first philosophy, whose object is entirely removed from matter and hence immutable, studies everything in the light of the most universal causes and for human beings is the highest, most

20 That is why Aristotle says further on (VI, 11, 1143 b 11) that we must always take into consideration the opinion of older or experienced people, even if they cannot justify that opinion by rational arguments. Their experience often lets them see rightly in these practical matters. "Intellectuals" who are so criticized in our time, are precisely hothouse philosophers who attempt to resolve the most particular problems of political and moral life in a purely abstract and theoretical manner without referring to the particular, existent conditions.

21 *Nicomachean Ethics*, X, 9, 1180 b 7.

22 *Nicomachean Ethics*, X, 9, 1180 b 10. From this, Aristotle concludes the superiority of private *paideia*, which is more easily adapted to the peculiarities of each subject.

23 For the distinction between the philosopher of nature and the mathematician, see, for example *Physics* II, 2, 193 b 22 ff; *Metaphysics*, II, 3, 995 a 15.

divine, and most inaccessible science.[24] Obviously, there are notable differences between these several disciplines. The name "science" which we give them is an analogous term not applied for the same reason or in the same way to each of them. It pertains to παιδεία to inform us about these differences. The πεπαιδευμένος is he who knows precisely what type of proof he should expect in each case. He does not expect from an orator the rigor which characterizes the geometer, any more than he would be content with probable arguments in mathematics.[25]

These considerations on the method of sciences especially explain the use of the word παιδεία in an important passage of the treatise *On the Parts of Animals*, which has sometimes given rise to serious confusion. In fact, in Book I, chapter one, (693 a 1, p. 643 McKeon edition) we read:

> Every systematic science, the humblest and the noblest alike, seems to admit of two distinct kinds of proficiency [ἕχις]; one of which may be properly called scientific knowledge [ἐπιστήμη] of the subject, while the other is a kind of educational acquaintance [παιδεία] with it. For an educated man [πεπαιδευμένος] should be able to form a fair off-hand judgment as to the goodness or badness of the method [τρόπος] used by a professor in his exposition. To be educated [πεπαιδεῦσθαι] is in fact to be able to do this; and even the man of universal education [τὸν ὅλος πεπαιδευμένον] we deem to be such in virtue of his having this ability.

The context sharply contrasts παιδεία with science, ἐπιστήμε. What characterizes παιδεία is still this aptitude or determination of the mind[26] in

24 Cf. *Metaphysics*, I, 2, 982 a 5 ff; VI, 1, 1026 a 7 ff.

25 *Nicomachean Ethics*, I, 3, 1094 b 24. See the parallel passage in *Metaphysics*, II, 3, 995 a 6 ff., where, appropriately, the problem is posed in the most general terms. In *Confessions*, VI, 4 (p. 91 Sheed translation) St Augustine will accuse himself: "I wanted to be as certain of things unseen as that seven and three makes ten," that is, of having wanted to obtain "the same sort of certitude."

26 The word ἕζις here designates the quality in virtue of which the subject is well or badly disposed in itself or in relation to something else. This is the second sense indicated in *Metaphysics*, V, 20, 1022 b 10; Cf. *Categories*, 8 b 27–29 a 12.

virtue of which the pupil is in a position to form a judgment on the procedure or method of an author who is explaining a question. Never having studied the subject thoroughly on his own, the πεπαιδευμένος does not have perfect or scientific knowledge and thus cannot declare himself directly and definitively on the truth or falsehood of the conclusions presented to him.[27] In this regard his position is inferior to that of his teacher. But he is no longer in a state of complete ignorance. In so far as he is sufficiently instructed about the principles and method of the science in question, he already has the means required to appreciate or judge (κρίνειν), from his more limited viewpoint, the explanation made by someone else.[28] This capacity can be restricted to one discipline or it can extend to all the branches of knowledge. The true πεπαιδευμένος is evidently the person who possesses this competence in all, or nearly all, domains.[29]

Accordingly, it would be mistaken to suggest, as has been done, that παιδεία is purely and simply identified with dialectic defined as being "able to reason from opinions that are generally accepted about every problem propounded to us,"[30] or to see in it the equivalent to what we sometimes call "general culture,"[31] without asking ourselves what precisely we

27 *De Partibus Animalium*, I, 1, 639 a 15. It is one thing, indeed, to criticize a conclusion and something else to criticize the method by which an author claims to arrive at this conclusion.

28 The *pepaideumenos* is always presented as having the power of "judging." Besides the text that we are commenting, see *Nicomachean Ethics*, I, 3, 1094 b 29; *Politics*, III, 6, 1282 a 7.

29 *De Partibus Animalium*, I, 1, 639 a 9; *Nicomachean Ethics*, I, 3, 1095 a 1.

30 *Topics*, I, 100 a 18–20 (p. 188, McKeon edition); cf. J.-M. LeBlond, *Aristote philosophe de la vie .Le livre premier du Traité sur les parties des animaux. Texte et traduction, avec introduction et commentaire*, Paris: Aubier, 1945, p. 129, for the reverse of the view we take here. According to our interpretation, *paideia* evidently includes dialectic. And more generally, we would have to say it includes logic, whose object is the method *common* to all science and whose knowledge is presupposed. But furthermore, it includes the method *peculiar* to each science, about which we have just been speaking.

31 Against P. Louis, *Aristote, Les parties des animaux*, text and translation, Paris, 1956, p. xxi, there is no reason to suppose that Aristotle directed himself here to an audience of cultivated men rather than students or tecnicians (see, in this same sense, LeBond, *Aristote philosophe de la vie*, p. 128, note 3). This is a

understand by this expression. In Aristotle's thought, the word takes on a precise sense in another way. The ancient translators understood this when they limited themselves to either simply transcribe it[32] or to render it by a periphrasis,[33] noting that the corresponding expression did not exist in their own language.

With this equipment, elementary perhaps, but quite clear and perfect in its order, the youth would advance steadily in the study of science properly so-called and perfect himself gradually as time permitted. The issue is obviously not to determine minutely, from this moment on, the content of a program, which can have many stages, The total knowledge that a student just emerging into philosophy can assimilate will depend on many factors:

completely mistaken interpretation of the sense of *pepaideumenos*. Aristotle begins quite simply, as is his custom, with the method or *paideia* of the science which he will treat, before entering into the heart of the matter. P. Louis's suggestion according to which three kinds of Aristotelian writings must be distinguished henceforth, the esoteric or acroatic works, the exoteric works, and the popular works, rests on the same error and it seems to us that it should no longer be held.

32 E.g., William of Moerbeke in this place.

33 See for example, William Ogle, *Aristotle On the Parts of Animals*, Translated with an Introduction and Notes, London: Kegan Paul and French, 1882, reprinted by Garland, 1987. Despite some inexactness, this remains the modern translation which seems to reproduce Aristotle's thought most faithfully: "Every systematic science, the humblest and the noblest alike, seems to admit of two distinct kinds of proficiency; one of which may be properly called scientific knowledge of the subject, while the other is a kind of educational acquaintance (*paideia*) with it. For an educated man should be able to form a fair off-hand judgment as to the goodness or badness of the method used by a professor in his exposition. To be educated is in fact to be able to do this; and even the man of universal education we deem to be such in virtue of his having this ability. It will, however, of course, be understood that we only ascribe universal education to one who in his own individual person is thus critical in all or nearly all branches of knowledge, and not to one who has a like ability merely in some special subject. For it is possible for a man to have this competence in some one branch of knowledge without having it in all." The author has clearly seen the problem presented by the interpretation of the term *paideia* in this text, even if he has not delved into it. Cf. William Ogle, *Aristotle, On the parts of Animals*, p. 141, note 1.

his native abilities, his previous education, the quality of his teachers, and his personal effort.[34] The essential thing is to see that between ἀπαιδευσία, or total absence of culture, and wisdom, which remains the privilege of a small number of particularly well endowed minds only achieved after long years of study, there is an important stage, situated at the beginning of the path which leads to the perfection of intelligence, and which ought to provide a youth with instruments thanks to which he will be able to throw himself into the pursuit of that wisdom.[35]

Since this initiation is ordinarily acquired during youth, the term παιδεία which Aristotle uses to designate it is fully justified and offers another example of the philosophical development which ordinary language frequently undergoes. The ancients were not used to the often pretentious jargon, almost always disconcerting for the layman, to which modern philosophers have accustomed us. Rather than continually forging new and strange expressions, they generally were content with the "words of the tribe," even if they sometimes gave them a technical meaning rather different from but always related to their primitive sense. Such a procedure has the undeniable advantage of permitting a beginner to base himself on notions which he has known for a long time, and which are rooted in completely familiar reality, in order to go beyond them. Ὕλη, elevated in the *Physics* to the rank of "prime matter," first meant the forest or the carpenter's lumber. The verb λογίζεσθαι, which would reappear under a different form in the famous "syllogism," characteristic of the third operation of the spirit, was first the very simple act by which the Greek child counted his marbles. Nothing prevents the philosopher from similarly taking over the word παιδεία to make it express a new phase of the complex education to which a young man must submit himself during the whole first part of his life.

* * *

34 On the three great principles of education, nature (φύσις), custom (ἔθος), reason (λόγος), cf. Aristotle, *Politics*, VII, 12, 1332 a 40; Plutarch, *De Educatione Liberorum*, 2, A.

35 The three stages are distinguished with the greatest clarity in *Politics*, III, 6, 1282 a 1 ff, where the issue is still the *pepaideumenos*.

Taken as a whole, a program like the one we have just sketched is much more diversified than our deliberately brief reflections would make one suspect. We have only kept the strictly philosophical part of Aristotelian παιδεία. To be complete it would be necessary to assume this vantage point to study the liberal arts, which the ancients considered as approaches to philosophy and thus immediately linked to it. Such an investigation would certainly bring us to better understand the nature of this ἐγκύκλιος παιδεία, as the best minds conceived it then: not as a collection of superficial knowledge, badly remembered and badly digested, but a whole, well defined and, at least in principle, well organized, having its proper finality and its relative perfection.[36] Even if the pupil who has undergone this type of training is only at the first stage of his intellectual development, there is no doubt that he is much better equipped for life or for the more profound studies which lie ahead, than the person who has piled up a jumble of disordered and chaotic knowledge. Provided with general principles upon which the different sciences are based, adequately informed about their respective methods and already to some degree broken in to handling these methods, he will be able to advantageously use the experience that time will bring, and in the long run will find the gradual mastery of those disciplines easier.

Among other things, it is because this education favors the flowering of intellectual virtues, because it aims at making a genuine ἕξις germinate in the young man's mind, that this education wins out over the sophists, those great innovators of the pedagogical revolution of the fifth century BC, which led to the elaboration of an ideal having for its goal precisely to form men, παιδεύειν ἀνθρώπους.[37] Instead of inculcating principles and systematically relating their ideas to them, the sophists were largely content with teaching by examples and practical exercises.[38] Such a method doubt-

36 By contrast, we can imagine the character in Sartre's *Nausea*, who as a young person had not received the education he had hoped for, and who had decided to make up for lost time by reading all the holdings in the municipal library ... in alphabetical order!

37 This is Protagoras's definition, according to Plato, *Protagoras*, 317 b, Cf. Aristotle, *De Elenchis Sophisticis*, 34, 183 b 36 ff.

38 Aristotle, *De Elenchis Sophisticis*, 34, 183 b 36 ff. On the methods of the sophists and their contribution to higher education, Henri-Irenée Marrou can be

less constituted progress over what existed previously, but it has the defect of stopping half-way. Aristotle[39] compares the method to that of a shoemaker who offers his client a number of shoes, among which the client can chooses what best suits him. Acting thus, the shoemaker is certainly useful, but if the buyer's feet come to hurt later, he will be forced to recur to the shoemaker again. There is another procedure, which consists in teaching the pupil the art of making footwear, thereby giving him the means to satisfy his own needs as they make themselves felt. In the intellectual order, the παιδεία which Aristotle recommends corresponds to this second alternative. The young student who has passed through this school and has received his instruction under a more universal form, is already in condition to act by himself and, should the case arise, to confront new difficulties without having to recur each time to the insights given by his teacher.

With the perspective of this notion of παιδεία the Aristotelian aporia about teaching philosophy to young people, with which we began, finds its most natural solution. That a young man is not yet a philosopher or a sage in the full sense of the word is self evident, and nobody will be surprised. It does not follow as a consequence that he is excluded from dedicating himself to the study of philosophy. Nothing prevents him from acquiring at this age the rudiments – the παιδεία – even if he only attains completion much later. Furthermore, there are good reasons to believe that the student who has not received the desired formation at the ideal moment when the mind awakens, will never reach the end of the long journey. Long before our modern psychologists, antiquity recognized the importance of these decisive, irreplaceable years. This is the only explanation of the dedication of Socrates to the elite Athenian youth, whatever the smirks of the multitude. Like every true philosopher, in love with the children of his kind, Socrates could have some hope of recruiting the candidates for wisdom and virtue in the palestras where they wrestled. A person whom education and habit have already formed or deformed, whose intelligence has received a crease that the years have only hardened, cannot easily be converted to new ways of thinking.

consulted, *A History of Education in Antiquity* (New York: Sheed and Ward, 1956, trans. George L. Lamb), pp. 48–57.

39 Aristotle, *De Elenchis Sophisticis*, 34, 184 a 2 ff.

There is no more dazzling example of this truth than the *Parmenides*, the unique dialogue, where for first and last time in the works of Plato, Socrates is presented as a young man who does not have the upper hand. Before the white-haired Eleatic, "one to be venerated" and also "awful,"[40] he refuses to completely commit himself to the discussions and ends by retreating into respectful silence. From that moment the conversation necessarily converts itself into a monologue, which closes abruptly, leaving the two adversaries further apart than ever. The idea merely insinuated at the start but which imposes itself more and more clearly as the conversation is pursued, is that old Parmenides, who is already reluctant to accept the role of defending his own position, would never agree to confront the "fearful ocean of words"[41] into which he must throw himself to be able to given an entirely new direction to his thought.[42]

However much wisdom is the ornament of mature years, in the measure in which it is accessible to mankind, it remains nonetheless the final

40 Cf. *Theaetetus*, 183 e 6 (p. 155, trans. H. N. Fowler, *Theaetetus, Sophist*, Cambridge, Mass.: Loeb Library edition, Harvard University Press, 1977). The praise is more apparent than real, as we see when we turn to the passage in the *Iliad*, book III, 172, from which it is taken. It is Helen who speaks, and the hero who is the "one to be venerated" and also "awful" is none other than Priam. He is aged when the Trojan War takes place and only plays a self-effacing role in it. Very soon he must humiliate himself and pay an exorbitant ransom for the corpse of his son Hector. Like Priam's kingdom, that of Parmenides approaches its end. So, the meaning of this encounter between Socrates and his elder (see similarly *Sophist*, 217 c) is clarified. Plato never chooses his quotations at random.

41 Parmenides, 137 a 7 (p. 235 Loeb Library edition, *Cratylus, Parmenides, Greater Hippias, Lesser Hippias*, trans. H. N. Fowler, Cambridge, Mass.: Harvard University Press, 1970).

42 About the need to unlearn before being able to learn, cf. St. Augustine, *Contra Academicos*, III, 17, 38 (p. 88, *Against the Academicians and The Teacher*, trans., with intro. and notes by Peter King, Indianapolis: Hackett, 1995): "Consequently, I suspect that Zeno, the first of the Stoics, was held in suspicion when he came to the school founded by Plato (then presided over by Polemo) after having heard and believed some of these doctrines. He didn't seem to be the kind of man to whom the Platonic teachings, sacrosanct as they were, should be disclosed and entrusted before he had unlearned [dedidicisset] the theories he had received from others and brought with him to the Platonic school."

blooming of ideas sown during adolescence.[43] In the last analysis, that is the reason why, like the devil in *Faust*, philosophers have always felt a love for the youth of the city, as mysterious as it is profound.

43 The same idea is found in St. Jerome, *Epistula 52*, 2–3, p. 414, 16 ff, Hilberg (*Corpus Scriptorum Ecclesiasticorum Latinorum*, vol. 54), who sees it as illustrated in the episode of the Sunamite, *III Kings*, I, 1 ff. This mysterious woman, virgin and spouse at the same time, who comes to share the bed of old King David, is wisdom, which must be cultivated from youth, but which is only truly possessed in a more advanced age's serenity and calm of passions.

Bibliography

Allers, Rudolf, "Microcosmus from Anaximandros to Paracelsus," in *Traditio*, 1944, pp. 338 ff.

Arnim, Hans Friederich August von, Leben und Werke des Dio von Prusa, Weidmannos, Berlin, 1898

_____ "Quelle der Überlieftrung über Ammonius Sakkas," in *Rheinisches Museum,* vol. XLII, 1887, pp. 278–285.

_____ *Stoicorum Veterum Fragmenta,* 3 vol., Leipzig, 1903–1905.

Arnou, René, "Platonismedes Pères," in *Dictionnaire de théologie catholique,* vol XII, co1. 2258–2392.

Bainvel, Jean Vincent, "Ame," in *Dictionnaire de theologie catholique,* vol I, col. 968–1006.

Bardenhewer, Otto, "Geschichte der altkirchlichen Literatur," vol. IV, *Das fünfte Jahrhundert,* Fribourg-en-Brisgau: Herder, 1924.

Bardy, Gustave, *L'Eglise et les derniers romains,* Paris: R. Laffont, 1943 "L'Eglise et l'enseignement in les trois premiers siècles," in *Revue des sciences religieuses,* 1932, pp. 1–28.

_____ "L'Eglise et l'enseignement au quatrieme siècle," in *Revue des sciences religieuses,* 1934, pp. 525–549; 1935, pp. 1–27.

_____ "L'enseignement au cinquieme siècle," in *Melanges F. Cavallera,* Toulouse, 1948, pp. 191–213.

_____ "Les origines des écoles monastiques en Occident," in *Sacris Erudiri,* vol. V, 1953, pp. 86–104.

Baumgartner, M., "Die Philosophie des Alanus de Insulis," in *Beiträge zur Geschichte der Philosophiedes Mittelalters, Texte und Untersuchungen,* II, 4, Münster, 1896.

Bavel, Tarcicius J. van, *Recherches sur la christologie de saint Augustin,* Fribourg: Éditions Universitaires, 1954.

Baynes, Norman Hepburn, "The Decline of the Roman Empire in Western Europe: Some Modern Explanations," in *The Journal of Roman Studies,* vol. XXXIII, 1943, pp. 29–35; reproduced in Baynes, *Byzantine Studies and Other Essays,* London, 1955, pp. 83–96.

Beutler, Rudolf, report of F. Bömer, "Der lateinische Neuplatonismus," in *Gnomon,* vol. xiii, 1937, pp. 552–558.

_____ "Olympiodorus," in P.-W., *R.E.,* vol. XVIII, I, col. 2II ff.

_____ "Porphyrios," in P.-W., *R.E.,* vol. XXII, I, col. 275–313 (on Porphyry and Claudianus Mamertus, cf. col. 293–294).

Bickel, E., "Inlocalitas," in *Kant-Festschrift;* Königsberg, 1924, pp. 19–26.

Bidez, Joseph, *Vie de Porphyre, le philosophe neo-platonicien,* Gand: E. van Goethem, 1913.

Bömer, Franz, *Der lateinische Neuplatonismus und Neupythagorismus und Claudianus Mamertus, Klassisch-philologisch Studien,* vol. VII, Leipzig: O. Harrasowitz, 1936.

Boyance, Pierre, *Le culte des muses chez les philosophes grecs,* Paris: E. de Boccard, 1936.

_____ *Études sur le Songe de Scipion,* Paris: Bordeaux, Feret & Fils, 1936.

_____ "Le platonisme à Rome, Platon et Ciceron," in les actes du *Congrès de Tours et Poitiers,* Paris: 1954, pp. 195–211.

Brehier, Émile, *Histoire de la philosophie,* 2 vol., Paris: F. Alcan, 1938–1949.

_____ *La théorie des incorporels dans l'ancien stoicisme,* Paris: J. Vrin, second edition 1928.

_____ *Chrysippe et l'ancien stoicïsme,* Paris: PUF, revised edition, 1951.

Cagnat, René, "Les bibliothequès municipales in l'empire romain," in *Memoires de l'Academie des Inscriptions et Belles Lettres,* vol. XXXVIII, 1909, pp. 1 ff.

Callahan, John Francis, *Four Views of Time in Ancient Philosophy,* Cambridge, Mass.: Harvard University Press, 1948.

Camelot, Pierre Thomas, "Les idées de Clement d'Alexandrie sur l'utilisation de la science et de la litterature profane," in *Recherches de science religieuse,* vol. XXI, 1931, pp. 38 ff.

Cappuyns, Dom H., review of Zimmermann, *Candidus,* in *Bulletin de théologie ancienne et médiévale,* vol. I, 1929–1930, number 127.

Cellier, D., *Histoire generale des auteurs sacres et ecclesiastiques,* 14 vols., Paris: new edition 1858–1863.

Chadwick, Henry, *Origen : Contra Celsum,* translated with an introduction and notes, Cambridge: Cambridge University Press, 1953.

Chadwick, Nora Kershaw, *Poetry and Letters in Early Christian Gaul,* London: Bowes, and Bowes, 1955.

Chadwick, Owen, *John Cassien, A Study in Primitive Monasticism,* Cambridge: Cambridge University Press, 1950, second edition 1968.

Chatillon, F., "Dracontiana," in *Revue du moyen âge latin,* vol. VIII, 1952, pp. 177 ff.

Cochrane, Charles Norris, *Christianity and Classical Culture, A Study of Thought and Action from Augustus to Augustine,* Oxford: Oxford University Press, second edition 1944.

Courcelle, Pierre Paul, *Les lettres grecques en Occident de Macrobe* à *Cassiodore,* Paris: E. Brocard, second edition 1948.

_____ *Recherches sur les* Confessions *de saint Augustin,* Paris: E. Brocard, 1950, 1968.

_____ *Histoire littéraire des grandes invasions germaniques,* Paris: Études Augustiniennes, 1948.

_____ "Litiges sur la lecture des *Libri Platonicorum* par saint Augustin," in *Augustiniana,* vol. IV, 1954, pp. 225–239.

_____ "Date, sources et genese des *Consultationes Zacchaei et Apollonii,*" in *Revue de l'histoire des religions,* vol. CXLVI, 1954, pp. 174–193.

_____ "Propos antichretiens rapportes par saint Augustin," in *Recherches Augustiniennes,* vol. I, Paris: 1958, pp. 149–186.

Couturier, C., "La structure métaphysique de l'homme d'apres Saint Augustin," in *Augustinus Magister,* vol. I, Paris: 1954, pp. 543–550.

_____ "Structure métaphysique de l'etre cree d'apres Saint Augustin," in *Recherches de philosophie,* vol. I, Paris: 1954, pp. 57–84.

Cumont, Franz, *Les religions orientales dans le paganisme romain,* Paris: E. Leroux, fourth edition, 1929.

_____ *Recherches sur le symbolisme funéraire des romains,* Paris: Paul Geuthner, 1942.

_____ *Lux Perpetua,* Paris: Paul Geuthner, 1949.

_____ "Comment Plotin détourna Porphyre du suicide," in *Revue des études grecques,* vol. XXXII, 1919, pp. 113–120.

Delhaye, Philippe, "Une controverse sur l'âme universelle au IXe siècle," in *Analecta Mediaevalia Namurcensia*, fasc. I, Lille and Namur: Centre d'Études Médiévales, 1950.

Deslisle, Leopold, *Le cabinet des manuscrits de la Bibliothèque Nationale,* vol. II, Paris: 1874; reprinted Amsterdam: Gérard T. van Heusden, 1969.

Diels, Hermann, *Doxographi Graeci,* second edit., Berlin-Leipzig: Walter de Gruyter, 1929. *Die Fragmente der Vorsokratiker,* 3 vol., sixth edit., Berlin: Walter Kranz, 1951.

Dodds, Eric Robertson, "The *Parmenides* of Plato and the Origin of the Neoplatonic One," in *Classical Quarterly,* vol. XXII; 1928, pp. 129–142.

Engelbrecht, August, "Untersuchungen über die Sprache des Claudianus Mamertus," in *Sitzungsberichte der Wiener Akademie,* vol. CX, Vienna: 1885.

Fabricius, *Bibliotheca latina mediae et infimae latinitatis,* 6 vol., Padua: 1754.

Festugière, André Jean, *L'ideal religieux des grecs et l'Evangile,* Paris: 1932.

_____ *La Révelation d'Hermès Trismégiste,* 4 vols., Paris: Lecoffre, 1944–1954.

_____ *L'Hermitisme,* Lund: C.W.K. Gleerup, 1948.

_____ *Personal Religion Among the Greeks,* Berkeley and Los Angeles: University of California Press: 1954.

_____ "Une source hermitique de Porphyre : l'egyptien du *De Abstinentia*" (II, 47), in *Revue des études grecques,* vol. XLIX, 1939, pp. 586 ff.

Fischer, (J. A.). – *Studien zum Todesgedanken in der alten Kirche; die Beiteilung des natürlichen Todes in der kirchlichen Literatur der ersten drei Jahrhunderte,* Munich: 1954.

Flórez, Enrique, *España Sacrada,* vol. XI, Madrid, 1753; Madrid: Hispanic Society of America, 1918.

Gandillac, Maurice de, *La sagesse de Plotin,* Paris: Hachette, 1952.

Geffcken, Johannes, *Der Ausgang des Griechisch-Römischen Heidentums,* Heidelberg: C. Winter, 1920.

Germain, A. C., *De Mamerti Claudiani scriptis et philosophia,* thesis, Montpellier, 1840.

Gilson, Étienne *Introduction à l'étude de saint Augustin,* third edit., Paris: Vrin, 1949. English translation, The Christian Philosophy of St. Augustine, New York: Random House, 1960

_____ *Thomas Aquinas and Our Colleagues,* Princeton, 1953.

_____ "Note sur un texte de S. Thomas," in *Revue Thomiste,* vol. LIV, 1954, pp. 148–152.

Gomperz, Heinrich Ἀσόματος in *Hermes,* vol. LXVII, 1932, pp. 155–167.

Grabowski, S., *The All-Present God, A Study in St. Augustine,* St. Louis and London: Herder, 1954.

Hack, R. K., *God in Greek Philosophy to the Time of Socrates,* Princeton: Princeton University Press, 1931.

Harleman, Eimar, *De Claudiano Mamerto gallicae latinitatis scriptore quaestiones,* Uppsala: A. B. Lundequistkabokhandeln, 1938.

Harnack, Adolf von, *Lehrbuch der Dogmengeschichte,* fifth edit., 3 vol., Tübingen, 1931–1932.

_____ "Zu Claudianus Mamertus, De statu animae Epilogus," (p. 196 Engelbrecht edition) *Zwei Fragen,* in *Texte und Untersuchungen, Neue Folge,* v, 3, pp. 147–148.

Henry, Paul, *Plotin et l'Occident,* Louvain: Spicelegium Sacrum Louvainense, 1934.

Jaeger, Werner, *Paideia, The Ideals of Greek Culture,* translated by Gilbert Highet, Oxford: Oxford University Press, 1939–1945.

_____ *The Theology of the Early Greek Philosophers,* Oxford: Clarendon Press, 1947.

Jammer, Max, *Concepts of Space,* Cambridge, Mass.: Harvard University Press, 1954.

Jonas, Hans, *Gnosis und spätantike Geist,* Gottingen: Vandeboeck & Rubrecht 1934.

Jones, L. W., *An Introduction to Divine and Human Readings by Cassiodorus Senator,* translated with an introduction and notes, New York, 1946.

Jullian, Camille, *Histoire de la Gaule,* 8 vols., Paris: Hachette, 1920–1926.

Karpp, Heinrich "Probleme altchristlicher Anthropologie. Biblische Anthropologie und philosophische Psychologie bei den Kirchenvätern des dritten Jahrhunderts," in *Beiträge zur Förderung christlicher Theologie,* vol. 44, 3, Gütersloh: C. Bertelsmann, 1950.

Kuijper, D., "Lienis regula," in *Vigiliae Christianae*, vol. VIII, 1954, pp. 50–60. Krause, Hans, *Studia Neoplatonica,* dissertation, Leipzig: Oswld Schmidt, 1904.

Labhardt, André, "Tertullien et la philosophie ou la recherche d'une position pure" in *Museum Helveticum,* vol. VII, 1950, pp. 150 ff.

_____ "Sur une page de Saint Jérome," in *Hommage et Reconnaissance, Recueil de travaux publics a l'occasion du soixantieme anniversaire de Karl Barth*, Neuchâtel and Paris: 1946, pp. 56–62.

Labriolle, Pierre, and Gustave Bardy, *Histoire de la litterature latine chrétienne,* 2 vols., Paris: Belles Lettres, third edition, 1947.

La Broise, René Marie de, *Mamerti Claudiani vita ejusque doctrina de anima hominis,* Paris: Retraux-Bray, 1890.

Lacombrade, Christian, *Synésios de Cyrène, hellène et chrétien,* Paris: Belles Lettres, 1951.

Laistner, Max Ludwig Wolfram, *Christianity and Pagan Culture in the Later Roman Empire,* Ithaca, New York: Cornell University Press, 1951.

Lambot, Dom D. C., editor, Ratramne de Corbie, *Liber de anima ad Odonem Bellovacensem, Analecta Mediaevalia Namurcensia,* 2, Namur and Lille: Godenne, 1951.

Leclercq, H., "Bibliothèques," in *Dictionnaire d'archéologie chrétienne et de liturgie,* vol. II, 1, Paris: 1910, cols. 842–904

Lenain de Tillemont, Louis-Sébastien, *Mémoires pour servir à l'histoire ecclésiastique des six premiers siècles,* 16 vols., Paris: 1693–1712.

Lot, Ferdinand, *La fin du monde antique et le debut du moyen âge*, Paris: A. Michel, second edition, 1951.

Loyen, André, *Sidoine Apollinaire et l'esprit precieux en Gaule aux derniers jours de l'empire,* (thesis), Paris: Belles Lettres, 1943.

_____ *Recherches historiques sur les panégyriques de Sidoine Apollinaire,* Pans: Champion, 1943.

Lubac, Henri de, *Catholicisme*, Paris: Éditions du Cerf, fifth edition, 1952.

Madoz, José, "Liciniano de Cartagena y sus cartas," *Etudios Onienses,* I, 4, Madrid, 1948.

_____ *Segundo decenio de estudios sobre patrística española,* 1941 - I 950, Madrid: Ediciones Fax, 1951.

Mandouze, André, "Saint Augustin et la religion romaine," in *Recherches Augustiniennes,* vol. I, Paris: 1958, pp. 187–223.

Manitus, Max, *Geschichte der lateinischen Literatur des Mittelalters,* 3 vols., Munich: Beck, 1911–1931.

Marrou, Henri-Irenée, *Saint Augustin et la fin de la culture antique,* 2 vols., Paris: E. de Brocard, second edition 1949.

_____ Μουσικὸς ἀνήρ, *étude sur les scenes de la vie intellectuelle figurant sur les monuments funéraires romains,* Grenoble: Didier et Richard, 1938.

_____ *Histoire de l'éducation in l'antiquité,* Paris: Éditions de Seuil, second edition 1950.

_____ *A Diognète, Sources Chretiennes,* 33, Paris: Éditions du Cerf, 1951.

_____ "Autour de la bibliothèque du Pape Agapit," in *Melanges d'archéologie et d'histoire publicés par l'École Française de Rome*, ~. XLVII~, 1931, pp. 124–169.

Mazzarino, Santo, *Aspetti sociali del quarto secolo, Ricerche di storia tardo-romana,* Rome: "L'Erma" de Bretschneider, 1951.

Merlan, Philip, *From Platonism to Neoplatonism,* The Hague: Nijhoff, 1953.

Mirmont, Henri de la Ville de, "L'astrologie chez les Gallo-romains," X; "Sidoine Apollinaire", XI; "L'astrologie in le De statu animae de Claudianus Mamertus," in *Revue des études anciennes,* vol. XI, 1909, pp. 301–327, Bordeaux: Feret & Fils, 1904.

Mommsen, E.T., "St. Augustine and the Christian Idea of Progress, The Background of the City of God," in *Journal of the History of Ideas,* vol. XII, 1951, pp. 346–374.

Moraux, Paul, "Recherches sur le *De caelo* d'Aristote, objet et structure de l'ouvrage," in *Revue Thomiste,* vol. LI, 1951, pp. 170–196.

Morin Dom Germain, "La lettre-préface du Comes, *Ad Constantium*, se rapporterait au lectionnaire de Claudien Mamert?" in *Revue Bénédictine,* vol. xxx, 1913, pp. 228–231.

Naumann, V. "Das Problem des Bösen in Tertullians zweitem Buch gegen Marcion," in *Zeitschrift für Katolische Theologie,* vol. LVIII, 1934, pp. 311–363 et 533–551.

Olivieri, A., "Osservazioni sulla dottrina di Filolao," in *Rivista Indo-greco-italica di filologia, lingua, antichità,* vol. v, 1921, pp. 29–46.

Pépin, Jean,"Saint Augustin et le symbolisme neoplatonicien de la vêture," in *Augustinus Magister,* vol. I, Paris: 1954, pp. 293–306.

Philippson, R., review of Franz Bömer, *Der lateinische Neuplatonismus,* in *Philologische Wochenschrift,* vol. LVIII, 1938, pp. 1033–1041.

Piganiol, André, *L'Empire chrétien,* Paris: Presses Universitaires de France, 1947.

Pirenne, Henri, "De l'état de l'instruction des laïcs a l'époque mérovingienne," in *Revue Bénédictine,* vol. XLVI, 1934, pp. 165–177.

Pitra, Jean-Baptiste, *Analecta sacra et classica spicilegio solesmensi,* vol. V, Paris-Rome: A. Jouby et Roger, 1888.

Pohlenz, Max, *Die Stoa, Geschichte einer geistigen Bewegung,* 2 vols, Göttingen: Vandenhoeck & Ruprecht, 1943.

Prestige, George Leonard, *God in Patristic Thought,* London: S.P.C.K., second edition 1952.

Quispel, Gilles, "Die Reue des Schöpfirs," in *Theologische Zeitschrift,* 1942, 2, pp. 151 ff.

Rehling, Bernard, *De Fausti Reiensi epistula tertia,* dissertation Münster, Monasterii Guestf.: ex Typographia Aschendorffiana, 1898.

Rehm, Walther, *Der Untergang Roms im abendländischen Denken, ein Beitrag zur Geschichtsschreibung und zum Dekadenzprobem,* Leipzig: Dieterich, 1930.

Roger, Maurice, *L'enseignement des lettres classiques d'Ausonea à Alcuin, introduction à l'histoire des écoles carolingiennes,* Paris: A. Picard, 1905.

Rohde, E., *Psyché, Le culte de l'âme ime chez les grecs et leur croyance à l'immortalité,* French translation by A. Reymond, Paris: 1952.

Roques, René, *L'univers dionysien,* Paris: Aubier, 1954.

Rüsche, Franz, *Blut, Leben und Seele,* Paderborn: Schöninghausen, 1930.

Salin, Edoard, *La civilisation mérovingienne d'apres les sepultures, les textes et le laboratoire, premiere partie, Les idees et les faits,* Paris: A & J. Picard, 1949.

Schanz, Martin von, *Geschichte der römischen Literatur bis zum Gesetzgebungswerk des Kaisers Justinian,* vol. IV: *Die römische Literatur von Constantin bis zum Gesetzgebungswerk Justinians,* 2 vols., Munich: C.H. Beck, 1914–1920.

Scherer, C., *Der Fuldaer Handschriften-Katalog aus dem* 16. *Jahrhundert,* in Franz Falk, *Beitrage zur Rekonstruktion der alten Bibliotheca fuldensis und Bibliotheca laureshamensis, Beiheste zum Zentralblat für Bibliothekswesen,* vol. XXVI, Leipzig: O. Harrossowitz, 1922.

Scherer, Jean, editor, *Entretien d'Origen avec Héraclide et les évêques ses collègues sur le Père, le Fils et l'ame,* Publications de la Societe Fouad I de Papyrologie, *Textes et Documents,* vol. IX, Cairo: Institut français d'archéologie orientale, 1949.

Schlitz, E. "La comparaison du symbol *Quicumque vult*" in *Ephemerides Theologicae Lovanienses,* vol. XXIV, 1948, pp. 440 ff.

Schmid, L., "Beiträge zur Geschichte der wissenschaftlichen Studien in sächsischen Klöstern," in *Neues Archiv sächsische Geschichte und Altertumskunde,* vol. XVIII, 1897, pp. 201–272.

Schmid, W., "Claudianus Mamertus," in *Realkxicon für Antike und Christentum,* vol,. III, columns 169- 179.

Schuhl, Pierre Maxime, *La fabulation platonicienne,* Paris: Presse Universitaires de France, 1947.

Schulze, Martin, *Die Schrift des Claudianus Mamertus, Presbyter zu Vienne, über das Wesen der Seele,* (dissertation Leipzig), Dresden: Rammingsche Buchdruckerei, 1883.

Schwartz, Eduardus, *Acta Conciliorum Oecumenicorum,* 4 vols., Berlin: Walter de Gruyter, 1914–1940.

Seznec, Jean, *The Survival of the Pagan Gods, The Mythological Tradition and Its Place* in *Renaissance Humanism,* translated by Barbara Sessions, New York: Pantheon, 1953.

Solignac, Aimé, "Analyse et sources de la Question *De Ideis*," in *Augustinus Magister,* vol. I, Paris: 1954, pp. 307–315.

_____ "Doxographies et manuels in la formation philosophique de Saint Augustin," in *Recherches Augustiniennes,* vol. I, Paris: 1958, 113–148.

Stevens, Courtenay Eduard, *Sidonius Apollinaris and His Age,* Oxford: The Clarendon Press, 1933.

Theiler, Willy, "Die Vorbereitung des Neuplatonismus," in *Problemata, Forschungen zur Klassischen Philologie,* vol. I, Berlin, 1930.

_____ "Porphyrios und Augustin," in *Schriften der königsberger gelehrten Gesellschaft,* vol. X, 1, Halle: M. Niemeyer, 1933.

Tresmontant, Claude, *Essai sur la pensée hébraïque,* Paris: Éditions du Cerf, 1953.

Trouillard, Jean, *La purification plotinienne,* Paris: Presses Universitaires de France, 1956.

_____ *La procession plotinienne,* Paris: Presses Universitaires de France, 1956.

van der Vyver, A., "Cassiodore et son oeuvre," in *Speculum,* vol. VI, 1931, pp. 244–292

Verbeke, Gérard, *L'évolution de la doctrine du pneuma du stoïcisme a Saint Augustin,* Paris-Louvain: Desclée de Brouwer, 1945.

Waszink, Jan Hendrik, *Tertulliani De Anima, edited with an introduction and commentary,* Amsterdam: J. M. Meulenhoff, 1947.

_____ "Aristoteles," in *Reallexicon für Antike und Christentum,* vol. I, columns 658–667.

Wilmart, Dom André, "L'opuscule inédit de Ratramne sur la nature de l'ame," in *Revue Bénédictine,* vol. XLIII, 1931, pp. 207–223.

_____ "Les Réponses de Priscien le philosophe sous le nom de Saint Augustin," in *Revue Bénédictine,* vol. XLIX, 1937, pp. 3–12.

Wissowa, Georg, *Religion und Kultur der Römer,* Munich: second edition 1912.

Wolfson, Harry Austryn, *The Philosophy of the Church Fathers,* vol. I, *Faith, Trinity, Incarnation,* Cambridge, Mass.: Harvard University Press, 1956.

Wuilleumier, Pierre, *Lyon, métropole des Gaules,* Paris: Les Belles Lettres, 1953.

Zeller, Eduard, *Die Philosophie der Griechen in ihrer geschichtlichen Entwicklung dargestellt,* vol. III, Leipzig: O. R. Reisland, tenth edition 1923.

_____ "Ammonius Sakkas und Plotinus," in *Archiv für Geschichte der Philosophie,* vol. VII, 1894, pp. 295–312.

Zimmermann, F., "Des Claudianus Mamertus Schrift *De statu animae libri tres,*" in *Divus Thomas* (Fribourg), vol. I, 1914, pp. 238–256;332–368; 470–495.

_____ "Candidus, ein Beitrag zur Geschichte der Früscholastik," in *Divus Thomas,* vol. VII, 1929, pp. 30–60.

Index of Names

Abelard Peter, 13
Aelius Aristides, 24
Aeschylus, 201
Alan of Lille, 12, 15, 217, 219.
Albert the Great, 16
Albinus, 146, 148, 159, 165
Alcuin, 3, 12, 22
Alexander of Aphrodisias, 18, 60, 74, 126, 128, 160, 146–147
Alexander of Hales, 16
Álvaro of Córdoba, 12, 13
Ambrose, St., 34, 50, 56, 64, 75,82, 107, 165, 172, 188, 190
Ammonius, son of Hermeias, 17
Ammonius Saccas, 131, 147, 214, 224
Anaximander, 143
Anaximines, 135
Apuleus, 7, 8, 978, 113
Archytas, 55
Aristotle, 15-16, 20, 23–24, 27, 33, 54, 72, 85, 88, 121–122, 127, 129, 145, 156, 199–202, 203–204, 208–209, 211
- *Categoriae*, 19, 206
- *De Anima*, 87, 105, 145, 154, 158
- *De Caelo*, 126, 145, 221
- *De Elenchis Sophisticis*, 210–211
- *De Generatione Animalium*, 127
- *De Generatione et Corruptione*, 126–127, 129
- *De Partibus Animalium*, 207–208.
- *De Plantis*, 127
- *Ethica Nichomachea*, 21, 33, 187, 199–200, 204–205, 207
- *Historia Animalium*, 202
- *Metaphysica*, 75, 202
- *Metereologia*, 127
- *Physica*, 144, 156, 203–204
- *Politica*, 126, 202
- *Rhetorica*, 6
- *Topica*, 129, 207

Arius Didymus, 146
Arnobius, 40, 45, 50, 67–69, 83, 107, 113, 127, 189
Arnobius the Younger, 46, 58.
Asclepius, 115
Athenagoras, 151
Augustine, St., 3, 6, 8–9, 12, 17, 31, 34, 42–43, 55, 58, 68, 72, 77, 82, 84–5, 93–95, 97, 107–108, 110–112, 117, 118–124, 126, 132–135, 136, 144, 151, 164–165, 171–172, 177–178, 180, 184, 188–189, 191, 194, 216, 218, 221
- *Contra Academicos*, 8, 18, 27, 154, 186, 212
- *Contra Epistula Fundamenti*, 177.
- *Contra Maximium Haereticum*, 109–110
- *Contra Mendacium*, 182
- *De Beata Vita*, 109
- *De Civitate Dei*, 7, 43, 46, 76, 78, 94–95, 108, 119, 122, 130, 132, 134, 137–138, 146, 152, 165 171–172, 178, 185, 190
- *De Cura pro Mortuis Gerenda*, 139
- *De Diversis Quaestionibus*, 94, 151

De Divinatione Daemonum, 51
D Doctrina Christiana, 4, 8, 32, 183
De Fide et Symbolo, 132, 134, 178
De Genesi ad Litteram, 58, 60, 78, 81, 86, 88, 90, 96, 109–112, 118, 130, 141, 151–153, 164
De Genesi ad Litteram Imperfectus Liber, 158
De Genesi contra Manichaeos, 184
De Immortalitate Animae, 144, 164–165
De Libero Arbitrio, 82, 119, 144, 178
De Mendacio, 184
De Moribus Ecclesiae Catholicae, 120–122, 158, 225
De Natura et Origine Animae, 58–60, 88
De Ordine, 18, 31, 121, 183, 187
De Quantitate Animae, 14, 36, 48, 93, 121, 144, 150, 164, 170
De Trinitate, 93, 111, 113, 165
De Vera Religione, 65, 189
Enarrationes in Psalmos, 165
Epistulae, 10, 136, 186
Retractationes, 51, 93, 189
Tratatus in Iohannis Evangelium, 114
Aulius Gellius, 5, 44, 88, 97, 128

Basil, St., 63, 69
Berenger, Peter, 13
Bernard, St., 14, 15, 24
Boethius, 1, 17, 64, 127, 185

Candidus of Fulda, 9, 11, 216, 224
Cassian, 12, 42–43,46, 50–52, 56–57, 59, 64–66, 70–71, 73, 75, 179, 190
Cassiodorus, 5, 11, 17, 47, 50, 136, 184, 190, 198, 219
Celsus, 6, 99, 185, 190
Chalcidius Chrysippus, 75, 82, 115, 126–127, 129–130, 146, 148, 159–160
Chrysostom, John, 34, 73, 81, 187
Cicero, 6, 17, 28, 60–61, 66, 69, 100, 165, 169, 202, 215
Cleanthes, 128
Clement of Alexandria, 64, 69, 74, 99, 147, 151, 189–190
Cleombrotus of Ambracia, 165
Consentius, 6, 184

Democritus, 144, 170
Dionysius of Halicarnassus, 23
Dionysius the Areopagite, 19, 135–136, 158
Descartes, René, 16
Diocles of Cnidus, 27
Diogenes Laertius, 61, 100
Diogenes of Seleucia, 146
Dion Cassius, 5

Ecdicius, 1, 3, 9, 136
Eucher, 3
Eusebius, 19
Eusebius of Caesarea, 117, 128, 138, 146, 148, 164
Eutropius, 19

Facundus, 141
Faustus of Riez, 12, 29, 32, 35–43, 45–50, 52, 55–57, 59, 61–65, 67, 69, 71, 73, 75, 106, 110, 113, 119, 142, 175, 179, 188, 193, 197
Favonius Eulogius, 115-117
Felix II, 141
Ferreolus, 6
Flavius Vopiscus, 5
Fredegisus, 196
Fronto, 7
Fulgentius of Rupsa, 58, 141

Galen, 74
Gennadius, 10-11, 46, 50, 113, 193
Gregory Nazianzus, 8, 16, 24, 33, 63, 69, 107.

Gregory of Nyssa, 32, 72, 108
Gregory the Great, 116, 187

Heraclides, 23
Heracides, bishop of Arabia, 74–75
Heraclitus, 143, 148
Hermannus, 13
Hermongenes, 6, 115
Hermophiles, 97
Herodotus, 33
Hesiod, 25, 55
Hierocles, 141
Hilary of Poitiers, 8, 13, 46
Hincmar of Reims, 153
Hippocrates, 74
Hippolytus, 115
Hugh of St. Victor, 15

Iamblichus, 104–106
Ireneus, St., 23–24, 45
Isidore of Seville, 4–5
Isocrates, 23, 27, 33

Jerome St., 3, 5, 8, 63–64, 72, 133, 213, 219
John Chrysostom, 81, 187
Julian the Apostate, 6
Justin, 14

Lactantius, 5, 16, 57, 67, 69, 74, 86, 147, 189
Libanius, 69, 104
Liber Testimoniorum, 42
Licinianus of Carthage, 11
Lucretius, 128
Lupus, 6
Lysias, 23. 28

Macarius, 59, 70
Macrobius, 101, 161–163, 166,
Majorian, 2
Mamertus. St., 9 n. 35
Marinus, 81
Martianus Capella, 113
Maximus of Tyre, 147, 185
Maximus the Confessor, 19, 106–108
Meditationes Piisimae de Cognitione Humanae Conditionis, 14
Mercator, Marius, 141
Methodius of Olympus, 21, 59
Mico of St. Riquer, 12

Naevius, 8.
Nemisius, 13, 16, 19, 75, 85–86, 93, 99, 122, 124–129, 131, 133, 135, 148–149, 156, 158, 160, 164
Nestorius, 70.
Numenius, 8, 14, 117, 138, 190.

Olympiodorus, 166, 215
Optatus of Milève, 7
Origen, 5–6, 43, 45, 47, 67, 74–75, 99, 147, 151–152, 180, 186, 189, 222, 216.
Ovid, 5, 64, 149, 151

Pelagius, 71
Peter of Celle, 13–14
Petreius, 7
Petronius, 5
Philo, 147
Philolaos, 153, 157
Philoponus, John, 19, 153
Plato, 10, 19, 23, 25–29, 33, 43, 59, 66, 69, 81, 88, 93–95, 97–98, 100, 102, 113, 116, 120–122, 128, 133, 145, 148, 150, 156, 159–160, 165, 167, 169, 175, 179, 185–186, 188–190, 192, 201, 212, 215, 217
  Cratylus, 22, 145, 212
  Gorgias, 27, 145, 175
  Euthyphro, 27, 33, 183
  Greater Hippias, 22, 212
  Laws, 25, 59, 81, 98–99, 112, 175, 204

Letter VII, 26
Parmenides, 22, 81, 116–117, 212.
Phaedo, 26–27, 43, 59, 81, 83, 93, 96, 98, 145,160, 163–166, 167, 169, 170–171, 178, 180, 183, 192
Phaedrus, 26–27, 183–185
Philebus, 25–26, 43, 144
Protagoras, 93, 210
Republic, 23, 25–26, 83, 98, 185
Sophist, 43, 100, 212
Statesman, 43
Symposium, 23
Theaetetus, 33, 100, 175, 212
Timaeus, 25, 34, 81–83, 99, 115, 145, 148, 158–159
Plautus, 8, 113
Pliny the Elder, 5, 212
Pliny the Younger, 7
Plotinus, 17, 19, 23, 74, 82, 85–86, 88, 90–92, 98, 100–106, 115, 117, 122, 125, 127–131, 133, 140–141, 145, 149–150, 153, 155, 160, 164, 166, 170, 175, 177–178, 179, 224
Plutarch, 7, 23, 51, 60–61, 69, 149, 151, 209.
Polemius, 19
Porphyry, 8, 10, 82, 86, 96, 103–104, 107, 127, 131–132, 141, 153, 158, 164, 166–167, 176, 179–180, 186, 192.
Posidonius, 146, 149
Priscian the Philosopher, 86, 106, 124, 125–126, 130–131, 156
Probus, 19
Proclus, 81–82, 101, 104–105, 127, 135, 148–149
Prudentius, 6
Psellos, 126–127, 153, 166
Pseudo-Aristotle, 59
Pseudo Hincmar, 12
Pseudo-Jerome, 105.
Pseudo Maximus, 60, 93
Pseudo-Primasius, 11, 136
Pythagoras, 143

Rabanus Maurus, 12
Ratramnus of Corbie, 12
Richard of Fournival, 15
Rufinus, 6
Ruricius, 32

Sallust, 7
Salvian, 10
Samson of Córdoba, 13
Sapaudus, 9, 10
Seneca, 146
Servius, 113
Severus, 7, 128
Sextius, 148
Sextus Empiricus, 60, 147
Sidonius Apollinaris, 1–5, 7, 9–10, 14, 18–19, 22, 32, 37, 62–63
Simplicius, 55, 92, 105–106
Socrates, 23, 28, 33, 54, 71, 183, 185, 211–213
Sophocles, 33
Soranus, 93
Stobaeus, 61
Symbolum Athanasianum, 136
Synesios of Cyrene, 195, 219

Tatian, 190
Tertullian, 6, 24, 42, 45–46, 57–58, 59–61, 67, 71–72, 88, 90, 93, 95, 99, 113, 128, 134, 189, 224
Themistius, 153
Theodorus Manlius, 172
Theophilus of Antioch, 151
Theophrastus, 98
Thomas Aquinas, 70, 85, 152, 154, 201, 218
Varro, 4, 7–8, 68, 95, 97, 122,
Victorinus, Marius, 92, 94, 112, 116–117, 139–140, 144, 171, 173, 180, 195

Vigilius of Thapse, 141
Vincentius Victor, 59
Virgil, 8, 89
Virgil the Grammarian, 195
Volusian, 123
William of Moerbeke, 208
William of St. Thierry, 14, 153

Xenophon, 23, 59, 145, 165

Zeno of Elea, 164, 212

Index of Terms

ἀβλαβής, 150
ἀγχίνοια, 33
ἀδιάστατος, 90
ἀλλοίωσις, 129
ἀλλότρια, 176
ἀπαιδευσία, 203, 209
ἄπονος, 150
ἁρμονία, 160
ἀσύγχυτος ἕνοσις, 129, 136, 137, 147
ἀσώματος, 43, 59, 128, 148
ἄτοπος, 90
Augustinism in Gaul, 9

βιαιοθάνατοι, 166

captive in *Deuteronomy*, 63–64
conservation, 150–151
continere 143, cf. συνέχειν
culture, 3, 6-7, 12, 33, 63–64, 69, 72–74, 99, 194–195–196, 198, 201–202, 209, 216, 220
culture, literary-oratorical, 22–23, 25–28, 31–32, 67, 216
culture philosophical, 17–23, 26, 28, 32–33, 62, 64, 66, 72, 95, 195

decadence, 3
δεινότης, δεινός, 33
dialectic, 9, 12, 20, 22, 24, 67, 70, 173, 181
divine government, 151
divinity of the soul, 46, 52, 100, 98–99, 106–108, 132, 193
dream, 4, 86, 100, 155

education, 4, 6, 21, 27, 125, 199, 201, 206, 208–211, 220
education, Christian, 4, 6, 21
ἐνκύκλιος παιδεία, 210
εἱμαρμένος θάνατος, 163
ἐνέργεια, 92, 148
ἕνωσις cf. ἀσύνχυτος ἕνωσις,
ἕζις, 206, 210
esotericism, 26, 185, 208; cf. Socratic rhetoric
εὐσχημοσσύνη, 94

funeral eulogy, 6

γνῶθι σεαυτόν, 97
gnostic, 69, 80, 99, 149, 185

heresy, 53, 65, 69

Idea, 61, 86, 90, 93, 95, 164, 168, 179
image of God, 14–15, 80, 92, 107, 110, 119, 139
Incarnation, 44, 99, 123–124, 131–138, 141 188, 224,
inconfusibiliter, 140–141
incorporeus, 46–50; cf. ἀσώματος

inlocalitas, 90, 215
inspiration, 191, 197
intermediaries, 137

κατάλγψις, 61
κρᾶσις, 128–129, 163
κρίνειν, 207

library, 4–6, 15, 187
lie, 44, 184–185

Manichaeism, 55, 132, 138, 158, 176–178, 225
medioximum, 113
μετάνοια, 150
microcosm, 143–144, 150, 154, 156–157, 214, 230
μικρολογί, 20–21, 23
minutiloquium, 23
μίξις, 127, 129
μουσική, 30

ὁμολογία, 164

pagan gods, survival of, 68, 223
παιδεία, 6, 30, 199–211
παράθεσις, 128
περιέχειν, 146
persona, 38–39, 123–125, 134–136, 139
philosophy, 12–13, 18–19, 20, 22, 25, 28–32, 34–35, 52, 56, 65–66, 68–69, 72–73, 75, 78, 82, 104, 107, 131, 151, 134, 165, 173, 179, 186, 188–191, 194, 195–197, 200, 203–204, 210
philosophy, teaching of, 1995, 199, 201, 205, 208, 211
philosophy, personifications of, 64
philosophia Christiana, 73; cf. culture, philosophical
πνεῦμα, 47, 88, 91, 146
potentia, 57, 81, 89, 92, 108, 139–140, 152, 158

religion of culture, 65
reminiscence, 41, 111
resurrection of the flesh, 67, 134
rhetoric, 6, 24–28, 30–32, 67, 107, 184; cf. culture, literary or oratorical
rhetoric, Socratic, 26, 182, 184

sensation, 91, 102, 158
sollertia, 34
sophistic, 30
soul, blood, 230
soul, impeccability of, 104
soul, invisibility of, 12, 42–43,47, 59–60, 109
soul, mutability of, 93, 101, 104–105, 112
soul, size of, 89, 149
soul, time in the, 102–103
spiritus, 43, 47, 57–58, 60, 89, 111, 113, 116, 173
stabilis motus, 114–116
status, 40–41, 48, 1113, 117
σύγχυσις, 129
suicide, 116, 162, 167, 217
συμπάθεια, 156, 164
συνέχειν, 150–151
συνοχή, 148

θάνατος, 159-160
transcendence, divine, 52, 84, 138
Trinity, 37, 42, 50, 92, 117, 139, 141, 197

unio inconfusa, 120, 125, 135, 139, 142